Food Justice Activism and Pedagogies

Food Justice Activism and Pedagogies

Literacies and Rhetorics for Transforming Food Systems in Local and Transnational Contexts

Edited by

Eileen E. Schell, Dianna Winslow, and Pritisha Shrestha

LEXINGTON BOOKS
Lanham • Boulder • New York • London

Published by Lexington Books
An imprint of The Rowman & Littlefield Publishing Group, Inc.
4501 Forbes Boulevard, Suite 200, Lanham, Maryland 20706
www.rowman.com

86-90 Paul Street, London EC2A 4NE

Copyright © 2023 by The Rowman & Littlefield Publishing Group, Inc.

All rights reserved. No part of this book may be reproduced in any form or by any electronic or mechanical means, including information storage and retrieval systems, without written permission from the publisher, except by a reviewer who may quote passages in a review.

British Library Cataloguing in Publication Information Available

Library of Congress Cataloging-in-Publication Data

Names: Schell, Eileen E., editor. | Winslow, Dianna, 1961- editor. | Shrestha, Pritisha, 1987- editor.
Title: Food justice activism and pedagogies : literacies and rhetorics for transforming food systems in local and transnational contexts / edited by Eileen E. Schell, Dianna Winslow, Pritisha Shrestha.
Description: Lanham : Lexington Books, 2023. | Includes bibliographical references and index.
Subjects: LCSH: Food writing. | Food in literature. | Food habits in literature | Social justice in literature. | Food supply--Social aspects. | Sustainable agriculture--Social aspects.
Classification: LCC TX644 .F665 2023 (print) | LCC TX644 (ebook) | DDC 808.06/6641--dc23/eng/20230127
LC record available at https://lccn.loc.gov/2022057909
LC ebook record available at https://lccn.loc.gov/2022057910

ISBN: 978-1-7936-5068-9 (cloth)
ISBN: 978-1-7936-5070-2 (pbk.)
ISBN: 978-1-7936-5069-6 (ebook)

Contents

Acknowledgments vii

Introduction: Framing Food Justice and Literacies for Rhetoric and
    Writing Studies 1
    Eileen E. Schell and Dianna Winslow

PART I 17

Chapter 1: Reclaiming Forgotten Literacies: Agency through Food
    Literacy 19
    Nabila Hijazi

Chapter 2: Building Sustainable Futures from Gastronomic Pasts:
    Cultural Heritage and the Rhetorical Value of Food 37
    Ellen Platts

Chapter 3: Flatbush Eats: Lessons about Food from a Community
    History Project 51
    Deborah Mutnick

Chapter 4: The Smell of the Other and Self-Alienation: A
    Mani(fold)festo of Race, Ethnicity, and Rhetorical (In)
    Accessibility to Food 71
    Bibhushana Poudyal and Mala Rai

PART II 83

Chapter 5: Seeds of the Diaspora: Using Creative and Collaborative
    Writing to Explore Critical Food Literacies with Black Youth 85
    OreOluwa Badaki

Chapter 6: "Rekindling Hope, Building Resilience": Critical
Agricultural Literacies and Food Justice on the Llano Estacado — 109
Callie F. Kostelich

Chapter 7: Once You Sell Us on the Service We Can Render:
Agricultural Public Relations, Feminist Food Literacies, and the
Rhetorical Power of Women in Ag — 129
Cori Brewster

Chapter 8: When the Land Writes: The Rhetorical and Reciprocal
Lives of Land and Plants — 149
Veronica House and Kelly Zepelin

Chapter 9: Food Justice, Citizenship Right, and Right to Food in
Nepal — 167
Pritisha Shrestha

PART III — 183

Chapter 10: Students Question the Academic Agrifood Industrial
Complex and Promote Food Justice — 185
Abby M. Dubisar

Chapter 11: From Food Security to Food Justice to Civic
Engagement: Building an Interdisciplinary Critical Pedagogy — 205
Deborah Adelman and Shamili Ajgaonkar

Chapter 12: Food Justice and Garden Writing in First-Year
Seminars at Bates College — 243
Stephanie Wade

Index — 263

About the Contributors — 269

Acknowledgments

This book would not have been possible without conversations begun in the Composition and Cultural Rhetoric (CCR) Doctoral Program at Syracuse University, the place where the three of us met as faculty and students and started the dialogue that led to this book. We are fortunate to have been able to continue to collaborate after Dianna graduated from Syracuse University and moved to the West Coast and Pritisha arrived in Syracuse after moving from Nepal to attend CCR. Our cross-generational conversations about food justice have provided us with a rich opportunity to pursue mutual interests and develop our ideas into this book.

We would like to thank the contributors who collaborated to produce this book. They have been wonderful to work with and have met all deadlines with dedication and resolve. Writing with passion and commitment about the sites of food justice activism and pedagogy, they will inspire and shape conversations in the field through this volume and beyond.

We offer, too, a special thanks to acquisitions editor Nicolette Amstutz at Lexington Books, who showed immediate interest in this project and encouraged its timely completion. We would also like to thank Jennifer Jeffery, an academic librarian at SUNY Potsdam and U.S. Coast Guard veteran, who assisted us with formatting and compiling the manuscript and index.

As for our individual acknowledgments:

Eileen would like to thank Dianna and Pritisha for the opportunity to imagine this volume and work over Zoom on a weekly basis. This was no easy feat, as we started this project in the midst of a pandemic and faced various losses and challenges along the way; our conversations always added a much-needed spark to Friday afternoons. Eileen would also like to thank her colleagues at Syracuse University and across the country who have encouraged and pursued scholarship on agriculture, food, and rural literacies over the years: Kim Donehower, Abby Dubisar, Charlotte Hogg, Adrienne Lamberti, Carolyn Ostrander, Kurt Stavenhagen, and Stephanie Wade.

Finally, the biggest thank-you goes to Eileen's parents Neva D. Schell and the late Robert E. Schell, brother Michael R. Schell, and late grandmother A. Elizabeth Schell, who inspired her to write about food and agriculture through their hard work as family farmers in eastern Washington State.

Dianna would like to thank Eileen for her patient and committed mentorship in graduate school and professional life over the years. Dianna has immense gratitude for her help in (re)imagining the social justice applications of rhetoric and writing and recognizing and nurturing a deep commitment to food and social justice. Dianna thanks Pritisha for widening her view to include global sites of food injustice and for her warm and welcoming acceptance of a fellow CCR grad. Like Eileen, she is full of gratitude for the colleagues listed above who continue to grow their work on critical food literacies and rhetorics; without all of you, this volume could not have emerged. Lastly, Dianna thanks her brother Rick Lytle, who encouraged this work of the intellect and heart; she cherishes memories of unauthorized play together in and post-harvest gleaning of a big commercial farm field behind the family home on the Southern California coast that started this exploration so long ago.

Pritisha would like to extend her immense gratitude to Eileen and Dianna for inviting her to this project and making her a part of this beautiful journey. Conversing with them during our weekly Friday afternoon zoom calls during the height of the pandemic offered a respite from the world and also promoted a feeling of resistance to addressing social injustices. Pritisha would like to also thank her CCR professors and friends, especially Dr. Krista Kennedy and Stephanie Jones. She also thanks her second academic home, the Food Studies Program (at Syracuse University). She felt wholeheartedly welcomed by Dr. Anne C. Bellows and Dr. Rick Welsch, whose works on global food policy and food justice inspired her to view social justice through the lens of food. She also thanks her Food Studies friends whose dynamic work on the food system and food justices further expanded her perspective of human relationships to food. Pritisha thanks her fellow South-Asian friend Bibhushana Poudyal, who has been a support system in academia. Last, but not the least, Pritisha would like to acknowledge her community back home in Nepal, especially the feminists and female activists at the grassroot levels whose lived experiences and relentless works and activism for social justice are truly paving the way for redefining how transnational feminism works, especially from the Global South.

Introduction

Framing Food Justice and Literacies for Rhetoric and Writing Studies

Eileen E. Schell and Dianna Winslow

Food is a basic human need, yet access to it, its production, and its equitable distribution, are by no means guaranteed. Food access is impacted by a wide range of influences, from the environment, drought, climate change, famine, and disease, to complex political forces, such as civil unrest, war, repressive regimes, fluctuating political trade agreements, racism, sexism, classism, and variable, often unjust public policies. Food insecurity and inequity often rest at the center of global conflicts, which, in turn, shape the ways that particular communities and bodies are granted or denied access to food. Our current historical moment of the ongoing global COVID-19 pandemic demonstrates many of the vulnerabilities and challenges of access to food in the United States and other nations.

In March 2020, as COVID-19 began to spread across the United States, many Americans masked up and went to their local grocery stores to stock up on shelf-stable food. For the first time in a long time, or ever, many saw empty grocery store shelves or signs rationing specific food and sundries as they pushed their carts down the aisles. Many shoppers, profoundly rocked by the sight of empty shelves, rushed to plant "victory" gardens, signed up for CSAs, visited farmers' markets, and ordered take-out from their favorite restaurants to help them stay afloat. Many hoarded food, hand sanitizer, and toilet paper and worried that one day they would see store closures. Some people who have always had to worry every day if a paycheck can stretch far enough to feed a family continued to worry about the choice between spending meager funds on food or on housing, heat, or medicine. Laid off and unemployed workers who had never visited a food pantry before lined up at church food banks and nonprofit food pantries to procure food and basic necessities. Many food pantries established on college campuses to address student food insecurity closed down their operations as colleges shifted to remote operations because of COVID-19–driven shutdowns. With the sudden absence of university basic needs support, these already at-risk students were forced to find alternative support structures (Janjou 2021).

As one third of the world's population went into lockdown (Galanakis 2020, 1) during the COVID-19 pandemic, people's physical and economic mobilities were limited at local, national, and international levels. This, in turn, increased the food insecurity experienced by vulnerable people across the globe and also disrupted supply chains. While certain portions of the world population saw their stock of food dry up, farmers from around the world found themselves with stockpiles of food that had no market as a result of the closing down of transportation and food industries. Thousands of meatpacking workers, farmworkers, grocery store employees, and food service workers were sickened by COVID-19, and some died due to a lack of corporate and industry efforts to safeguard their health. Additionally, ripple effects in agricultural production were felt most by migrant workers who were laid off or whose earnings were slashed, which made them and their families back home more vulnerable. Many consumers began to think more about where their food came from and how the labor of essential workers brought it to them, realizing that we couldn't eat without these workers and their labor. Thanking and applauding essential workers, as many did, though, is not enough. They deserve better wages, benefits, and a safer food system in which to work, and the pandemic heightened those ongoing labor issues.

While the effects of COVID-19 have been devastating to human health and have highlighted already existing racial, class, gender, and geopolitical disparities, food insecurity and failed structures in the food system have also shown us how unjust and how vulnerable our food infrastructure is and was in the first place. Just as the pandemic has exposed weaknesses in our health care systems, we have learned more about the weaknesses and gaps in our national and global food systems, labor conditions, and supply chains. The domino effect of the pandemic and subsequent lockdown called out to us as researchers and scholars to address the methods, methodologies, and activist strategies and discourses we can use to engender new ways to continue fighting injustices in the food system.

As many public commentators and food justice advocates have argued, changes to the food system coming out of the crisis moment of the pandemic as well as climate crisis can and should be profound. How can we create a food system that is more just, sustainable, secure, equitable, local, and robust? How can we create a food system that allows all of us, not just some of us, to eat healthy food and that eliminates the racialized, gendered, and classed food access disparities that food justice activists have rightfully called out for decades? How can we create and maintain a system of local and regional family-farm-centered agriculture that does not harm the environment and that also adapts to changing environmental conditions due to climate change? These are not new questions, but they are ones that food justice scholars and teachers and agricultural advocates have been asking for decades as food injustice has long been present prior to the pandemic and the noticeable effects of climate change.

To address these vital questions, this edited volume *Food Justice Activism and Pedagogies: Literacies and Rhetorics for Transforming Food Systems in Local and Transnational Contexts* brings together scholars in the field of rhetoric, composition, and writing studies to address food as a topic of inquiry and a matter of social justice. As contributors argue in this collection, the work of literacies and rhetorics for transforming food systems allows for the analysis and rethinking of the practices of everyday life and encourages dissenting perspectives that allow people to critically engage with shaping food systems that sustain all communities. Scholars in this collection, along with long-standing food activists and community educators, also advocate that food learning be taught and engaged at all levels of schooling and in society, including college courses and community settings. This work is especially important during the COVID-19 pandemic, postpandemic era, and in the midst of climate crisis as activists, scholars, and teachers develop pedagogies in schools and colleges that help prepare the younger generation to address the exigent needs and issues of food systems plagued by food insecurity, racialized food injustice, climate change, and food policies that discount food sovereignty.

The contributors to this collection draw on food justice rhetorics and literacies and critical food literacies in their scholarship and teaching to investigate and address these flawed and unjust food systems. Critical literacy is knowledge built around complex, inquiry-driven activities and practices that uses language and literacy to question the status quo, pay astute attention to power inequities and domination, and creatively imagine socially just alternatives (Shor and Pari 1999, 3–5; Shor, 1999). We connect critical food literacies to the food justice movement in which eaters, growers, and policymakers interrogate our food systems and actively engage in transforming them to become more just and sustainable systems for all. In concert with critical food literacies, the term *food justice* is an important concept for this volume. Food justice rhetorics and literacies seek "to challenge and restructure the dominant food system," and provide "a core focus on equity and disparities and the struggles by those who are most vulnerable." Food justice also establishes "linkages and common goals with other forms of social justice activism and advocacy—whether immigrant rights, worker justice, transportation and access, or land use" (Gottlieb and Joshi 2013, vi).

The co-editors of this volume represent three different generations of food studies and literacy/rhetoric scholars, with each of us coming from complex positions and histories within the food system and different geopolitical locations, although we share the common space of having worked at Syracuse University. Eileen grew up on a third-generation family apple and pear orchard in eastern Washington state and lived and worked inside family farm agriculture until she went off to college. Once she left the farm and was in college, she continued work in the food system as a part-time restaurant worker, waiting tables and bartending while working on her degrees. As a faculty member, she began to teach and write about food in 2001 when her family left farming full-time and began to lease their orchards. In her published work, she began to grapple with the changes in the family farm system due to globalization and corporate consolidation. Dianna grew up next to a large farm near Oxnard, California, and spent hours gleaning in the farm fields. She married early in life and raised a family, cultivating a large garden and cooking with home-grown produce. When she attended graduate school in the Composition and Cultural Rhetoric (CCR) program at Syracuse University, she got involved in Community-Supported Agriculture, volunteering at the organization Community-Supported Agriculture, Central New York (CSA-CNY). Her dissertation focused on the collaborative work that she and students did in a research writing course that was connected to the work of CSA-CNY. She remains active in promoting and supporting food and environmental studies scholarship and teaching through her work at the Center for Teaching, Learning, and Technology at Cal Poly, San Luis Obispo. Pritisha came to Syracuse University from Nepal to study in the CCR program and brought a keen interest in food studies and human rights, specifically women's right to food and citizenship in Nepal and globally. She became a student not only in the CCR program, but also in the Interdisciplinary Food Studies program at Syracuse. She has become active in the local food foraging scene in Syracuse and frequently posts and microblogs on social media about food; her work on gender, citizenship, and food policy in Nepal promises to be central to transnational feminist food scholarship.

Likewise, the authors in this volume also have complex histories with food studies scholarship and teaching. Across their chapters, they engage in a wide range of inquiries around critical food literacies and food justice in their teaching, scholarship, and community engagement. Striving to highlight and alleviate injustices in the food system, they engage in inquiry about food justice and the environment, land access and use, health, immigration, worker rights, economic and community development, cultural integrity, and social justice (Gottlieb and Joshi 2013, xii). Our project joins with a growing body of scholarship on food rhetorics and literacies in rhetoric and writing studies.

FOOD STUDIES IN THE FIELD OF RHETORIC AND COMPOSITION

To date, rhetoric and literacy scholars have begun to address rhetorics of food and farming mainly through special issues of journals themed around food and farming. *College English* published a special issue on food writing in 2008 (Schilb), which included articles addressing food memoirs, organic agriculture, and the "slow food" movement. A special issue of *Pre/Text* (2013) on food theory co-edited by Jeff Rice and Jenny Edbauer Rice explores "the connection between critical theory and food" with an emphasis on understanding how food functions rhetorically, with articles addressing a range of issues, from global warming and its effects on farming systems, food and popular culture, and the rise of new industries such as craft brewing. Adrienne Lamberti edited a special issue of the rhetoric journal *POROI* in 2015 that focuses on the rhetoric of food, with essays analyzing the rhetoric of representations of food in literature, the rhetorics of vegetarian diets, and racialized food rhetorics.

The *Community Literacy Journal* has taken up the issue of food in relation to questions of community literacy and food justice, publishing two special issues addressing food and connected themes. The autumn 2015 special issue on "Community Food Literacies" featured a diverse array of topics, including food labeling, agricultural literacies, community cookbooks, and permaculture, among other topics. A fall 2019 issue on "Reciprocity in Community-Engaged Food and Environmental Justice Scholarship "explored topics connected to food justice in communities of color and also questions of reciprocity as a method within community literacy projects and scholarship." The special issue co-editors Dawn Opel and Donnie Johnson Sackey (2019) ask: "What notions of reciprocity guide 'successful' partnerships around food and environmental justice? What can community organizations teach us about how we as researchers engage with them to address food and environmental justice issues?" (2). The contributions to this 2019 special issue address those questions, connecting them to issues taken up at the 2017 Conference on Community Writing's Food and Environmental Justice Deep Think Tank (DTT). Our book project builds on this important work while also offering an expansive overview of how our field can connect and extend this work to address food justice rhetorics and literacies across a range of sites in both local, national, and transnational contexts.

Scholars of feminist rhetorics and food rhetorics have examined and valued women's rhetorical traditions and literacies connected to domestic labor, including food-themed topics such as cooking and cookbook traditions; growing and sharing food; and bodily norms, practices, and rituals connected to eating and food production and preparation. *Food, Feminisms, Rhetorics,* edited by Melissa Goldthwaite, brings a gendered and feminist lens to food studies, addressing traditions of cooking and recipes, feminist food writing, food practices and traditions, and bodily rhetorics and norms connected to food (Goldthwaite 2017, 5–8). Bringing feminist rhetorical lenses to food, Goldthwaite and contributors address questions of representation, power, bodily norms, and labor, pointing to the significance of food and food-connected activity as a subject worthy of scholarly notice and a feminist rhetorical topic of inquiry (Goldthwaite 2017, 4–5). Abby Dubisar's insightful work on gender, food, farming, and peace activism has also begun to appear with frequency, not only in Goldthwaite's collection, but in multiple journal articles addressing women engaged in agricultural practices and peacemaking activities connected to food in *Peitho* (2016b), *Rhetoric Review (*2017), and the *Community Literacy Journal* (2016a) among others. This volume draws on and cites this important feminist work while connecting work in feminist activism and inquiry with the larger intersectional food justice and environmental justice movements.

Food literacy, rhetorics, and food-themed writing courses have been featured not only in some of the special issues, edited collections, and articles mentioned above, but they have made the national news. Steven Alvarez's "Taco Literacies" writing course at the University of Kentucky and St. John's University has caught the attention of both scholars in our field and the national media (Hansen 2016). As Alvarez noted in an interview with the *Huffington Post*: "This class allows our students to explore the issues of immigration, inequality, workers, intercultural communication, and literacy through the prism of food" (qtd. in Hanson 2016). Alvarez's course outline and syllabus, published in *Composition Studies,* and his approach to the materiality and transnational flows of food has sparked widespread interest around studying cultural foodways, labor, and power relations in the food system. Given the wide interest in this work, Alvarez along with Casey Kelley also sponsored a 2019 Rhetoric Society of America workshop focused on "Foodways Rhetorics." This volume is influenced by Alvarez's analysis of cultural foodways and his analysis of the transnational circulation of food.

Scholars concerned with ecocomposition and environmental rhetorics and communication have sought to understand ways that environmental questions and concerns about land use, natural resources, and fossil fuel and energy usage are important to studies of writing and rhetoric and the writing classroom and vice versa. Derek Owens' *Composition and Sustainability: Teaching for a Threatened Generation* (2001) and Christian Weisser and Sidney Dobrin's *Natural Discourse: Toward Ecocomposition* (2002) provide useful perspectives on how the environment and sustainability can be brought to bear as topics of inquiry and paradigms for composing in rhetoric and writing studies. Dobrin and Weisser argue that composition studies provides a unique site for allowing students to explore discourses of sustainability as well as connections between nature and discourse. Exploring questions of rural sustainability, Kim Donehower, Charlotte Hogg, and Eileen Schell address agrarian rhetorics and literacies connected to food and farming systems in *Rural Literacies* (2007). They analyze the historical and contemporary discourses about rural literacies, including representation of small family farm agriculture and rural communities and students, and examine how to engage topics of rural literacies in the writing classroom, offering a concluding chapter on addressing food and sustainability as a topic of inquiry in writing courses. The edited collection, *Reclaiming the Rural* (co-edited by Donehower, Hogg, and Schell 2011), continues the conversation about rural literacies and offers an examination of the issue of land economies and rhetorics with three chapters addressing agricultural literacies, water rights, and representations of farmers. Like these authors, we demonstrate how a critical understanding of discourses on agriculture and the environment have relevance to the broader goals of connecting the writing done in classrooms and communities to social action.

A connected stream of food inquiry has come from rhetoric scholars in communication studies, who have been engaged in the study of food and farming rhetorics in varied ways. Tarla Rai Peterson was one of the earliest communication scholars to address agriculture and sustainability and study the representations of farmers as environmental stakeholders. Since Peterson's work was first published (see also Peterson and Choat 1998), scholarly interest in communication studies and food has expanded, resulting in a series of essay collections that examine food as an area of human communication such as *Edible Ideologies* (LeBesco and Naccaratto 2008) and *Food As Communication: Communication as Food* (Cramer, Green, and Walters 2011). The co-edited collection by Joshua Frye and Michael Bruner, *The Rhetoric of Food: Discourse, Materiality, and Power* (2012), offers a valuable series of essays on politics, culture, lifestyle, identity, advertising, environment, and economy with respect to food. They argue that their project promotes "readers' understanding of the role of rhetoric in mediating our perceptions of why discourse, materiality, and power are interwoven as well as the prospects for imagining reconstituted relations with the earth, each other, culture, power, and ourselves—through food" (2012, 3). Our edited collection also explores this nexus of discourse, materiality, and power and expands it to consider the wider networks surrounding these concepts, especially in relation to questions of labor, access, and justice.

Perhaps the book that best bridges work in agricultural rhetoric/writing studies and communication studies is Adrienne Lamberti's *Talking the Talk:*

Revolution In Agricultural Communication (2007). She offers a qualitative study of the communication practices of the Beginning Farmer Center, an Iowa State University Extension program housed under the Leopold Center for Sustainable Agriculture. Lamberti's study, like Peterson's work, considers the on-the-ground perspectives and knowledge of farmers in the debates over current practices and the future of agriculture. In her second edited collection, *Cultivating Spheres: Agriculture, Technical Communication, and the Publics* (2018), Lamberti continues her qualitative work to illustrate the public and discursive evolution of agricultural changes that significantly affect cultures and societies.

These articles, special issues, and books/collections indicate that scholars in rhetoric and writing studies are beginning to not only engage the topics of food studies and food justice but are also starting to contribute to and shape the larger dialogues within interdisciplinary food studies. This collection further opens spaces to consider critical food literacies and food justice rhetorics and literacies and critically interrogates the politics, ethics, economics, and rhetorics of food systems locally, nationally, and transnationally. In doing so, we expand the conversation about food in relation to questions of social and environmental justice.

Food Justice Rhetorics and Literacies in Action

The chapters in the first section of this volume connect questions of culture and community to food justice and food sovereignty, emphasizing the ways in which specific community stakeholders are fighting for food justice in their neighborhoods and communities and as they enter the country as new Americans. In neighborhoods threatened by gentrification and the ravaging effects of the pandemic, community members are fighting to maintain their cultural foodways and ensure cultural and economic survivance. Food can be a site for cultural survivance and opportunity, but it can also be a site of contestation, conflict, and potential discrimination.

In chapter 1, "Reclaiming Forgotten Literacies: Agency through Food Literacy," Nabila Hijazi argues that Syrian refugee women living in the Washington, D.C., area exercise rhetorical agency and food justice as they draw upon their knowledge of Syrian cooking traditions to pursue opportunities as food entrepreneurs. Hijazi argues that refugee women, many of whom hail from rural areas of Syria, gain agency and power through their food literacies and entrepreneurial efforts as microbusiness owners, supporting and providing for their families. She argues that their actions as purveyors of specific food literacies and as entrepreneurs disrupt the cycle of stereotyping and stigmatization that have often been used to portray refugee women as unproductive, passive, and dependent on male partners or on the government and local agencies for support and survival. Hijazi examines how these women's food literacy practices and efforts toward food justice sustain their families and communities and demonstrate resilience, autonomy, and agency as they negotiate traditional gender roles and new economic, social, and political futures.

Ellen Platts, in "Building Sustainable Futures from Gastronomic Pasts: Cultural Heritage and the Rhetorical Value of Food," addresses how community members in Tucson, Arizona, are addressing food insecurity and sustainability through becoming a Creative City of Gastronomy and a member of the UNESCO Creative Cities Network (UCCN). The UNESCO Creative Cities Network (UCCN) recognizes cities that have placed specific creative fields—including gastronomy—at the center of their plans for sustainable development. She examines how the framework of cultural heritage can be a rhetorical tool with uneven effects, especially when the traditional food practices of several distinct and overlapping communities are included under the banner of "heritage" foodways. She argues that cultural heritage may empower dominant social groups while minimizing those taken up by marginalized indigenous and Latinx communities. Drawing on ethnographic fieldwork undertaken in community gardens, mutual aid projects, and urban farms in Tucson, Arizona, Platts examines how "heritage" can become a rhetorical strategy for influencing the movement toward food justice and social justice more broadly rather than as a site of cultural appropriation and exploitation.

Also focusing on the connection between food and culture, in "Flatbush Eats: Lessons about Food from a Community History Project," Deborah Mutnick addresses how food justice operates within the space of Flatbush-Prospect Lefferts Gardens, a diasporic West Indian neighborhood, which has been recently designated New York City's "Little Caribbean." While food in the neighborhood is a productive component of the culture, it is also rapidly becoming a site where gentrification occurs. The rise of upscale coffee shops, bars, grocery stores, yoga studios, and restaurants has begun to alter the cultural makeup of the community and threatens long-standing businesses, which have already been threatened by the COVID-19 crisis. Residents have also faced increasing food insecurity, which has led to efforts to create grassroots food distribution, a renewed focus on community gardening, and fresh food box programs sourced from local farms. Mutnick argues that food is vital to understanding the forces of change and resistance that imperil the integrity and identity of Flatbush-Lefferts Gardens. Her chapter addresses the development, processes, artifacts, and public impact of the Flatbush Eats Project on the Flatbush-Prospect Lefferts Gardens neighborhood, drawing conclusions about the rhetoric and politics of food justice, literacy, and pedagogical theory and practice from the project themes of food distribution, food insecurity, and the environment.

In chapter 4, "The Smell of the Other and Self-Alienation: A Mani(fold)festo of Race, Ethnicity, and Rhetorical (In)Accessibility to Food," Bibhushana Poudyal and Mala Rai address the cultural bias against food smells, developing a rhetorical framework that addresses what they refer to as " the smell of the Other." Their chapter documents incidents of "food smells" or cooking odor discrimination that they and others have experienced in their living situations and daily interactions. They document the impact that these remarks, gestures, and overt acts of discrimination have had on their sense of identity and the ways in which these forms of discrimination and singling out lead to feelings of alienation and shame. Representing multiple examples from South Asia and the United States on the relationship between racism, ethnicism, and shaming around food smells, they argue for the need to examine the concept of "the smell of the Other" through feminist and decolonial rhetorical frameworks attentive to the interconnections between racism, ethnicism, food justice, and self-alienation.

The chapters in the second section of the book offer case studies of food justice work among specific communities of stakeholders, including youth interns of color working on a community farm, a regional nonprofit organization in Texas that is shaping food justice initiatives, a conference connected to women farmers in Washington state, small farmers and foragers in Colorado, and in relation to global policy issues such as women's right to food in Nepal. Together these chapters give us strategies and practices for addressing food justice initiatives in relation to different community sites, emphasizing the ways in which that work is situated by the specific positionalities and material conditions of specific stakeholders and regional and geopolitical locations.

In chapter 5, "Seeds of the Diaspora: Using Creative and Collaborative Writing to Explore Critical Food Literacies with Black Youth," OreOluwa Badaki addresses a collaborative storytelling project she worked on with a group of eight Black high school-age students working at a community farm rooted in African Diasporic farming traditions. In her chapter, she highlights the creative and critical citizenship practices that the youth interns exhibit as they engage in a collaborative screenwriting project that addresses themes of Afrofuturism, food justice, slavery, and freedom struggle. Drawing from interview and focus group data that Badaki collected, she co-constructed screenplay scripts with the interns that highlight themes, questions, and insights connected to food, health, food justice, racial justice, and environmental justice. The scripts have not yet been filmed, though we have done table reads with community members. Through analyzing the collaborative storytelling project that students engaged in, she addresses the critical ways in which these young people are providing helpful insights for educators and researchers interested in securing healthier, safer, and more just and sustainable futures.

In chapter 6, "'Rekindling Hope, Building Resilience': Critical Agricultural Literacies and Food Justice on the Llano Estacado," Callie F. Kostelich provides a case study of how Ogallala Commons, a nonprofit organization based in Nazareth, Texas, supports local foodshed movements and food justice initiatives. Ogallala Commons operates along the Ogallala Aquifer, spanning from Texas to the Dakotas, and their mission to "rekindle hope and rebuild resilience" is grounded in their "12 Key Assets of the Commonwealth." Examining the Ogallala Commons' initiatives to educate the public and support local food production in order to reinvigorate regional food systems, Kostelich analyzes the organization's methods and methodologies for sponsoring agricultural literacies and food justice, arguing that the nonprofit models ways to set up and engage more equitable, accessible, and sustainable foodshed movements that address the needs of both producers and consumers. At the same time, Kostelich points to gaps and flaws in the nonprofit's strategies, emphasizing the ways that all of us as citizens can take up this work across our lives in connection to different organizations.

In chapter 7, "Once You Sell Us on the Service We Can Render: Agricultural Public Relations, Feminist Food Literacies, and the Rhetorical Power of Women in Ag," Cori Brewster addresses food justice activism and pedagogy by analyzing the annual Women in Ag workshop hosted by the Washington State University's Extension Service. Brewster argues that the workshop is one of the many contemporary sites of rhetorical education that has emerged for women working in agriculture, partly in response to neoliberal transformations of the agricultural sector that have transferred an increasing and often unpaid portion of rhetorical labor and responsibility to individual farm women. As Brewster argues, farm women in the United States have been differently trained and enlisted over the past century to speak for and from the farm. Looking closely at the methods employed in this particular site of rhetorical education, Brewster analyzes the tacit, intersecting theories of rhetoric, gender, whiteness, and labor that underlie this conference. She also addresses the rhetorical challenges and openings that such a workshop presents for progressive food and farm groups (such as the Western Organization of Resource Councils and Oregon Rural Action, on whose board she serves). Brewster concludes with the implications for community-engaged research and teaching and for community organizing around food and farm justice that might more fully center and amplify more diverse voices of "women in ag."

In chapter 8, "When the Land Writes: The Rhetorical and Reciprocal Lives of Land and Plants," Veronica House and Kelly Zepelin expand the conception of reciprocity to include nonhuman elements such as plants and soil as partners in the work of food literacy, food justice, and food accessibility.

They ask how food literacy changes when stakeholders consider the land, the plants, and the soil itself as "writers," whose rhetorical lives teach us about ourselves, our health, the ecosystem, and possibilities for a more just food system. By highlighting some of the innovative work happening with foragers and farmers in a local foodshed in the state of Colorado, they offer an approach to food system work that incorporates the land and plants themselves as "writers" that help all of us understand what is just and possible within our ecological systems.

In chapter 9, "Food Justice, Citizenship Right and Right to Food in Nepal," Pritisha Shrestha analyzes how the "Right to Citizenship" as prescribed by the 2015 Constitution of Nepal is interlinked with the "Right to Food" as envisioned by the United Nations Declaration. Although the constitution of Nepal guarantees the Right to Food to every citizen of the country, she examines how citizenship rights, which are based on discriminatory acts against women, impact achieving the Right to Food and food justice. Drawing on interview narratives from local feminist activists, policymakers, and the people who are struggling to obtain their citizenship cards, she analyzes why it is imperative to actively lobby and put pressure on the government to ensure the "Right to Food" as a human right in Nepal, an important struggle for food justice.

The third section of this volume considers pedagogies and practices of food justice as they are taken up across K–12 and higher education. Each chapter provides an important site of inquiry for considering school-based food justice activist projects and pedagogies, providing readers with concrete ideas and strategies for engaging in food justice work in educational settings.

In chapter 10, "Students Question the Academic Agrifood Industrial Complex and Promote Food Justice," Abby M. Dubisar examines a case study of genetically modified banana research at a Midwestern land grant institution. This institution solicited women students to take part in a banana-feeding study, and those who consented to participate in the study would be paid $900 to eat the GMO bananas; they would also have their blood tested to measure their bodies' reactions. Dubisar interviewed three student activists who organized a critical response to the banana study and its broader transnational agrifood contexts. Significantly, the students that she interviewed asked questions related to colonialism in Africa, single-solution technological interventions to food systems, food sovereignty, and the study's relationship to food justice. Her analysis of the interview data, informed by grounded theory and agricultural and food literacies research, showed that the students were both enabled and constrained by their status as students as they worked to engage public discussions of the consequences and sustainability of the research their university conducted. Dubisar argues that the students' use of public opportunities for discussion and engagement, the endorsement of their ideas by publics beyond campus who shared their concerns, and their postgraduate reflections on how and why students should critically engage their university's research practices offer rich examples of ways that students have mobilized in relation to food justice.

University curricula that take up food and agricultural issues are increasingly prominent in university settings, and in some cases, college faculty have engaged in this work for decades. This is the case in chapter 11, "From Food Security to Food Justice to Civic Engagement: Building an Interdisciplinary Critical Pedagogy," where Deborah Adelman and Shamili Ajgaonkar describe and analyze an interdisciplinary, cross-campus food pedagogy that they have developed over the past two decades at DuPage College, a community college in the western suburbs of Chicago. The two authors have taught an interdisciplinary course together as scholars/teachers in the fields of Environmental Biology and Film Studies. Their interdisciplinary seminar explores personal practice towards food system issues on a national and global level, drawing on scientific texts, feature films, and documentaries. In 2003 they added an experiential component by founding the Community Education Farm, an on-campus service-learning site, which provides organic produce to the on-campus food pantry. From this initial imagining of the course, they revamped it to address an organizing framework of food security—the human right to have access to nutritious and safe food—to one of food justice. They argue that while food justice overall provides a more relevant framework, they advocate for a particular definition of food justice that is broader than an anthropocentric concept of human rights. To truly be a system that is just, they argue that the concept of food justice must go beyond the concept of human rights to include elements of human responsibility to the entire ecosphere.

In the final chapter, "Food Justice and Garden Writing in First Year Seminars at Bates College," Stephanie Wade describes the ways in which she draws upon concepts of permaculture and antiracist pedagogies to design classes around the theme of food justice. Her courses integrate community engagement throughout the semester: assigning multigenre public writing rooted in cultural rhetorics, teaching about linguistic justice and code meshing, and modeling inclusive citation practices. She argues that in her courses, she is "interested in literally breaking up concrete and asphalt, in cultivating healthy soil, and in growing gardens of vegetables, flowers, and other plants to feed neighbors and create sustainable habitats for all people, for pollinators, other insects, birds, rabbits, and more." Yet she is also interested in "breaking up the ideological concrete and asphalt of modernist thought and conventional literacy pedagogies that constrain healthy thinking, inhibit diversity, and feed the school-to-prison pipeline." Her classes bring together the critical work of garden-based writing pedagogies with innovative writing assignments and give readers a model for thinking through K–12/college community partnerships.

Across the volume, contributors offer readers different entry points into food justice as an area of inquiry and social action in higher education, in community spaces, and in relation to larger interventions in food systems and food policies locally, nationally, and globally. Contributors offer varied insights about the ways the work of food justice can take place and how rhetoric and literacy scholars can be direct partners, or at least allies and accomplices, in this work. We encourage readers to draw upon the varied contexts, examples, theories, and lived experiences and practices represented here to think through the ways in which they can engage in food justice work in their classrooms, universities, communities, and activist sites of intervention. Together we can work actively toward a more just food system.

REFERENCES

Alvarez, Steven. 2016. "Taco Literacies: Ethnography, Foodways, and Emotions Through Mexican Food Writing." *Composition Forum* 34 (2016). http://compositionforum.com/issue/34/taco-literacies.php.

Cramer, Janet, Carinita P. Greene, and Lynn M. Walters, eds. 2011. *Food as Communication: Communication as Food*. New York: Peter Lang.

Dobrin Sid, and Christian Weisser. 2002. *Natural Discourse: Toward Ecocomposition*. Albany: SUNY Press.

Donehower, Kim, Charlotte Hogg, and Eileen Schell. 2007. *Rural Literacies*. Carbondale: Southern Illinois University Press.

———, eds. 2011. *Reclaiming the Rural: Essays on Literacy, Rhetoric, and Pedagogy*. Carbondale: Southern Illinois University Press.

Dubisar, Abby M. 2017. "Toward a Feminist Food Rhetoric." *Rhetoric Review*, 37, no. 1: 118–30.

———. 2016a. "'If I Can't Bake, I Don't Want to Be Part of Your Revolution': CODEPINK's Activist Literacies of Peace and Pie." *Community Literacy Journal* 10, no. 2: 1–18.

———. 2016b. "Linking Rural Women Transnationally: Iowa's 'First Lady of the Farm' and Post WWII Ethos." *Peitho: Journal of the Coalition of Women Scholars in the History of Rhetoric and Composition* 19, no. 1.

Frye, Joshua, and Michael Bruner, eds. 2012. *The Rhetoric of Food: Discourse, Materiality, and Power*. Routledge.

Galanakis, Charis M. 2020. "The Food Systems in the Era of the Coronavirus (COVID-19) Pandemic Crisis." *Foods* 9, no. 4: 523.

Goldthwaite, Melissa, ed. 2017. *Food, Feminisms, Rhetorics*. Carbondale: Southern Illinois University Press.

Gottlieb, Robert, and Anupama Joshi. 2013. *Food Justice*. Boston, Mass.: MIT Press.

Hanson, Hillary. 2016. "There's a 'Taco Literacy' Course, But It's about More Than Food." *Huffington Post* 29 no. 1. https://www.huffpost.com/entry/taco-literacy-college-class_n_56ab8cc5e4b00b033aaec716.

Janjou, Elmira. 2021. "Staying Home, Staying Alive: Campus Food Pantry Student Clients' Experiences during the COVID-19 Pandemic." *Journal of Applied Social Science.* https://journals.sagepub.com/doi/full/10.1177/19367244211035671.

Lamberti, Adrienne. 2007. *Talking the Talk: Revolution in Agricultural Communication.* Nova Science Publication.

———, ed. 2015. "Special Issue: A Forum on the Rhetoric of Food." *POROI Journal: Project on the Rhetoric of Inquiry* 11, no. 1: https://ir.uiowa.edu/poroi/vol11/iss1.

———, ed. 2018. *Cultivating Spheres: Agriculture, Technical Communication, and the Publics.* N.p.: Open Library of Humanities.

Lebesco, Kathleen, and Peter Naccarato, eds. 2008. *Edible Ideologies: Representing Food and Meaning.* Albany: SUNY Press.

Opel, Dawn, and Donnie Sackey, eds. 2019. "Special Issue: Reciprocity in Community-Engaged Food and Environmental Justice Scholarship." *Community Literacy Journal* 14, no. 1 (Fall): 1–93.

Owens, Derek. 2001. *Composition and Sustainability: Teaching for a Threatened Generation.* Urbana, IL: National Council of Teachers of English.

Pennell, Michael, ed. 2015. "Special Issue: Community Food Literacies." *Community Literacy Journal* 10, no. 1 (Autumn): 1–98.

Peterson, Tarla Rai. 1986. "Conceptual Metaphor in Soil Conservation Service Rhetoric and Farmers' Responses." PhD dissertation, Washington State University (Interdisciplinary Studies).

Peterson, Tarla Rai, and Christi Choat Horton. 1998. "Rooted in the Soil: How Understanding the Perspectives of Landowners Can Enhance the Management of Environmental Disputes." In *Landmark Essays on Rhetoric and the Environment*, ed. Craig Waddell, 165–94. Mahwah, NJ: Hermagoras Press.

Rice, Jeff, and Jenny Edbauer Rice, eds. 2013. "Special Issue: Food Theory." *PRE/TEXT: A Journal of Rhetorical Theory* 21, no. 1–4: 1–220.

Shor, Ira. 1999. "What Is Critical Literacy?" *Journal of Pedagogy, Pluralism, and Practice* 1, no. 4 (Fall): 2–32. https://digitalcommons.lesley.edu/jppp/vol1/iss4/2.

Shor, Ira, and Caroline Pari, eds. 1999. "Introduction." In *Critical Literacy in Action: Writing, Words, Changing Worlds/A Tribute to Paulo Friere.* Portsmouth, NH: Boynton/Cook.

Schilb, John, ed. 2008. "Special Focus: Food." *College English* 70, no. 4 (March): 345–436.

PART I

Chapter 1

Reclaiming Forgotten Literacies

Agency through Food Literacy

Nabila Hijazi

Norman Denzin argues that "critical personal narratives are counternarratives, testimonies, autoethnographies, performance texts, stories, and accounts that disrupt and disturb discourse by exposing the complexities and contradictions that exist under official history" (Denzin 2009, 455). In accord with Denzin, I argue that the narratives of Syrian refugee women, currently living in the Washington, DC, region, challenge the dominant definition of literacy. I posit that Syrian refugee women exercise agency through food literacy, which is defined as "a set of skills and attributes that help people sustain the daily preparation of healthy, tasty, affordable meals for themselves and their families. Food literacy builds resilience because it includes food skills (techniques, knowledge, and planning ability), the confidence to improvise and problem-solve, and the ability to access and share information" (Desjardins and Kawartha 2013, 6). I adopt the definition of *agency* as "the ability of minimally competent members of a society to apply cultural schemas creatively to new contexts and situations, coupled with the ability to reinterpret and mobilize resources" (Gallagher 2012, 7). Assessing Syrian refugee women's food literacy choices and gendered experiences highlights their ability to leverage available resources in ways that create a space for their lives and their Syrian culture and thus preserve food sovereignty and cultural foodways that did not have a recognizable presence before the coming of the Syrian refugee community or the transnational literacy work Syrian refugee women have embodied in Western contexts and spaces. Syrian refugee women's food literacy practices, while leading to cultural survivance, are acts of food justice. These women preserve cultural foodways and ensure economic survival amidst the vital work of cooking and selling traditional

Syrian food, allowing food justice to emerge in their communities. In the face of economic hardships, Syrian refugee women financially sustain their families and achieve food sovereignty through embodying Syrian food literacies. This radical alternative allows traditional and culturally appropriate food literacy practices to materialize and thrive.

This chapter supports the argument that Syrian refugee women are exercising rhetorical agency in the dominant culture as they invest in food literacy which empowers them to pursue new educational and employment opportunities. According to Karen Culcasi, "Mainstream migration and refugee discourses often frame refugees as living in 'limbo' and merely waiting to return home" (Culcasi 2019, 466). However, "despite rather dire circumstances, displaced people continue various 'homemaking' practices, including recreating familiarity, improving their material conditions, and imagining a better future" (Culcasi 2019, 466). These women take on additional roles in caring for family members and maintaining the family and the community. Their food practices defy the notion that refugee women are victims, vulnerable, dependent, acquiescent, and passive in decision-making. Their actions and decisions reflect Peter Hitchcock's idea in his book, *Dialogics of the Oppressed*: "The oppressed are victims of social injustice; their significance, however, does not reside in the fact of their victimization but in the possibility that their agency will transform their lived relations" (Hitchcock 1993, 8). Syrian refugee women generate resisting discourses and take initiative in their everyday lives. Even though their practices do not conform to Western definitions of female empowerment, they show "cultural continuity," which refers to the spread of cultural heritage from one generation to another and includes the means by which that transmission is done—"the process of maintaining and passing on traditional knowledge" (Lenette, Maror, and Manwaring 2019, 752). They participate in a transnational migration of food literacy—while crossing borders and communities. Analysis of their everyday practices helps clarify how these women claim agency and enact food sovereignty and justice through embodying and reliving rural and food literacies in a new context and culture and through sustaining their cultural and economic livelihoods.

METHODOLOGICAL DESIGN

This IRB[1] empirical study, which uses robust qualitative methods to describe Syrian refugee women's gendered literacy practices as they move West and settle in a country that has a different language and culture from their own, focuses on the on-site literacy class (RESLA) which I co-organized and managed in the spring of 2017. Being a member of a local mosque's board of education, I was invited by the mosque's religious leader, the Imam, to create several programs, including literacy programs, for refugee men and women, especially Syrians, as the community helped many Syrian refugees relocate and resettle. RESLA stands for Refugee English as a Second Language Adult. We named the program RESLA because it sounds like the word (رسالة) in Arabic, which has several positive and powerful meanings and connotations: a written or typed letter that is sent in an envelope by mail. رسالة represents literacy and communication and resonates with refugees who love to contact their relatives overseas to inform them about some of the most intimate details of their lives.

I analyze data that come from interviews[2] that were done organically at several places, including the mosque and Syrian refugees' houses. My interviewees are RESLA refugee female students; they identify as Syrian Sunni Muslims. They come to this local mosque for various reasons: praying, receiving charities and spiritual and emotional support, accompanying their children for Quranic and Arabic classes, participating in festive Islamic events such as Eid[3] parties, and attending ESL literacy classes—to name a few. During the spring 2017 semester, I was able to coordinate and run RESLA, the ESL literacy class, which met weekly on Wednesdays, 9:30 am to 12:00 pm. Students were ten female refugees: eight Syrians and two Iraqis, whose ages varied between twenty-five and forty-five. The participants come from different parts of Syria; some come from rural areas while others come from suburbs or cities. All speak Arabic, mainly the Syrian and Iraqi dialects. Their education level varies: the two Iraqis were college students back in Iraq but were unable to attain their college degrees because one got married and became busy with marital responsibilities while the other's education was disrupted by the internal conflict and the violence in Iraq. Of the Syrian women, one has a high school diploma, two have ninth-grade level education, and the rest have little to no literacy in their first language, Arabic, because they lived in rural areas and did not attend school at all.

Due to cultural pressure, assumed gender roles (most women are stay-at-home mothers and housewives), and the need to work at an early age, especially in rural areas, literacy in their native language was basic for many refugees, especially women: "One reason proposed for girls' low attendance in schools relates to . . . families requiring girls' labor in the home" (Abdi 2007, 202). Bigelow and Schwartz consider gender to be one of the major factors for limited or no literacy, i.e., education for many refugees. They claim that "gender may influence opportunities for formal schooling and literacy development . . . schooling for girls is not a family or societal priority" (Bigelow and Schwartz 2010, 2). All of the female students are stay-at-home mothers and housewives. As mothers, they have always placed the highest priority on taking care of their children, while making their education secondary at most. None of them has a full-time job, though some have been able to work and make money through service jobs like babysitting, catering, or sewing. All of the women in this study reside in the same state and neighborhood and have their children living with them. Of the ten students who enrolled in the RESLA program, four agreed to be interviewed. However, the focus of this chapter is mainly on one: Fatima,[4] known as Umm Mustafa[5] within the Syrian community.

Syrian refugee women preserve elements of their cultural practices yet navigate the dominant culture resulting in "upward mobility . . . through supportive governmental and social policies" (McBrien 2005, 331). The historical narrative that defines Syrian refugee women in terms of deficits in education, language, and employment is challenged by the stories of my research subjects. When I started my volunteer work with these women, I subconsciously adopted historian Julie Roy Jeffrey's approach when she wrote about the pioneer generation of the westward migration: "My original perspective was feminist. I hoped to find that pioneer women used the frontier as a means of liberating themselves from stereotypes and behaviors that I found constricting and sexist. I discovered that they did not" (Jeffrey 1979, xv-xvi). I found out the hard way that these Syrian refugee women did not and do not necessarily want, even in this country, to abandon the literacies they had learned; rather, they utilized them to sustain their families and achieve economic mobility. A nuanced and critical analysis of the lives and experiences of these women suggests that they, while retaining certain cultural practices and ethnic markers of their native country and not necessarily seeking higher education, gain agency and power through sustaining and using multiple types of literacy, especially *food literacy*, to achieve cultural continuance. The complexity and richness of their food literacy practices disrupt gender stereotypes and complicate gendered dynamics. Their food literacy experiences in the United States help us understand how these women have drawn upon their cultural contexts and foodways to survive and sustain their families while achieving food sovereignty—their right to healthy and culturally appropriate food.

Rural Literacies: Food Literacies

Rural literacy allows for "sustainability" in rural communities. Since my Syrian refugee women interviewees come from rural parts of Syria, it is important to consider the type of literacy they had and its potential effect on their productivity and financial sustainability. Umm Mustafa, for instance, was born and raised in the rural parts of Syria and never had any formal schooling. In a Western definition of literacy, she is considered illiterate, but according to the surrounding environment and the context she was raised in, she is considered very literate. In their book, *Rural Literacies*, Kim

Donehower, Charlotte Hogg, and Eileen Schell identify the problems inherent in understanding rural literacy and the traditional misrepresentations of this type of literacy. They define rural literacies as "the particular kinds of literate skills needed to achieve the goals of sustaining life in rural areas—or, to use [Deborah] Brandt's terms, to pursue the opportunities and create public policies and economic opportunities needed to sustain rural communities" (2007, 4). They conceptualize the word *sustain* in relation to the word *sustainability,* which is defined as meeting "the needs of the present without compromising the ability of future generations to meet their work needs" (qtd. in Donehower, Hogg, and Schell 2007, 5). Rural literacy aims at increasing the economic productivity of rural regions (Ferrell and Howley 1991, 371).

Several scholars have called for expanding the field to recognize and legitimize those literacy practices deemed nonacademic and to see how social, cultural, and economic factors have affected literacy learning in certain communities. They acknowledge the existence of wider definitions of literacy beyond the walls of classrooms and academia and that literacies are plural and include sets of material skills that operate rhetorically and symbolically in knowledge-making. Thus, rural literacy moves beyond the stigma of being deficient or "'lacking': lacking education, lacking economic opportunities, [and] lacking cultural opportunities" (Donehower, Hogg, and Schell 2007, 14). However, "the predominant representations of rural literacy in popular culture have been those of extreme deficiency" (Donehower 2007, 37). Under this stereotype, people who come from rural areas are considered *illiterate,* enforcing *rural otherness.*

Even though free public education is available in Syria, primary school attendance in rural areas frequently remains far below the national average; dropout rates are high at the secondary level, especially among girls. Many young Syrians, mainly living in rural areas, do not see education as a means to meet labor needs. For them, education does not necessarily lead to stable employment or employment that would meet their immediate economic, rural needs; therefore, many drop out of school (COR Center 2014). Of course, the situation is more extreme with females, many of whom do not see the impetus behind education since they have been taught by their families that a woman's role is to be the best housewife and mother one can be. They are taught the skills they need to flourish in domestic spaces while supporting their male relatives, especially husbands, fathers, and brothers, in the fields. The skills they learn and excel in pertain mainly to domestic work. Nonetheless, Syrian refugee women have found autonomy and strength with these skills, especially during the Syrian civil war and after they came to the United States. Umm Mustafa, for example, found a rewarding employment opportunity through building a small-scale family business, in which she offers homemade food for sale. In her Syrian rural, domestic space, she learned how to make different types of authentic Syrian food, while using natural ways of preservation, since she and her family did not have regular access to basic amenities like clean water and electricity. She learned how to make different types of pickles and jams and preserve them, regardless of the surrounding temperature.

Syrian women use unique ways of making jams, pickles, pepper molasses, and other authentic Syrian foods. Using organic, natural methods has made her products more desired in the United States, especially, with the demand for organic food. To "sustain" the tradition she grew accustomed to and to acquire the needed income once in the United States, she relied on her rural literacy and skills to start a small business, "sustain" it, expand it, and succeed in it. She even utilized her family members' skills in her business. Her husband is the one who goes to wholesale markets to buy the materials she needs in large quantities since that job requires considerable strength. He helps her pack her products and deliver them to her customers, including residents, small businesses, and nonprofit organizations. Rural women may need training in key success factors in selling food products, especially production standards, branding, marketing, and bookkeeping to ensure that they can earn a profit from processing food. They need access to resources and knowledge to improve their skills and capabilities. Therefore, her eldest son, Mustafa, a high school student, does bookkeeping on a small scale, since he knows more English than both of his parents. He handles branding and marketing as well and utilizes social media outlets to promote his mother's products. He uploads pictures on Facebook, Instagram, and WhatsApp, an application that is highly popular in the Syrian community. His mother and father follow his lead and reach out to wider audiences, seeking more customers and soliciting more interest and orders. They attend local events to promote their products as well. I have personally helped her advertise and sell her products. Anytime local mosques have social events, we reserve a table for her to showcase and sell her products.

When I asked Umm Mustafa about the skills she gained when she grew up in one of the rural communities of Syria, her recent family dynamics, and survival mechanisms, and the roles she plays in both private and public paradigms, she replied:

> When we came to America, all I wanted was just to focus on my children getting an education. However, after a few months and even a few weeks, reality hit us hard, that we needed to work to support ourselves. Government funding was limited, and government-sponsored agencies have made it clear that after six months of arriving in America, we have to be on our own. We dreaded the fact that we do not speak English, and we figured there was no way for us to learn

it that fast, considering that I do not have an education in my native language, Arabic. (Umm Mustafa 2019)

That is why she had to think of ways to support her family, since her husband, even though he speaks and writes in Arabic, does not speak English, or have the proper education or even a high school diploma to have a decent-paying job. In Syria, he worked on his farm and made money from his farm's produce and crops. The only way for her and her family to survive and thrive is to extend her maternal, domestic role into public spaces. Umm Mustafa indicated how cooking, catering, and making Syrian jams, bread, Jubna (cheese), labneh, makdous, hummus, baba ghanoush, falafel, fatayer (meat, cheese, za'atar), stuffed grape leaves and zucchini, kibbeh, and sweets[6] are skills that help her sustain herself, her family, and even her community and preserve the authenticity of her Syrian culture. She indicated that she and other Syrian women in her community had to make a hard choice to work within their domestic terrain to support their families. She said:

> When I grew up in Syria, my parents, who strongly held on to our Syrian rural traditions, taught me that my husband is my heaven and hell and my home is my eternal space in life; I, the wife and mother, have to do what it takes to make my family's life work. Divorce was never an option for us [even though Islam allows it, giving women their full rights when divorced]. Any time I argued with my husband, I was never encouraged by my parents to leave my house. Rather, they would argue with me and ask me to go back and amend the situation, even if my husband was at fault. I was always taught that women can always think of ways to survive and make life work. And, the best woman, wife, and mother is the one who makes numerous sacrifices for her family. Thus, I had to think hard about the best ways to survive after we've lost everything and left everything behind. So, if I fail in this country, I fail my family forever; I fail my heritage. The best way to survive is to use my home skills like my cooking skills. After you and other organizations indicated that there would be demand for our Syrian food, and suggested we should try, I decided to take advantage of the situation. After several events and the multiple orders we got, I knew I could improve my family's situation by selling Syrian food. (Umm Mustafa 2019)

Like many rural women, she is a key agent for achieving the transformational economic and social change needed for sustainable development.

Umm Mustafa is one of many Syrian refugee women who empower themselves through the utilization of their rural literacies and skills; these skills are empowering not only to their well-being and their families but also to the overall economic productivity of the Syrian refugee community. Umm Mustafa represents women-led entrepreneurship and women's connections to high-value markets. She and other Syrian refugee women doing similar work demonstrate leadership and participation in their communities and promote their agency—defying the dominant narrative that women who come from rural areas and possess rural literacies, especially refugee women who do not speak the main language of the host country, English, are unproductive and dependent on their male partners or governmental systems for support and survival. By embodying Syrian food literacies, Syrian refugee women have proven what many food justice advocates have asserted: "the cultivation and distribution of culturally identified foods can provide opportunities for economic growth . . . [and] links between food and cultural identity can serve as sources of wealth for their communities, providing culturally relevant underpinnings for green economic growth" (Alkon and Agyeman 2011, 11). Through Syrian food practices, these women are intimately performing and sustaining their Syrian identity, culture, and community. They practice "cultural continuity" through honoring their Syrian rural practices and bringing them to life in a place where non-Western cultural traditions are defamed and excluded—ultimately, exercising food sovereignty and moving beyond a marginalized status into a negotiation position.

After coming to the United States and being able to utilize their rural expertise, these women are becoming literacy *sponsors* who are working to benefit themselves, their families, and their communities, ultimately giving and securing power. I extend Brandt's definition of sponsorship, showing how these women are enacting and adopting self-sponsorship from their domestic terrain. Their literacy practices highlight not only their agency but also bring a new definition of *sponsors*. Brandt defines *sponsor* as "any agents, local or distant, concrete or abstract, who enable, support, teach, or model, as well as recruit, regulate, suppress, or withhold literacy—and gain advantage by it in some way" (Brandt 1998, 166). The agency is attributed to an outside agent, not to the person whose literacy is being affected. I argue, however, that besides outside sponsors, including me, these refugee women perceive their use of these literacies as self-sponsorship: re-enacting their literacy practices and determining the most efficient decisions and actions needed in their unique situations. These decisions and practices enable not only their families but also their own—as women, wives, and mothers—survival in the diasporic space.

Umm Mustafa is one of many Syrian refugee women who, with no prior business or entrepreneurial skills, has become a successful microbusiness owner, supporting and providing for her family. Her experience helps to disrupt the cycle of "stereotyping and stigmatization" that is perpetuated by popular media, which holds that rural people lack literate skills (Donehower 38). What is fascinating about Umm Mustafa and her counterparts is that they are successful not only within their community but also outside it, in the surrounding Western communities that have a strikingly different language and culture. Their food literacy practices affirm "how images of women as victims have been transformed into images of survivors and responders taking on the task of ensuring household and community safety and survival" (Leyesa 2019, 17). Umm Mustafa's enactment of her authentic Syrian food literacies further confirms women's contribution "to local and national economies and to food production and to achieve food security and improved nutrition, in particular in poor and vulnerable households" (UN CSW 62).

Syrian Food Literacy: Making a Place

Syrian refugee women's sustenance of their rural and food practices has made these practices move beyond the confinement of the walls of their rural Syrian communities to other far places and nations. Before the Syrian refugee crisis and the settlement of Syrian refugees in Canada and the United States, Syrian cuisine or even the Syrian organic, natural ways of cooking, canning, or making jams were hardly known among Westerners. With Syrian refugees starting several small businesses and effectively employing their rural literacy practices, they have been able to strategically engage in food literacy, allowing for Syrian cuisine to make a place for itself. Being active participants and vital agents in sustaining their rural practices and eventually new lives and communities, Syrian refugee women have proven that women's contributions are significant. These women present themselves as "liberated rather than limited" (Fink 1992, 2). They have been able to negotiate gender lines and provide for their families, refusing to be trapped by the dominant view of an agrarian tradition that places women in the backseat, in a state of subordination and marginalization. Even though they are not necessarily crossing gender lines by staying true to their gender roles as mothers and wives, they are, however, becoming productive from their domestic space. Their gendered practices complicate the binary construct of working and succeeding in either public or domestic spaces.

Back in Syria, these women were considered illiterate. They were representative of the "Jeffersonian" ideology: their contributions were not considered significant; they do not have seats at the table or do not contribute to the conversation, and their main role in life is to do domestic work and comfort and support men (Fink 1992, 19). Taking a more active role in their new community and refugee situation, they establish and decentralize power. Men, like Umm Mustaf's Husband (Abu Mustafa) and her son Mustafa, are not superior, as the normative narrative implies; rather, Umm Mustafa is vigorous, fully involved, and not only participating in but strongly capable of decision-making. Her engagement and enactment of rural food literacies resist the masculinist thinking and superiority attached to their image. Utilizing their rural literacy allows these women to honor their rural Syrian heritage and to present it positively, empowering themselves and incentivizing their children to celebrate their rural Syrian heritage. By enacting rural literacies, these women have not reinscribed narrow roles for women or relied on preservationist narratives; rather, these literacies have functioned as "a tool of self-expression, self-actualization, resistance, even accommodation and power" (Williams-Forson 2006, 2). These women make it possible to maintain connections to their life back home while securing economic mobility: securing cultural continuity and survivance, food sovereignty, and women's empowerment.

The rural literacy practices, artifacts, and products created by Syrian refugee women are omnipresent and ubiquitous in the community where these refugees are currently living. When I interviewed Umm Mustafa, she showed me the various types of food she prepares and explained the steps she takes, and the nutrition fact labels she makes with the help of her son. We tasted and tested many of her products. As a Syrian woman who lived up to high school age in the suburbs of Damascus in Syria, I was raised to learn and embody domestic roles and excel in domestic jobs which Umm Mustafa proudly employs and celebrates. Every summer, my family used to spend days taking care of one of our farms in Ghouta,[7] an irrigated agricultural area in the Damascus countryside. We used to collect different crops ranging from fruits like apricots, peaches, and plums to vegetables like eggplants, cucumbers, tomatoes, and okra. My mother taught me the natural ways to make different types of jams, pickles, and makdous, for example, from these products, which would sustain us during the winter season when these items would not be available. Having this experience and knowledge of preservation, which I continue to practice in my own domestic space, allowed me to bond with Umm Mustafa and other Syrian refugee women as we talked about the natural, organic methods to make healthy food. As I interviewed these Syrian women, I could not help but realize the literacy synergy we have.

My previous experiences growing up and identifying with the same issues and values allowed me to relate to Syrian refugee women, especially since I have not abandoned what I learned in Syria. I became a familiar face. I found myself in Steven Alvarez's position and replicating his research practice: "I am participating in the literacy practices I write about, and my closeness to these communities indicates the depths of respect and direct contact I invest into community literacies and what the communities invest in me" (Alvarez, "Latinx and Latin American Community Literacy Practices en Confianza" 2017, 219). The bonding experience with these women allowed me to ground my research in "trust, respect, and sustainability en confianza . . . [which] translates literally as 'confidence,' but in practice confianza means reciprocating a relationship where individuals feel cared for. [It] involves exchanging mutual respect, critical reflection, caring and group participation. Confianza is dialogical trust, acceptance and confirmation between researchers and communities" (Alvarez, "Latinx and Latin American Community Literacy Practices En Confianza" 2017, 219–20).

My interactions with Syrian refugee women motivated me to see how their gendered literacy practices can bring these women to the forefront, locating and acknowledging what has been ignored of the rural past, while legitimizing these practices. In my frequent, ongoing interactions with them, we shared meaning-making processes: construing, understanding, and making sense of the brutal life events that as Syrians we have endured. During the interviews, we had flashbacks about these women's experiences in Syria during the war and how their rural practices sustained them as they were held hostage in their towns and were deprived of any supplies or amenities going in or out. As Cynthia Cockburn states, war affects women from the "bedroom to the battlefield" (Cockburn 1998, 8). Women are active on battlefields and experience war in less visible and more intimate sites like the body, the bedroom, and the household (Culcasi 2019, 465). Umm Mustafa described how she and other women in the same town bore the burden of food shortages and had to preserve the scarce food supply they were left with to sustain everyone during that vicious time. She mentioned how before the war, they would give corn cobs for livestock feed. However, during the war, they urgently felt the need to preserve every tiny piece of food they had. For instance, instead of using corn cobs for livestock feed, after peeling and drying the corn, they ground the whole corn using a manual stone grain grinder to make flour for batters and dough that would feed as many people as possible. This job required strenuous physical work, and the flour produced was coarse, which made kneading the dough more difficult since everything was done by hand. She said,

> When our town was under siege, a few of my female neighbors and I would get together and split the jobs. We would take turns splitting the dry corn into pieces and eventually grinding them, making doughs and eventually bread. We would share the scarce milk supply the livestock gave us and make dairy products that would survive with no electricity like Syrian white cheese and labneh balls.[8] We preserved every small grain of salt we had as it was our natural preservative, preserving our food and a source of natural medicine. (Umm Mustafa 2019)

For them, salt was a source of sustenance and survivance, preserving their food, healing their bodily wounds, and figuratively preserving whatever is left from their lives. And, the sound of the manual stone grain grinder became a consoling therapy that would help these women forget or imagine forgetting the noise of bombs and gunshots.

Umm Mustafa's narrative further confirms that "[w]omen are the first to suffer the impacts of the lack of water and food because they are the ones who have to look for solutions. They have to travel long distances in search of water for their families. They are also the first to go without food so that their children and husbands can eat" (Leyesa 2019, 21). These stories showcase the "gendered realities" and the chapters of hard domestic life these women skillfully utilized to sustain the life of the community that endured some of the ugliest, bloodiest, and hardest days of their lives. The literacy practices they utilized to survive, like the use of corn, for example, were extended to the new context, the Western context; therefore, it is essential not to have these "gendered realities." Even though they were not taught to value their female voices or contributions, it is still necessary to acknowledge the adaptations they have made to sustain their families.

The artifacts Umm Mustafa is making are an example of food literacy produced by Syrian refugee women, who have created a lived experience that should not be ignored, forgotten, or erased. For these Syrian refugee women like Umm Mustafa, food making and preserving have become more than a means of sustenance; it is a constant, lived practice and reminder of the rich and diverse culture that has been displaced or destroyed by the Syrian civil war. Their work in this country, which stems from their home-cooking skills, and which was previously considered minor domestic chores, has given them a chance to share their stories and recipes, preserve their culture, ensure a sense of food justice, and ultimately empower themselves as they establish their place, which has been forgotten or ignored.

Migration of Literacies through Food Literacy

In recent years, after the arrival and settlement of Syrian refugees in the D.C. region, there has been a steady interest in Syrian food and cuisine. Popular interest in the transnational migrations of Syrian food connected to multilingual, transnational, and cross-cultural issues is starting to emerge. Many nonprofit agencies are sponsoring Syrian refugees and immigrants. For example, "Mozaic,"[9] founded in 2014, is one of several nonprofit organizations which has helped Syrian refugee families in the D.C., Maryland, and Virginia (DMV) area. One of its projects is "SafarTas,"[10] which was founded to create opportunities for refugees and immigrants in the DMV area and to allow the American community to taste the authentic recipes that originate directly from Syria. The concept of food and the choice of names for these projects evoke a sense of nostalgia and connection to home, and, at the same time, create a name for Syrian food in Western contexts. For instance, the word "Mozaic" has an important connotation in Syrian culture, as Syria is home to some of the oldest mosaics ever found. Artists in the region use small pieces of colored stone and glass to create large images of daily life, animals, or complex geometric shapes. The word "SafarTas" has a more important connotation, especially in rural cultures. A safartas, a tiffin carrier that functions like a lunchbox, is opened by unlocking a small latch on either side of the handle. It is generally made from steel or aluminum and is widely used in Syria, especially in agrarian areas where farmers would bring lunch with them because it safely contains the food in separate compartments and keeps it fresh and hot. It comes in two or three tiers. It was and still is one of the main kits that are used as containers to carry a packed meal.

As a child, I remember carrying it to the farms where my brothers and father would be working. Mozaic and SafarTas use the same idea to recreate the essence of the Syrian home and normalcy. This is what they wrote on their website:

> Mozaic has created SafarTas to help recruit these chefs and identify a market for their special recipes. The start was very successful when we identified a market for catering among friends and families. Soon, the word spread so quickly to the point where Mozaic started receiving catering orders for big events. That is when we decided to establish this business in the state of Virginia to recruit these

Figure 1.1. Drawing of a *safartas*, a tiffin carrier that functions like a lunchbox. Credit: Artwork by Walaa Hijazi.

chefs and help connect them to the open market while facilitating the opportunity for everyone to enjoy real authentic rich Syrian food.

The name is doing both: introducing a new cultural concept to the American public as well as promoting a sense of familiarity, nostalgia, and comfort, essentially bridging the gap between the two cultures. Safartas was used in Syria as an efficient system that regularly delivers hot lunches to farmers; similarly, it is used in the metropolitan area to deliver catered Syrian food to American customers. Umm Mustafa, doing multiple jobs for SafarTas, mentioned getting constant orders from regular and repeat customers. Syrian women are grateful for the work Mozaic has created for the Syrian refugee community and commented on how they did not think that something very basic like safartas, something regularly used in Syria, in mostly agrarian places, would become this reputable in the United States and among various communities, whose cultural values differ.

These words with their important connotation and connection to Syrian culture create a level of authenticity for Syrian food in an American context. Steven Alvarez introduced the notion of "taco literacy," which refers to examining and connecting Latino immigrant communities through the seemingly simple acts of eating. He explains that

> food is also very much an emotional element of immigrants' experiences. Food can sustain affective connections and build publics across borders and languages. These important, emotional networks should not be overlooked. Rather, composition classes can access them by engaging students in a sensorial literacy that includes embodied, emotional experiences—like eating and thinking about eating—experiences that activate students' imaginations and fire their will to act. (Alvarez 2016)

Alvarez emphasizes that the influence of Mexican food in the United States is "deeply connected to local intercultural experiences that extend beyond disciplines, genres, and national borders" (Alvarez 2016). Similarly, through my research, I have come to discover the deep emotional connections to food shared transnationally among Syrian immigrants and refugees across the United States. SafarTas and the food Syrian refugee women make is a way to connect with cultural literacies from people's home countries; it allows for transnational migration and for preserving the culture of those who migrate. These women are achieving success through displacement, which speaks volumes about the agency and resilience they show in this country. Through the displacement of Syrians and the migration of Syrian refugees, most importantly refugee women, Syrian literacy practices, particularly food, have crossed borders. Sharing Syrian food with community members became a humanizing opportunity for coming together to learn from, especially as anti-immigrant sentiment toward Syrians, especially refugees, and increasingly hateful and dehumanizing rhetoric connected to xenophobic policies have increased and become emotionally distressing.

COOKING: MORE WAYS OF DECISION MAKING AND FOOD SOVEREIGNTY

The food literacy practices presented in this chapter challenge this characterization by showing how these practices prove economic functioning and productivity as well as cultural continuity and community development. This chapter adds to the scholarly attention that has been directed towards what David Bell (2006, 154) calls the "transnational rural" or the way the rural can be imagined globally. It confirms the idea that ruralities circulate across nations and geographical regions. Like "motherhood and apple pie [that are] symbols for which wars are fought [and that] spring from an American identity grounded in pure, honest, rural values" (Fink 1992, 11), the rural literacy practices of Syrian refugee women, including the fatayer and the sweets, stem from a rich Syrian culture that is making a name for itself in Western lands through these women. Syrian refugee women did not come to the United States to abandon their Syrian culture and identities but to honor them and to improve their lives. Uprooted Syrian refugee women's pasts and intense life experiences affect their identities and the choices they make. Tensions that arise from their refugee experiences open a space for agency. In listening to them and observing their literacy practices, I demonstrate how these women retain and maintain agency, cultural foodways, and cultural survivance through their food literacies and entrepreneurship. Their food practices, consistent with their cultural identities and embedded in community networks, act as a project that legitimizes their place and empower them to perform community existence, care, and belonging; they are recipes asserting identity and agency through food performance, security, justice, and sovereignty.

REFERENCES

Abdi, Cawo Mohamed. 2007. "Convergence of Civil War and the Religious Right: Reimagining Somali Women." *Signs* 33, no. 1: 183–207. https://www.journals.uchicago.edu/doi/abs/10.1086/518393.

Alkon, Alison Hope, and Julian Agyeman. 2011. *Cultivating Food Justice: Race, Class, and Sustainability*. Food, Health, and the Environment. Cambridge: MIT Press.

Alvarez, Steven. 2016. "Taco Literacies: Ethnography, Foodways, and Emotions through Mexican Food Writing." *Composition Forum* 34. https://compositionforum.com/issue/34/taco-literacies.php.

———. 2017. "Latinx and Latin American Community Literacy Practices En Confianza." *Composition Studies* 45, no. 2: 219–21. https://compstudiesjournal.com/fall-2017-45-2.

Bell, David. 2006. "Variations on the Rural Idyll." In *Handbook of Rural Studies*, edited by Paul Cloke, Terry Marsden, and Patrick Mooney, 149–60. London: SAGE.

Bigelow, Martha, and Robin Lovrien Schwarz. 2010. *Adult English Language Learners with Limited Literacy*. Washington, DC: National Institute for Literacy.

Brandt, Deborah. 1998. "Sponsors of Literacy." *College Composition and Communication* 49, no. 2: 165–85.

Cockburn, Cynthia. *The Space Between Us: Negotiating Gender and National Identities in Conflict*. London: Zed Books, 1998.

Culcasi, Karen. 2019. "'We Are Women and Men Now': Intimate Spaces and Coping Labour for Syrian Women Refugees in Jordan." *Transactions of the Institute of British Geographers* 44, no. 3: 463–78. https://doi.org/10.1111/tran.12292.

Cultural Orientation Resource Center (COR Center). 2014, November. "Refugees from SYRIA." http://www.culturalorientation.net/learning/backgrounders.

Denzin, Norman K. 2009. *Qualitative Inquiry Under Fire: Toward a New Paradigm Dialogue*. Walnut Creek, CA: Left Coast Press.

Desjardins, Ellen, and Hailburton, Kawartha. 2013. *"Making Something Out of Nothing": Food Literacy among Youth, Young Pregnant Women, and Young Parents Who Are at Risk for Poor Health*. Food Literacy for Life. https://foodsecurecanada.org/sites/foodsecurecanada.org/files/food_literacy_study_technical_report_web_final.pdf.

Donehower, Kim. 2007. "Rhetorics and Realities: The History and Effects of Stereotypes about Rural Literacies." In *Rural Literacies*, edited by Kim Donehower, Charlotte Hogg, and Eileen Schell, 37–76. Carbondale: Southern Illinois University Press.

Donehower, Kim, Charlotte Hogg, and Eileen E. Schell. 2007. *Rural Literacies*. Studies in Writing & Rhetoric. Carbondale: Southern Illinois University Press.

Ferrell, Susan T., and Aimee Howley. 1991. "Adult Literacy in Rural Areas." *Journal of Reading* 34, no. 5: 368–72.

Fink, Deborah. 1992. *Agrarian Women: Wives and Mothers in Rural Nebraska, 1880–1940*. Studies in Rural Culture. Chapel Hill: University of North Carolina Press.

Gallagher, Sally K. 2012. *Making Do in Damascus: Navigating a Generation of Change in Family and Work*. 1st ed. Contemporary Issues in the Middle East. Syracuse, NY: Syracuse University Press.

Hitchcock, Peter. 1993. *Dialogics of the Oppressed*. Minneapolis: University of Minnesota Press.

Jeffrey, Julie Roy. 1979. *Frontier Women: The Trans-Mississippi West, 1840–1880*. 1st ed. American Century Series. New York: Hill and Wang.

Lenette, Caroline, Apuk Maror, and Serena Manwaring. 2019. "Mothers & Daughters: Redefining Cultural Continuity through South Sudanese Women's Artistic

Practices." *Journal of Intercultural Studies* 40, no. 6: 751–71. https://doi.org/10.1080/07256868.2019.1675618.

Leyesa, Daryl L. 2019, November. "Women's Resistance against Authoritarianism in Brazil, the Philippines, and Rojava (Northern Syria)." In *Right to Food and Nutrition Watch*, no. 11: 17–25.

McBrien, J. L. 2005. "Educational Needs and Barriers for Refugee Students in the United States: A Review of the Literature." *Review of Educational Research* 75, no. 3: 329–64.

Umm Mustafa. 2019, February 21. Interview with author.

Williams-Forson, Psyche A. 2006. *Building Houses Out of Chicken Legs: Black Women, Food, and Power*. Black Women Writers Series. Chapel Hill: University of North Carolina Press.

NOTES

1. Data collection for my IRB-approved study took different stages. Before I started planning for the literacy class, I was involved in organizing community events at the mosque, welcoming the new groups of refugees and helping them settle in, furnishing their houses, helping with groceries, and translating documents. Due to cultural and language familiarity, I became close to many of them, who started expressing interest in enrolling their children in Quran and Islamic studies classes.

2. I conducted the interviews in Arabic, mainly the Syrian dialect. A formal question-and answer interview format is rigid; therefore, my interviews took the form of a dialogue. Since these women's English proficiency was basic, the IRB office required that I translate all of the recruitment and consent forms to Arabic.

3. Eid represents Muslim festivals, in particular Eid al-Fitr (the religious holiday celebrated by Muslims worldwide that marks the end of Ramadan, the Islamic holy month of fasting) and Eid al-Adha (the second of the two Islamic holidays; it corresponds with the height of the Hajj, the pilgrimage to Mecca).

4. The first official interview took place on February 21, 2019. Fatima is a pseudonym. She and her family arrived in the United States in October 2015. She is in her late thirties. She has three boys, the oldest Mustafa a high school student and two in middle school. Even though she didn't receive any schooling at all, Umm Mustafa has an in-house catering business.

5. In Arab cultures, mainly Syrian cultures and more specifically rural and suburban cultures, married women with children are addressed by "Umm" plus the name of the eldest child, mainly the male child. "Umm" means the mother of. If the family does not have male children, they use the name of the eldest daughter. Fatima's eldest son's name is Mustafa (pseudonym), so she is called Umm Mustafa (mother of Mustafa). In these cultures, it is an honor to address married women with children this way. Fathers are addressed by "Abu," which means the father of.

6. For images of the different Syrian food Umm Mustafa makes and sells, see the website of "SafarTas," a business project that was founded by Mozaic, a nonprofit organization, that helps Syrian refugees in the DMV area utilize their culinary

skills and sell authentic Syrian food to the American community: https://safar-tas.org/gallery-2. Umm Mustafa is one of their chefs. She sells some of her products through them.

7. Ghouta (غُوطَةُ دِمَشْقَ) is a countryside area in southwestern Syria that surrounds the city of Damascus along its eastern and southern rim. It has become well known in the West, due to enduring the infamous chemical attack by the Assad regime.

8. Labneh is sack yogurt; it is yogurt that is strained to remove most of its whey, resulting in a thicker consistency than unstrained yogurt, while preserving yogurt's distinctive sour taste. Labneh balls are made by making labneh extra thick and then drying under the sun to make it firm and last longer. It is one of Umm Mustafa's products that is in high demand.

9. For more information about this nonprofit organization, see its Facebook page: https://www.facebook.com/MozaicDMV.

10. For more information about the project, see this link: https://safar-tas.org/about-us.

Chapter 2

Building Sustainable Futures from Gastronomic Pasts

Cultural Heritage and the Rhetorical Value of Food

Ellen Platts

In December 2015, Tucson, Arizona, was recognized by the United Nations Educational, Scientific and Cultural Organization (UNESCO) Creative Cities Network (UCCN). As Tucson thus became an official Creative City of Gastronomy, a new initiative was born based on a gastronomy marked by "the influences of Native American, Northern Mexican or Sonoran, Mission-era Mediterranean, and American Ranch-Style Cowboy food traditions, among others," and "ancient food preparation practices and cooking techniques unique to southwestern North America, as part of our intangible heritage" (Nabhan et al. 2015, 5). The UNESCO Creative Cities Network (UCCN) recognizes cities that have placed specific creative fields at the center of their plans for sustainable development. Practices within these fields are conceived of as cultural heritage both by the UCCN and by the cities that nominate themselves to join.

In this chapter, I explore how the traditional heritage food practices of several distinct and overlapping communities are presented as one city-wide Tucsonan gastronomy within this institutional framework. Heritage has been described as "that part of the past which we select in the present for contemporary purposes . . . and choose to bequeath to the future" (Ashworth and Graham 2005, 7). This definition emphasizes the production of heritage through selection and urges an interrogation of the "contemporary purposes" for which heritage is used. As Michel-Rolph Trouillot reminds us, the production of heritage and historical narratives takes place in a broad range of everyday contexts. Trouillot emphasizes that through examining the silences in the narratives created through this production, we can "discover the differential exercise of power that makes some narratives possible and silences others" (Trouillot 1995, 5). As Cheryl Glenn argues, silence, whether forced or chosen, carries meaning (Glenn 2002, 262). Trouillot further notes that "not all [silences] are deliberate or even perceptible as such within the time of their production" (Trouillot 1995, 152–53). Exploring the ways in which silences are created in recent history and contemporary moments creates opportunities for addressing these problems and remedying harm. Glenn argues that silence itself can be a rhetorical strategy that at its best invites listening and conversation on a more equal footing. Identifying silences may then create opportunities to listen, reflect, and make necessary changes.

With these concepts in mind, what food heritage is being produced through the City of Gastronomy designation in Tucson, and what silences has this production created? In tracing out the connections between the UCCN, economic development, cultural heritage, presentations of food, and concerns of food justice, I draw on a theoretical approach to cultural heritage as a rhetorical tool to explore how food heritage in Tucson has been presented and perceived as one unified gastronomy. In this chapter, I explore the rhetorical strategies that support this shift and examine how this move supports the goals of the Creative City of Gastronomy, while deflecting other narratives. However, I argue that this same process of narrative creation also opens up possibilities to pursue alternative strategies as a tool for imagining and pursuing more just food systems.

HERITAGE AND RHETORICAL PERSUASION

Heritage is not a static description of what is, but rather a set of ideas that seek to "mobilize people and resources, to reform discourses, and to transform practices" (Hafstein 2012, 502). As a dynamic and changing set of categorizations, heritage narratives can be created by anyone, from the top down and bottom up alike. Heritage functions as a reflexive way for us to relate to and imagine ourselves and our futures (Kirshenblatt-Gimblett 2004, 52–65). This reflexivity also makes it possible for many imaginations to take place that "disrupt the official representation of who and what we are and what it is we do" (Hafstein 2012, 514). In this way, heritage is a form of persuasion, ripe for rhetorical strategy.

Heritage as persuasion works by inspiring audiences to act on an issue, mobilizing the past as "a standpoint, a performance, a metaphor, an ironic juxtaposition, an alternative vision, or a competing narrative for making strategic moves in broader struggles" (Samuels 2015, 7). Kathryn Lafrenz Samuels argues that the multiple rhetorical strategies identified by Aristotle—emotional (*pathos*) and trust-based (*ethos*), in addition to logical argument (*logos*)—are particularly useful for understanding how heritage is used to persuade (Samuels 2018, 115–20). Trust in the speaker, or *ethos,* is central to rhetorical uses of heritage, especially as it relates to conceptions of expertise. As heritage managers and those who seek to use heritage speak on heritage and interact with communities, issues of trust are paramount. How might a community decide that the speaker is trustworthy? This relies upon building relationships between the speaker and the community, a process that rhetoric assists "by accommodating itself to the particular, substantive, beliefs and desires of the listeners it addresses" (Beiner 1983, 116). Of relevance to the case discussed in this chapter, when cloaked in the institutional weight of an international body such as UNESCO, the speaker carries a particular kind of expertise. When an administrative body as large and institutionalized as UNESCO labels a particular activity, knowledge, place, or thing as heritage, it becomes transformed, reforming "existing customs, habits, pastimes, and expressions" into "objects of conservation through plans developed by local, national, and international experts with reference to officially sanctioned criteria of excellence" (Hafstein 2012, 511). This transformation creates tension between the administrative body perceived as an outsider, and the communities being often spoken for. These tensions extend through the process of drawing upon these kinds of designations as a strategy to create heritage narratives within particular frameworks.

SHIFTING PRIORITIES: THE UNESCO CREATIVE CITIES NETWORK

The UCCN was initiated in 2004 with the goal to "unlock the creative, social and economic potential of cultural industries held by local actors" (UNESCO 2013). Currently, the UCCN includes 295 cities from over 90 countries recognized in the seven creative fields of crafts and folk art, design, film, gastronomy, literature, music, and media arts. The UCCN supports cities as they "[strengthen] the value chain of local creative economies" in each of these fields in order to "make creativity a driver and an enabler for sustainable urban development" (UNESCO 2014).

This marks a shift from traditional approaches to heritage at UNESCO, an organization that also carries out better-known heritage work through the 1972 Convention Concerning the Protection of the World Cultural and Natural Heritage and the 2003 Convention on the Safeguarding of the Intangible Cultural Heritage. Though economic purposes have long fueled desires for UNESCO recognition (Meskell 2018), the UCCN reveals a different approach to heritage. Unlike World Heritage and the Intangible Heritage lists, participation in the UCCN is an explicit and sanctioned move towards using cultural heritage for development.

The 2003 Convention defines *intangible* cultural heritage as the "practices, representations, expressions, knowledge, skills—as well as the instruments, objects, artefacts and cultural spaces associated therewith—that communities, groups and, in some cases, individuals recognize as part of their cultural heritage" (UNESCO 2003). In appointing a City of Gastronomy to the UCCN, UNESCO looks for "local know-how, traditional culinary practices, and methods of cooking that have survived industrial/technological advancement," and a "tradition of hosting gastronomic festivals, awards, contests, and other broadly targeted means of recognition" (Pearson and Pearson 2016, 168). These guidelines map onto the definition of intangible cultural heritage. Through designation, the UCCN labels this intangible cultural heritage as worthy of attention and resources for the purposes of development. When intangible cultural heritage practices of food are recognized through this framework, they are positioned as gastronomy, a discursive field where styles of food production and consumption are negotiated—and often made very appealing to foodie tourists (Richards 2015, 5–17).

Intangible heritage is embodied within *people*, not places or things. Intangible heritage itself is a process of creative engagement in relationships between people, places, and practices passed down through generations. Drawing upon intangible heritage reorients the focus towards the process and the community, and not the object or place itself. Overemphasis of the economic value of this embodied knowledge, through strategies such as urban redevelopment and tourism, can lead to the counterproductive co-option or destruction of these subtle resources if inclusive strategies are not undertaken (Ross 2017, 31–56). When these resources center upon food, this kind of valuation impinges upon concerns of food justice, an issue to which I now turn by way of analysis of rhetorical strategies from the City of Gastronomy.

METHODS: AN ETHNOGRAPHY OF THE CITY OF GASTRONOMY

This chapter is part of an ethnography of Tucson as a City of Gastronomy that examines the UNESCO designation and how people use cultural heritage to imagine just and sustainable futures. Over the course of twenty total months of fieldwork in Tucson, my research practice included participation in community gardening, food distribution with mutual aid groups, and observing community organizing and nonprofit board meetings. Online and in-person interviews, participant observation, and archival research inform this project as I document the networks of people, funds, food resources, and ideas that have emerged from the City of Gastronomy designation. While conducting fieldwork in Tucson, I identified an intersection of issues of urban development, challenges such as climate change and food injustice, and intangible heritage—a certain something about surviving and thriving in a tough desert landscape. As a white woman born and raised on the green East Coast of the United States, I had much to learn from those who carried that heritage. Imbued within those intersecting ideas, concerns, and hopes, in the conversations I had, I felt the possibility of something different for the future—a goal for myself, my friends and communities in Tucson, my loved ones elsewhere, and the broader community of people in which I exist.

The themes described in this chapter focus on the connections between the rhetoric of gastronomy, concerns of food justice, and where the city of Tucson may be headed in the future. This chapter draws primarily from rhetorical analysis of documents authored by City of Gastronomy representatives and is supplemented with data drawn from interviews with residents of Tucson familiar with the designation. Per IRB protocol, pseudonyms are used for all interview participants.

MAKING GASTRONOMY OUT OF FOOD

The application process for Tucson's City of Gastronomy designation was initiated by then–City of Tucson historic preservation officer Jonathan Mabry and Gary Nabhan, an internationally recognized nature and food writer, ethnobotanist at the University of Arizona, and co-founder of Native Seeds/SEARCH, a seed bank that preserves heritage seeds. The process was then carried on by the local government in partnership with the University of Arizona. The motivation for submitting this application is described by Mabry, now Executive Director of the Tucson City of Gastronomy nonprofit organization, as increasing recognition of Tucson's agricultural and food heritage on a global scale, promoting Tucson as a culinary tourism destination, and facilitating international exchanges of best practices for using food heritage for sustainable economic development (Di Giovine et al. 2017, 210).

Tucson City of Gastronomy representatives define their understanding of gastronomy through the UCCN framework as being "more [broad] than just the cooking style of a particular area, extending it to food traditions as living cultural heritage" (Mabry 2020, viii). This "living cultural heritage" is linked to a number of data points to back up the claim to a long history of traditional foods and food knowledges. The most often-stated argument for Tucson's gastronomy is that the region has an agricultural history developed over

4,000 years, supplemented by a "300-year tradition of vineyards, orchards, and livestock ranching" (Nabhan et al. 2014, 5). Linking this history with the economic aspects of gastronomy that are central to the UCCN framework, more data is called forth: the application cites the 2,350 farms and ranches, 55 community and school gardens, and the 2,500-plus restaurants and drinking establishments in the region; the 14 percent of Tucson-area jobs provided by the food sector; and the number of programs to provide food for those in need that serve "190,000 individuals and families every year" (Mabry 2020, ix).

The response to the City of Gastronomy designation from some Tucsonans indicates that the rhetoric in the air about Tucson's history and current position is not persuasive to everyone. One of the major concerns about the designation is co-option—in which heritage practices that belong to a particular group have been brought into this designation without due diligence and inclusion throughout the process of applying for and managing the designation. Of particular concern is a lack of specific acknowledgment of the central contributions of the Tohono O'odham people, who are the farmers in this region that have tended to agriculture for the over four thousand years cited in the designation.

During an interview, I asked Marina, a Chicana former chef and current director in a community-focused nonprofit organization, specifically about this issue. She said, "It's not just about the O'odham experience, but it's also about the Black experience, and the Chinese experience, and about the cultural melding of the Mexican or whoever that is at this point. I mean, what is Mexican in this land?" In asking, "what is Mexican in this land?" she reflects upon histories of settler colonialism in what is now called southern Arizona, piecing together the histories of different groups coming together in this region under systems of violence and colonialism. Tucson community organizers Claudio Rodriguez and Nelda Ruiz, leaders of the grassroots group Regeneración, also highlight the ways in which they see this co-option as problematic. They argue that the designation should include "admission and support for the actual people preparing and picking foods and crops, and an acknowledgment of Mexican and Tohono O'odham people for preserving their foods, and recognition of the displacement that has happened here, on these lands that we call home" (Rodriguez and Ruiz 2016, 183–84). Averting this acknowledgment is seen to shift Mexican and Indigenous foodways into a broader Tucsonan gastronomy that is seemingly more accessible to Anglo communities and tourists.

This perception of what the City of Gastronomy designation is doing, and not doing, can be linked back to rhetorical moves made within the application materials. Within these materials and subsequent descriptions of the City of Gastronomy, Tucson's culinary heritage is described as "culturally layered" and as a "unique blend" (Mabry 2020, viii; Nabhan et al. 2014, 5).

The application describes Tucson's gastronomy as a blended one that mixes Native American, Sonoran, Spanish, and Ranch-Style Cowboy food traditions (Nabhan et al. 2014, 5). Wild plant harvesting, ancient food preparation practices, and cooking techniques are all considered to be part of a broadly Tucsonan intangible heritage and "are perceived as a source of identity and vitality for the people who live here" (Nabhan et al. 2014, 8). Within the application, the four-thousand-year agricultural history is not associated with the specific Indigenous groups who tended to that agriculture, the Tohono O'odham Nation and the Pascua Yaqui Tribe. This positions the history and traditions of particular communities as belonging to Tucson as a whole, and all of "the people who live here." The perception by community members that Mexican and Indigenous food traditions have been co-opted into a city-wide Tucsonan heritage is one possible reading of these materials, and importantly, one that has been selected by Tucson residents. While the application makes it clear that there are many cultural origins of these foodways, the collection of them together into one heritage creates a silence. Grouping together the diverse cultural origins of these foodways while not addressing the disparate consequences of historical trauma on distinct communities hides the marginalization and struggle of the communities who carry these traditions, evidenced by the concerns and critiques of Tucsonans not involved with the designation.

In the context of Tucson as a City of Gastronomy, the combination of specific cultural food practices under the banner of a city-wide heritage is also seen as a move to transform these practices into tools for development usable by others. As Marina said to me, in Tucson "we construct these ideas on the backs of ideology, and remembrance of these folks. But we don't actually support the folks that we have these ideas around. Even in the City of Gastronomy, part of the biggest thing is 4,100 years of continuous agriculture. And yet, how is this impacting the O'odham people, in any way, shape, or form?" In another interview, Dan, the chef and owner of a high-end bistro focused on incorporating traditional Mexican recipes, described it with an air of exasperation: "What is this again? It's some white people, somebody else, from somewhere else that came here to study the culture of the brown people that always been here, wrote a paper about it, applied, got this designation, and are enriching other white people off of it. You know, that's really kind of how I see it."

These Tucsonans have identified the silence within the City of Gastronomy narrative and are interrogating it. While not necessarily seeing themselves in the way the designation is being used, they do see themselves in the histories at the core of it. Identifying this gap creates an opening for possible changes in the future use of the designation, but, as Dan noted, this possibility may run into barriers due to the significant economic value the designation has already generated. Recasting certain food practices as part of a blended, city-wide gastronomy imbues them with the value needed for economic uses. For example, restaurants can now become Tucson City of Gastronomy-certified, an initiative that promises increased exposure to visitors through promotion by the tourism organization Visit Tucson, increased media coverage, and exclusivity in the Tucson restaurant community through the use of the City of Gastronomy brand (Tucson City of Gastronomy 2021). This process of valuation has succeeded, indicated by the $25 million per year increase in free media coverage since the designation and the 30 percent growth in lodging occupancy rates from 2016 to 2018 (Mabry 2020, ix). At the same time, this rhetorical move deflects from not-so-savory histories of settler colonialism, poverty, and food insecurity that do not appeal to foodie tourists and creates profit that is not equitably distributed to those who have carried food traditions for millennia.

FOOD JUSTICE IN THE CITY OF GASTRONOMY

This transformation of food into gastronomy is critical for the stated goals of the City of Gastronomy, such as promoting tourism, but its impacts on food justice concerns are less clear-cut. Though Tucson has been recognized for its gastronomy, many residents are not well-served by the food system as it stands. The organization Feeding America found that in 2019, Pima County, where Tucson is located, had a food insecurity rate of 13.3 percent (Feeding America 2021). The impact of the COVID-19 pandemic on the food system increased food insecurity across Arizona and within Pima County, with uneven distribution of insecurity across racial groups, and higher proportions of new and persistent food insecurity affecting non-white households (Owen et al. 2021). These challenges are exacerbated by gentrification resulting from development pressures in Tucson's downtown and surrounding areas, emerging out of a long history of urban renewal and racialization of the cityscape (Otero 2010).

These concerns are mentioned by City of Gastronomy rhetoric, which presents the designation as an economic booster that will "help us build a more sustainable, resilient, and secure food system based upon traditions, innovation, and food justice" (Nabhan et al. 2015, 4). The City of Gastronomy designation emphasizes the importance of the private sector in revitalizing the food system and the food economy, evidenced by one of the motives for application: "Designation will galvanize talents and creativity among our chefs, farmers, ranchers, educational institutions, nonprofit organizations, and businesses to make Tucson the cultural center and tourism destination for Southwest Borderlands cuisine" (Nabhan et al. 2015, 4). The transformation of specific food practices in Tucson into a citywide gastronomy designed for foodie tourists and used for economic development within the UCCN framework emphasizes market-based solutions to food insecurity that align with the emphases of the City of Gastronomy designation, rather than thorough abolishment of underlying systems of oppression in pursuit of food justice.

An example of this focus is the short-lived Mayor's Commission on Food Security, Heritage and Economy. Appointed for the first time in 2015, commissioners advised the mayor's office on ways to "increase access to healthy foods, increase demand and markets for locally produced foods, improve local food distribution, reduce food waste, expand composting and other uses of food waste, expand food industry job opportunities, and expand food entrepreneur support" (City of Tucson 2017). The description of the commission reiterates the emphasis on food security efforts in a market-based framework, especially in its emphasis on creating demand for local foods, expanding food-related job opportunities, and increasing support for entrepreneurship. Within the meetings, red tape surrounding the commission's scope made it difficult for commissioners to hold frank conversations about the complex topic of food justice (Mendelson 2017). Further complicating the commission's abilities to address this topic was the history of its creation. Tucson applied for the City of Gastronomy designation twice, in 2014 and 2015, winning the designation the second time. After its first rejection, UNESCO representatives suggested that the city was not chosen because it did not have a food commission in place. Then-Mayor Jonathan Rothschild "[shared] that the commission was formed in direct response to the application for the designation, standing as the singular piece missing from a complete and successful application" (Mendelson 2017, 41). As of the time of this writing in 2022, the commission is defunct due to a continual lack of quorum in commission meetings, indicating the infeasibility of addressing food justice concerns through this mechanism, and casting doubt upon the original purpose of the commission itself.

As Julian Agyeman and Jesse McEntee argue, any campaign that claims it is fighting for food justice and yet "re-creates conventional exchange-value markets that fetishize profit and commodification of food" will continue to focus only on the symptoms of food insecurity, and not the root of the issue, which is based in structural racism and classism (Agyeman and McEntee 2014, 217). Food justice is a form of social justice that requires consideration and movement on all forms of inequality and oppression (Cadieux and Slocum 2015; Sbicca 2018). Addressing only concerns of economic and physical access to food, which could be solved through private sector investment, does not get to the heart of the issue. Food justice requires a recognition of past and present conditions of structural inequality and explicitly calls out how these conditions affect contemporaneous food systems. Focusing primarily on economic support creates another silence by drawing upon the food heritage that has long been central to the lives and livelihoods of the residents of Tucson and the surrounding region while not addressing the historical harm that accompanies that heritage.

PURSUING POTENTIAL: REFRAMING FOOD AND HERITAGE NARRATIVES

While institutions such as the UCCN frame heritage narratives towards the ends of sustainability through economic development, ongoing creative and engaging activity between the people that form the core of intangible cultural heritage provides opportunities for taking up a new vocabulary. The embodied nature of an intangible cultural heritage of food means that these practices live within communities and are regenerated when people cook the food they like and can afford to eat every day and teach their families and children these traditions. This everyday nature of food creates opportunities for reframing separate from institutional rhetoric. This reframing is happening in Tucson, both in concert with and pushing against the City of Gastronomy designation. In continued conversation with Marina, she said that "as long as it doesn't try to be this monochromatic smattering of 'this is Tucson,' but that it's this rich mosaic and patterning of so many contributing forces," the City of Gastronomy designation has immense potential. But when I asked her what her ideal city of Tucson would look like, both as a City of Gastronomy and beyond, she simply said, "Everybody would have enough. Everybody would have enough so that they can start to dream about what it would look like to thrive." Addressing core disparities that exist within this so-called City of Gastronomy is the first step that must be taken.

These are complicated stories, with actors and narratives that are continually changing. Through supporting, funding, and advocating for the communities that hold these stories, however, the City of Gastronomy designation could play a crucial supporting role, different from the path it is now seen to be traversing. The currently perceived path is seen to be a "rah rah rah thing," as Dan put it, focused on bringing in tourists and external funds—a path that gives him "very muddied feelings." While tourist dollars come into Tucson businesses, it is not clear to residents that that money is then invested in the community. The City of Gastronomy is not perceived to be for local residents, but instead primarily for visitors. But the resources and prestige behind the UCCN presents an opportunity to create what Marina described as "living, thriving communities that are localized and connected . . . that are innovating and remembering and rethinking and striving for a more just and equitable society." In thinking about their dreams for Tucson, other interviewees saw the City of Gastronomy designation as a potential meeting ground for networks of city support and community mutual aid to ensure that everyone has enough to eat, to build economies of scale for local businesses and farms, and to ensure continued investment in community resources. Realizing these opportunities and bringing them to life is a long-term project, the pathways of which are only hazily articulated by the keepers of the City of Gastronomy designation. Many of these goals are more actively pursued by community groups focusing on mutual aid, free grocery distribution, home gardening, eviction protection, and an increased minimum wage, to name but a few of the dynamic areas of action in Tucson. Supporting these existing advocacy and mutual aid efforts with the cultural and economic cachet of the City of Gastronomy designation would go a long way to actualize the possibilities described here.

What should come now is a further reframing of the narrative around what and who the City of Gastronomy designation is for and centering and supporting the voices calling for these efforts to reframe. This narrative should interrogate the historical and geographical frameworks that cause food injustice in the first place. Considering these frameworks emphasizes the agency of communities to decide what kind of food they need and desire, and to navigate the food geographies accessible to them (Kato 2013, 369–91). This would be a crucial step towards remedying the harm caused by silencing in this designation thus far. The themes described in this chapter illustrate potential pathways for better incorporating food justice concerns into the work of the City of Gastronomy, a topic I take up further in other writing. Future research could more deeply examine how the food system in Tucson is shaped by structural power and historical context, highlighting openings for moving towards a more just food system and guiding the direction of organizations that aim to contribute to such a system.

CONCLUSION: IMAGINING ALTERNATIVE FUTURES

As COVID-19 changed what fieldwork looked like, I started spending more and more time online, immersing myself in the networks found on platforms like Facebook and Instagram. In closing this chapter, one particular Instagram post comes to mind, a clear and effective reframing of food concepts toward an alternative path. Posted by Flowers & Bullets, an urban farming cooperative founded to support underserved Chicanx, Mexicanx, and Latinx communities on Tucson's south side, the image is of black text on a white background. It reads, "We must stop seeing food security as the pathway to eradicating hunger. It reduces food to an economic commodity when food is the basis of culture, of life itself. Food sovereignty is the pathway to imagining something fundamentally different. Something better" (Flowers & Bullets 2021). This is an explicit reorientation of the rhetoric of food security and economic development to one centered in the life and the imagination of something new. It is rooted in the intangible cultural heritage practices of food, which are based "in a people's body of deep historical—yet flexible and evolving—experience in particular places" (Niles 2018, 346). By not presenting precisely what the "something better" may look like in this call to thought, the post encourages reflection and imagination—a productive silence that invites one to contribute. This regenerative rhetorical possibility aligns with the evolving nature of cultural heritage, where the past is held close and yet continually dreamed, described, and drawn upon anew.

REFERENCES

Agyeman, Julian, and Jesse McEntee. 2014. "Moving the Field of Food Justice Forward through the Lens of Urban Political Ecology." *Geography Compass* 8, no. 3 (March): 211–20. https://doi.org/10.1111/gec3.12122.

Ashworth, G. J., and Brian Graham. 2005. "Senses of Place, Senses of Time and Heritage." In *Senses of Place: Senses of Time*, ed. G. J. Ashworth and Brian Graham, 3–12. Burlington: Ashgate.

Beiner, Ronald. 1983. *Political Judgement*. London: Methuen.

Cadieux, Kirsten Valentine, and Rachel Slocum. 2015, December 1. "What Does It Mean to Do Food Justice?" *Journal of Political Ecology* 22, no. 1: 1–26. https://doi.org/10.2458/v22i1.21076.

City of Tucson. 2015, May 5. "Commission on Food Security, Heritage, and Economy." City of Tucson Office of the City Clerk. https://www.tucsonaz.gov/files/clerks/uploads/bccfiles/19300.pdf.

Di Giovine, Michael, Jonathan Mabry, and Teresita Majewski. 2017. "Moveable Feasts: Food as Revitalizing Cultural Heritage." In *Heritage in Action: Making the Past in the Present*, ed. Helaine Silverman, Emma Waterton, and Steve Watson, 201–16. Cham: Springer.

Feeding America. 2021. "Food Insecurity in Pima County, 2019." Map the Meal Gap. http://map.feedingamerica.org/county/2017/overall/arizona/county/pima.

Flowers & Bullets. 2021, February 20. Instagram photo. https://www.instagram.com/p/CLiY8nehjxM.

Glenn, Cheryl. 2002. "Silence: A Rhetorical Art for Resisting Discipline(s)." *JAC* 22, no. 2: 261–91.

Hafstein, Valdimar T. 2012. "Cultural Heritage." In *A Companion to Folklore*, ed. R. F. Bendix and G. Hasan-Rokem, 500–519. Malden: Blackwell.

Kato, Yuki. 2013. "Not Just the Price of Food: Challenges of an Urban Agriculture Organization in Engaging Local Residents." *Sociological Inquiry* 83, no. 3: 369–91. https://doi.org/10.1111/soin.12008.

Kirshenblatt-Gimblett, Barbara. 2004, May 1. "Intangible Heritage as Metacultural Production." *Museum International* 56, no. 1–2: 52–65. https://doi.org/10.1111/j.1350-0775.2004.00458.x.

Lafrenz Samuels, Kathryn. 2015. "Introduction: Heritage as Persuasion." In *Heritage Keywords Rhetoric and Redescription in Cultural Heritage*, ed. Kathryn Lafrenz Samuels and Trinidad Rico, 3–28. Boulder: University Press of Colorado.

———. 2018. *Mobilizing Heritage: Anthropological Practice and Transnational Prospects*. Cultural Heritage Studies. Gainesville: University Press of Florida.

Mabry, Jonathan B. 2020. "Foreword." In *A Desert Feast: Celebrating Tucson's Culinary Heritage*, by Carolyn J. Niethammer. Southwest Center Series. Tucson: University of Arizona Press.

Mendelson, Jaclyn Haley. 2017. "Food Justice Policy and the UNESCO City of Gastronomy: How the Designation Can Lay a Positive Foundation for the Future of the Food System of Tucson, Arizona." Bachelor's, University of Arizona.

Meskell, Lynn. 2018. *A Future in Ruins: UNESCO, World Heritage, and the Dream of Peace*. New York: Oxford University Press.

Nabhan, Gary, Vanessa Bechtol, Jonathan Mabry, and Rafael de Grenade. 2014. "Tucson, Arizona: An International Culinary Destination." Santa Cruz Valley Heritage Alliance. http://www.santacruzheritage.org/files/file/CityGastronomy_Web.pdf.

Nabhan, Gary, Rafael de Grenade, Jonathan Mabry, and Vanessa Bechtol. 2015, July 4. "Creative Cities Network Application Form: Tucson." City of Tucson. https://www.tucsonaz.gov/files/pdsd/COG_Application_Tucson-signed.pdf.

Niles, Daniel. 2018. "Agricultural Heritage and Conservation Beyond the Anthropocene." In *The Oxford Handbook of Public Heritage Theory and Practice*, ed. Angela M. Labrador and Neil Asher Silberman. Oxford: Oxford University Press.

Otero, Lydia R. 2010. *La Calle: Spatial Conflicts and Urban Renewal in a Southwest City*. Tucson: University of Arizona Press.

Owen, Gigi, Eden Kinkaid, Laurel Bellante, and Sean Maccabe. 2021. "State of the Tucson Food System Report: Assessing the Impacts of the COVID-19 Pandemic in Southern Arizona 2020–2021." Tucson: University of Arizona Center for Regional Food Studies. https://crfs.arizona.edu/sites/crfs.arizona.edu/files/2020–21%20State%20of%20the%20Tucson%20Food%20System%20Report.pdf.

Pearson, David, and Thomas Pearson. 2016, April 2. "Branding Food Culture: UNESCO Creative Cities of Gastronomy." *Journal of International Food & Agribusiness Marketing* 28, no. 2: 164–76. https://doi.org/10.1080/08974438.2015.1035472.

Richards, Greg. 2015, July 15. "Evolving Gastronomic Experiences: From Food to Foodies to Foodscapes." *Journal of Gastronomy and Tourism* 1, no. 1: 5–17. https://doi.org/10.3727/216929715X14298190828796.

Rodriguez, Claudio, and Nelda Ruiz. 2016, November 11. "Barrio Sustainability: Giving Back to the 'Hood and to the Earth." *Edible Baja Arizona Magazine*.

Ross, Sara Gwendolyn. 2017, February. "Development versus Preservation Interests in the Making of a Music City: A Case Study of Select Iconic Toronto

Music Venues and the Treatment of Their Intangible Cultural Heritage Value." *International Journal of Cultural Property* 24, no. 1: 31–56. https://doi.org/10.1017/S0940739116000382.

Sbicca, Joshua. 2018. *Food Justice Now! Deepening the Roots of Social Struggle*. Minneapolis: University of Minnesota Press.

Trouillot, Michel-Rolph. 1995. *Silencing the Past: Power and the Production of History*. Boston: Beacon Press.

Tucson City of Gastronomy. 2021. "Restaurant Certification." https://tucson.cityofgastronomy.org/restaurant-certification.

UNESCO. 2003, October 17. "Convention for the Safeguarding of the Intangible Cultural Heritage." UNESCO. https://ich.unesco.org/en/convention.

———. 2007. "UNESCO Creative Cities Network." UNESCO. https://unesdoc.unesco.org/ark:/48223/pf0000156026.locale=en.

———. 2016. "UNESCO Creative Cities Network: Creativity for Sustainable Urban Development." UNESCO. https://en.unesco.org/creative-cities/sites/creative-cities/files/E%20UCCN%20leaflet.pdf.

Chapter 3

Flatbush Eats

Lessons about Food from a Community History Project

Deborah Mutnick

More than twenty of us are participating in the first of eight Flatbush Eats writing workshop sessions in early 2021 via Zoom, a mix of editor/coaches and writers, including representatives from two of our project partners, CaribBeing and the Maple Street Community Garden. About an hour into the meeting, Nadia Ketoure tells us her story. Unlike Dali Adekunle, who was born in Nigeria and has just confessed that she "can't stand cooking," which she associates with "patriarchal expectations," Nadia says she loves to cook. She is from Tunisia and moved to Canada at age fifteen. As a small child, she recalls complaining to her mother that there was no readymade food in the refrigerator. Then, in Canada, she recalls, her parents shopped at Costco where they got "delicious orange-colored chips," introducing her to junk food and causing her to gain weight. Five years later, she became more conscious of her diet and started exercising. Now a mother of three studying nutrition, she declares, "When I look at a product, for me it represents more than just the product; it represents the person who made it. It represents the love, the soil, and taking care of the environment. . . . For me, there's no peace without good food. There's no revolution without good food, there are no rights without good food"—by which I think she means that ample, nutritious food is a fundamental right and necessity in her vision of a better world.

A BRIEF HISTORY OF THE VOICES OF LEFFERTS COMMUNITY HISTORY PROJECT

I start with Nadia's impassioned call for "good food" as a human right and her insight into the labor, love, and soil concealed in the commodified product to set the scene of Flatbush Eats and underscore the problem of productive as well as distributive relations in struggles for food justice. Dalia's resistance to the patriarchal order that places women in the kitchen also suggests an implicit critique of women's traditional role in social reproduction on a daily and generational basis through unpaid labor. In this chapter, I describe how Flatbush Eats coalesced midway through the COVID-19 pandemic, partly in response to exigencies of unemployment, illness, and hunger. It was also inspired by the solidarity that sprang up in Flatbush-Prospect Lefferts Gardens (Flatbush-PLG) and elsewhere in the form of mutual aid, community fridges, and soup kitchens. It reflects longstanding interest among team members—one in particular, from Guyana—in food as a cultural barometer of taste, tradition, social trends, history, and identity. And it was shaped by a collective process of grant-writing and envisioning that goes beyond a cultural focus to recognize food justice as a community priority. To convey the full reach of Flatbush Eats, however, I need first to relate the genesis of the Voices of Lefferts Community History Project (VoL), which brought us all together in the same virtual room (https://voicesoflefferts.org).

I helped start VoL in the mid-2010s in the Flatbush-PLG neighborhood of Brooklyn, New York, where I have lived since the mid-1990s. Since the project's inception, which I continue to direct, it has evolved to feature a free writing workshop for community members that culminates in the publication of an issue of *Voices of Lefferts: The Flatbush-PLG Community Writing Journal*; an oral history program that collects oral histories and trains residents to interview friends and neighbors, thereby widening our reach; and public events that bring our work to local audiences through author readings and art and photography exhibits. VoL's overarching mission is to document and preserve the history of the neighborhood in the words and images of the people who live here. While open to any topic that pertains to neighborhood history and culture, VoL is committed to fostering dialogue about the issues that called it into being: local manifestations of global processes of gentrification, dispossession, and the perpetuation of racial and class inequality as seen most recently in the disproportionate impact of the pandemic on essential frontline workers of color. The effects on these forces can be seen in the 2010 U.S. Census, which revealed that PLG's Black population decreased by 25.5 percent between 1990 and 2010 while the number of white residents increased by 127 percent from 2,390 in 2000 to 3,035 in 2010. Unofficial

Figure 3.1. Nadia Ketoure shopping for food at the Grand Army Greenmarket in Brooklyn. Credit: Neil Carpenter.

demographic reports show that the white population has more than tripled since then.

The unprecedented and unparalleled documentation of America by the 1930s New Deal Federal Writers' Project (FWP) and its pluralistic, inclusive values inspire and define VoL's mission to collect, preserve, and publicize the words, voices, and images of Flatbush-PLG residents and their stories. Funded by Humanities New York, the Brooklyn Arts Council, Citizens Committee NYC, the Prospect Lefferts Gardens Neighborhood Association (PLGNA), the Lefferts Manor Association, and Long Island University, the project is also allied with Greenlight Bookstore and PLG Arts, a group founded more than a decade ago to support local writers and artists and to create community programming. The bookstore, in particular, has played a major role in sustaining VoL, selling journal issues for six dollars a copy, hosting author readings for each issue, and promoting the journal in store displays and on its website. Also explaining the project's longevity and capacity for community-building is its inclusive, collective process and diverse team—in race, ethnicity, gender, age, time in the neighborhood, income, and type of housing—composed of coach/editors, many of whom first participated as writers and published in the journal, who pair up with writers throughout the drafting, revising, editing, and proofreading process, as well as photographers, copyeditors, and a graphic designer.

Before returning to Flatbush Eats, it will be helpful to explain a few key aspects of neighborhood history that define VoL's critical-dialogic ethos with respect to tensions that resurfaced during the 2020 pandemic between longtime, predominantly Black, working-class residents, including a large Caribbean community, and mostly younger, white newcomers in mutual aid efforts to alleviate hunger and deliver food and other necessities to housebound neighbors. VoL adopted the hyphenated name "Flatbush-PLG" in recognition of ongoing, often bitter debates about the neighborhood's identity. Within the borders of what became known as Prospect Lefferts Gardens in the late 1960s sits Lefferts Manor, a twelve-block, landmarked district of brownstones and limestones built by a descendant of the once slave-owning Lefferts family starting in the late nineteenth century. When I moved to the neighborhood in the mid-1990s, the prices of these homes were still reasonably low; they have since risen, in many cases, to $2 million plus. The surrounding neighborhood is far less affluent with a median household income of $57,090 for renters and $63,370 for homeowners as of 2018. Many longtime residents call the neighborhood "Flatbush" while relative newcomers know it as PLG, a name that only began to catch on in the late 1990s, when it was on the cusp of gentrifying, abetted by one real estate story after another about "discovering" a neighborhood that tens of thousands of people already called home.

In fact, the name "Prospect Lefferts Gardens" was coined in 1969 by founders of the neighborhood association PLGNA, an interracial organization whose mission is to promote and sustain racial justice and racial and economic diversity. To do so, the association sought to redraw PLG's boundaries to make it more inclusive and more financially viable in the aftermath of 1960s urban unrest and white flight. Throughout the rest of the twentieth century, African American and Afro-Caribbean populations increased as white families fled the city, real estate companies used redlining and blockbusting tactics to drive out white homeowners who sold below market rate, and realtors sold at inflated prices to middle-class Black families denied access elsewhere. Despite PLGNA's good intentions, for many residents whose families may have lived here for generations, the moniker PLG spells gentrification. As prospective homebuyers and renters, especially young, white college graduates, artists, and graduate students priced out elsewhere in the city, began flocking to Flatbush-PLG in the early 2000s, a twenty-four-story luxury glass tower was proposed adjacent to the subway station half a block from Prospect Park. In addition to being architecturally out of scale and dissonantly modernist in design, the glass tower would have been a hazard to migratory birds.

There was strong community opposition to the proposed building, but it was the 2008 financial crash rather than the will of the people that ultimately stopped its development. Even so, as an "as of right" project safeguarded by former Mayor Bloomberg's massive rezoning plan, developers were allowed to bypass approval by community boards and other local stakeholders. Consequently, by the time they lost their funding, construction workers had already started to excavate the site, leaving a giant hole in the ground, a hazardous eyesore that obstructed entrance to the subway station for years. In 2014, another proposed project a few blocks away met with similar opposition. This time, however, with no financial crisis and the loss of a lawsuit filed by community groups protesting the development and the shadows it would cast on the park, the twenty-three-story building was completed two years later with a typical 80–20 split between market and affordable rates, plus tax abatement for the developer. The two-story frontline, in keeping with adjacent buildings, houses Greenlight Bookstore and a nursery school; the tower is set back from the street. A former principal at the development company who now lives in PLG has donated to VoL and other local groups. Gentrification continues apace.

FLATBUSH EATS: FOOD, SURVIVAL, CELEBRATION

Flatbush Eats, an idea that had been in the wings of VoL for years, took center stage in fall 2020 with a successful application for a Humanities New York (HNY) Action Grant—the project's third HNY grant. The initiative owed its title and some of its vision to a never-published FWP collection called *America Eats,* derailed by the onset of World War II, which has only recently attracted more attention from writers and scholars, including an online collection of

FWP artifacts hosted by Michigan State University called *What America Ate: Preserving America's Culinary History from the Great Depression* (https://whatamericaate.org). Although knowledge of *America Eats* influenced our conceptualization and gave us the title of Flatbush Eats, our interest in the topic grew out of repeated references to food in VoL workshops, particularly by our Guyanese team member, Andrea Phillips-Merriman, who took every opportunity to remind us of its centrality to our essential cultural, historical, political, and biological wellbeing, individually and collectively. It was her brilliant invocations of food in her feedback to authors and her insistence on its critical importance to any cultural history that convinced us to take up the topic, a focus that only crystallized once we decided to apply for the HNY grant and started collaboratively and generatively drafting the narrative.

"Flatbush Eats: Food, Survival, Celebration" thus reflects a convergence of the project's goals and our neighborhood cred, abiding interest in the topic of food, and the local and global transformations wrought by the pandemic, especially those related to food, hunger, and social inequality. As we wrote the grant narrative, it became clear that the pandemic had already begun to change our thinking about food. Still in the midst of a year of tragic loss of life, jobs, and economic and food security, food appeared at the center of the crisis in numerous respects from underlying systemic problems of factory farming in relation to the virus to food shortages to food lines rivaling those in the Great Depression to the disproportionate impact of COVID-19 on low-income communities of color. The subthemes listed in the grant proposal (the pleasures, production, distribution, culture, social reproduction, quality, availability, and ecology of food) reflect our lived experience in the neighborhood as we bore witness to the sharply rising curve of COVID cases, hospitalizations, and deaths; adjusted to lockdowns and school and business closures; learned to work remotely; ate more takeout food; starting cooking more than many of us had ever before done; and worried about our neighbors facing hunger, locally owned restaurants going out of business, frontline food workers' safety, food shortages and empty shelves in supermarkets, and price gouging by companies like Uber Eats.

Lessons from the Field: Sowing the Seeds for Flatbush Eats

In September 2021, the first of two special issues of Flatbush Eats was still in production. The Delta variant was the dominant strain of the virus. The country had returned to school, work, and other normal routines at the same time it had not. Most of the writing that came out of the workshop was rooted in powerful personal stories of food: making roti in Brooklyn as a point of entry

Figure 3.2. Tending squash in the Maple Street Community Garden. Credit: Nancy Treuber.

to family and Caribbean history; reminiscing about the "Great Hunger" in Ireland in light of recipe notes for hot sauce by relatives of the Irish author's Antiguan wife; and other stories rooted in the Gullah Islands off the coast of

South Carolina, Senegal, Tunisia, Palestine, Ukraine, Grenada, and a hill at a Wisconsin home overlooking the Chequamegon Bay off Lake Superior.

VoL's new focus on food has appealed, on the one hand, to food lovers, cooks, and culturalists, and on the other, to the community's heightened awareness and anxiety about food in relation to COVID-19: food insecurity, food deserts, widespread hunger, food shortages, and dangerous conditions experienced by poorly paid, undervalued frontline workers. These problems raise key questions about the underlying causes of worsening environmental and social conditions, widespread hunger and malnutrition, even in a rich country like the United States, and the elemental role food plays in human existence. Contemporary ecosocialist thinkers provide convincing answers to those questions, starting with a recovery of Karl Marx's environmental critique, much of which pertains to food and agriculture. In *Capital*, Marx wrote, "All labor is originally first directed towards the appropriation and production of food" (qtd. in Foster 2016, 25). He further observed, "[A] rational agriculture is incompatible with the capitalist system (although the latter promotes technical improvements in agriculture), and needs either the hand of the small farmer living by his own labour or the control of associated producers." The cascading, cumulative effects of industrial agriculture, together with processes of urbanization, industrialization, and the globalization of capital, culminated in the anthropogenic crisis of the mid-twentieth century that has come to be known as the "Great Acceleration." These forces of production in the postwar era have driven climate change, concentrated wealth in the hands of a few, and created "the bestiary of pathogens now in circulation" (Wallace et al. 2020, 19).

Bearing in mind this historical material analysis was vital to planning and implementing Flatbush Eats and, more broadly, food justice pedagogies and activism. In each context, an ecosocialist perspective offers insights into the root causes of food injustice and associated environmental and social problems. It reveals complex ecological and social relations of production that drive accumulation and dispossession in the face of mounting threats of violent storms, wildfires, heat waves and other consequences of climate change as well as ethnic and racial tensions exacerbated by intensifying social and economic inequities. In my introduction to the first of the two special issues, I wrote about a Jewish-owned restaurant in the neighborhood named Kulashkat. The owner Yagil Kadosh had posted a story in the PLG Facebook group about antisemitic vandals who smashed the restaurant's outdoor dining space. At the time, the pandemic was subsiding in Brooklyn but more violence had erupted in the Middle East that had left dead 250 Palestinians, including sixty-six children, and thirteen Israelis, two of whom were children. Kadosh could have ranted about the damage but instead he called for unity and declared that he depends on and patronizes Black- and Palestinian-owned businesses in Flatbush. I then observed:

> When the Voices of Lefferts project team decided to launch Flatbush Eats, we imagined we would collect an infinite number of stories like this one, for next to water, food is the most essential of all human needs. It sits at the center of history, culture, and survival. This past year and a half, the global pandemic taught us how fragile our systems of care, transport, commerce, and delivery of those essential needs can be. It exposed the cracks in local, national, and international political economic systems, revealing even more starkly the racial and class antipathies and disparities that spared the rich and left masses of working and poor people vulnerable to the deadly virus and the cascading effects of its socioeconomic consequences. (Mutnick 2021)

These interconnections among food, industrial agriculture, climate change, pathogens, and social equality form a "hidden substratum" of the metabolism or interaction between nature and humanity, the essential relations of production that expose the contradictions of capitalism that its associated social and political institutions work so hard to mystify. As John Bellamy Foster (2016) puts it, "Food has become a core contradiction of contemporary capitalism" (1). Foster explains Marx's concept of a "metabolic rift" between nature and humanity derived from his study of the rise of 19th century capitalist food systems and industrial agriculture, the depletion of nutrients from the soil, food contamination and artificial scarcity, and generally poor nutrition of the English working-class. Food, of course, is fundamental to any society. In underinvested or disinvested urban centers, food is also a sign of gentrification and real estate predation as upscale coffee shops, bars, restaurants, and supermarkets open to serve a whiter, more affluent class, threatening long-time residents and commercial tenants with displacement.

In Flatbush-PLG, this sign of "urban renewal"[1] threatens a greater degree of racial and class diversity than exists in most urban neighborhoods, a diversity that community members have self-consciously, if never altogether successfully, fought to achieve and preserve. COVID-19 hastened the closure of some food businesses, including Black-owned restaurants and shops, and plunged many local residents into food insecurity. It also gave rise to grassroots mutual aid efforts even as it intensified racial and class inequalities and lay bare the environmental depredation of industrial food production. More broadly, the "explosion of interest" in food justice observed by Robert Gottlieb and Anupama Joshi (2010, ix) between their initial research in 2007 and publication of their book on the topic three years later reflects deepening concerns about the global nexus of industrial agriculture, factory farming, deforestation, disappearing small and medium-sized farms, obscene levels of social inequality, poverty, unequal access to nutritious food, and climate change.

These realities are reflected locally in Flatbush-PLG in the existence of three community gardens (and many more, as well as urban farms, in New York City), along with composting efforts, school-based food and garden initiatives, and the emergence of mutual aid groups and farm/food stand operations, all of which attest to local manifestations of the global food justice movement. As Silvia Federici explains with respect to the politics of food, "It is a mistake for left movements to underestimate, practically and analytically, the importance of agricultural work in today's political economy and, consequently, the transformative capacity of the struggles that farmers are making on this terrain" (Federici 2009). She goes on to emphasize the contribution of such work to the Marxist concept of social reproduction, the self-perpetuation of forms of human existence that entail both institutional necessities like housing, schools, and hospitals, and the necessary but typically unpaid or underpaid, undervalued activities that sustain life from generation to generation, including caregiving of all kinds, cleaning, cooking, and, in some places, subsistence farming. Food justice/sovereignty movements can be seen here in Brooklyn, across the U.S., and worldwide, particularly in the Global South, in lower-income, marginalized countries in Africa, Latin America, and South Asia.

The participants in the Flatbush Eats writing workshop have roots in South Carolina's Sea Islands, Guyana, Trinidad, Ireland, and Tunisia among other places. Their stories about food reflect histories of farming, famine, African culture, slavery, and colonization. They may not theorize food in relation to climate change or pathogens, but they make clear the significance of traditions and generational knowledge of food as cultural inheritance, the ritual side dish of rice, for example, a cash crop in antebellum South Carolina that originated in Africa, cultivated by the slave labor that built Southern wealth. Relatedly, in her book on agricultural resistance and the Black freedom movement, Monica M. White (2019) recovers the history of collective resistance and resilience among dispossessed Black Southerners who remained in the post-agricultural Jim Crow South where they grew crops for their own sustenance, created alternative structures in the face of harsh, often violent repression to meet their collective food, education, health care, and employment needs, and provided safe harbor for 1960s civil rights activists. This research was inspired by and meant to inform the urban agriculture and food justice movement that White chronicled as an activist and ethnographer in Detroit, where she "witnessed an enormous resurgence of urban agriculture in the city ... led by black and brown urban farmers descended from migrants from southern states who had sought better living conditions through work in the automobile industry even as they retained a historical connection to agriculture" (White 2019, 20).

Other Black food justice activists and farmers include Leah Penniman, who sets out in her book *Farming While Black* to correct her "miseducation" about her own relationship to the land and the history of Black agriculture in "a reverently compiled manual for African-heritage people ready to reclaim our rightful place of dignified agency in the food system" (Penniman 2018, 8). Penniman quotes a passage in Toni Morrison's (1977) *Song of Solomon*, resolving to honor the directive "to pass it on" (Penniman 2018, 10) personified as Macon Dead's Georgia farm that "spoke . . . like a sermon" to the old men reminiscing about their youth with the novel's protagonist Milkman Dead: "See? See what you can do? . . . We live here. On this planet, in this nation, in this country right here . . . Nobody staring in my home . . . Grab this land! Take it, hold it, my brothers, make it, my brothers, shake it, squeeze it, turn it, twist it, beat it, kick it, kiss it, whip it, stomp it, dig it, plow it, seed it, reap it, rent it, buy it, sell it, own it, build it multiply it, and pass it on—can you hear me? Pass it on!" (Morrison 1977, 235). These deeper values of reverence for the land—this planet—and responsibility to pass it on to the next generation resonate powerfully with everyday experiences of the dispossessed and their posterity as well as contemporary food justice movements and community gardens like the Maple Street Community Garden featured in a photographic essay by VoL photographer Nancy Treuber. Noting that this urban garden is surrounded by a chain-link fence and gate, Treuber writes:

> The gate opens from a Brooklyn street to a garden of stories and histories; a place but also a collection of memories. These stories connect us to a plot of land, where the simple, wearing, repetitive tasks of tending—digging, raking, planting, watering, weeding, harvesting—blossom into a mélange of recipes and histories and voices. The garden is fertile soil for these stories. (Treuber 2021, 34)

The focus in Flatbush Eats on urban gardens, food, community, and recovery of lost stories and histories in the midst of the pandemic spawned an idea for a collaborative project—the Parkside Food and Culture Collective—to bring healthy food to the neighborhood together with an already existing composting site on a corner of Prospect Park and several cultural organizations. Supported by a small grant from Citizens Committee NYC, the collective launched "The Parkside Commons" in October 2021 to expand an already existing, grassroots composting and recycling operation every Sunday morning outside the park to include Nadia's food stand, storytelling, musical performances, spoken word, and oral history interviews. VoL is contributing a free library for sharing books, articles, and children's

Figure 3.3. Jess Meyer in the Maple Street Community Garden. Credit: Nancy Treuber.

literature about food, ecology, and other topics, equipped with a mail slot into which people can drop letters, stories, poems, drawings, and recipes that will become part of our archive and shared with the wider community. The Commons thus illustrates another concretization of an already existing if nebulous food justice network in one neighborhood that aims to contribute to a more sustainable urban environment and improve food quality, access, and security as a public good, echoing Henri Lefebvre's (2000) famous assertion of the people's "right to the city."

THE BENEFITS AND CHALLENGES OF MUTUAL AID

That right—to the city—has been severely challenged since the pandemic began in 2020, accentuating local disparities in exposure to the virus as blue-collar frontline workers reported to jobs in health care and food industries while white collar workers mostly got to stay home and work remotely. The interrelatedness of climate change, loss of biodiversity, and social inequality emerged starkly in alarmingly high rates of illness, death, job loss, and hunger among the most vulnerable members of our society. Among few bright spots in an extraordinarily bleak time, mutual aid groups sprang into existence in the Flatbush-PLG and many other neighborhoods worldwide from Brooklyn to Rojava, Syria, to Taiwan to Southern Africa to Greece to Brazil (see Sitrin and Colectiva Sembrar 2020). In Flatbush-PLG, the groups included new organizations like Flatbush United Mutual Aid and already established ones like Equality for Flatbush, a grassroots people-of-color-led group, and People In Need (PIN), a nonprofit founded in 2015 to assist low-income families that speak a variety of languages, and through individual interest, often expressed in social media posts—all looking for ways to mitigate the disastrous events unfolding in the first months of the pandemic.

According to the *New York Times*, over eight hundred mutual aid groups formed nationwide as stopgap measures during the pandemic, including more than one hundred in New York State, half of which are in New York City (Fraytas-Tamura 2021). Their main focus at the height of the pandemic was food access and delivery to unemployed, elderly, disabled, ill, and other people in need. The widely reported disproportionate impact of the pandemic on people of color and essential, low-wage frontline workers revealed already existing cracks in a neoliberal system whose ravages often appear as food deserts in working-class and working poor communities, including Flatbush, besieged by diabetes, obesity, hypertension, and other avoidable diseases that then put them at higher risk for contracting COVID. Mutual aid groups in Flatbush-PLG and surrounding neighborhoods pooled resources, recruited volunteers, fulfilled requests for food shopping and delivery, and started stocking community fridges.

As many commentators have recently observed, mutual aid has a long history starting with Peter Kropotkin's (1902) theorization of cooperation—an anarcho-socialist answer to a social Darwinian, survival-of-the-fittest emphasis on competition as an inherent tendency of human beings and other species. Other important antecedents include the programs created by the Black Panther Party and the Young Lords from free breakfasts for children to sickle cell anemia testing to daycare centers to neighborhood cleanups. Similarly, radical movements like Occupy Wall Street, its offshoot Occupy Sandy, and occupations of public spaces in the summer of 2020 across the U.S. during Black Lives Matter protests, demonstrate the efficacy of mutual aid in providing collective care, politicizing activists, developing capacities, and building solidarity in wider struggles for social and food justice. Under the banner "solidarity not charity," such projects can be understood, according to Dean Spade, "as frontline work in a war over who will control social relations and how survival will be reproduced, especially in the face of worsening crises" (Spade 2020, 147). For the food justice movement and related literacies, the possibilities of mutual aid, both its ethos of solidarity and its idealistic, prefigurative politics of building the society it envisions in a capitalist-dominated world, provide important lessons about political organizing methods and strategies.

On the one hand, this spontaneous mutual aid work has provided material relief, especially through food distribution, and demonstrated the potential for rebuilding a strong left movement better able to challenge state power. As Nancy Romer argues about the food justice movement in general, noting that recent uprisings like Occupy Wall Street have been derailed without long-term strategies and organizations, "The more we build grassroots organizations of trust and shared experience, communities of learning and analysis, experiments in structure and action, develop leadership of those most oppressed by the system, and most importantly, create alliances and broad strategic approaches, the more our movements will sustain us in the future" (Romer 2014, 6). On the other hand, mutual aid is also prone to volunteerism if not charity, despite Spade's caveat, and susceptible to the vicissitudes of movements like Occupy. Gus Breslauer puts it this way: " . . . [T]he truth is, mutual-aid isn't a challenge or threat to the social order which produced hunger and precarity. The state is largely indifferent or even welcoming to it. In a world where the working class is increasingly being told to fend for itself, can we continue to call this 'solidarity' with any honesty?" (Breslauer 2020) Many community fridges created this past year in New York City are now empty (Freytas-Tamura 2021), though at least two in Flatbush-PLG have not only survived but also thrived. One local mutual aid group suffered from internal conflicts that led to a temporary halt in deliveries; another experienced a disconnect between mostly young, white volunteers and older, longtime residents of color in need.

This latter group, the one born of social media users eager to help allay widespread suffering, also felt the stress of "toxic personalities" and anarchist principles of decentralization and horizontal, leaderless consensus-building that led to a refusal to use any Google products for fear of data surveillance by immigration or other authorities. The decision to avoid collecting data and to use complex digital programs to organize deliveries meant the group had no records and communication was controlled by a few individuals who knew consumer relationship systems (CRS) and related software applications. At its height, according to one activist, the group had a core of twenty-two organizers, two of whom were nonwhite, and some four hundred peripheral volunteers, 75 percent of whom were white, who served about one thousand majority nonwhite, working-class neighborhood residents. An internal crisis led to a "pause" of operations in mid-2020 and a series of virtual meetings to "co-create a compelling purpose and vision" going forward. Such efforts build capacity, however slowly and sporadically, through grassroots activism in which people accrue knowledge and skills necessary for long-term movement-building, but they also highlight the failure of neoliberal states to eradicate poverty, hunger, and social inequalities that became painfully evident during the pandemic in the struggle to meet basic nutritional needs.

THE WAY OUT IS NOTHING SHORT OF BIRTHING A WORLD

In community programs created by more established political organizations like the Black Panthers, mutual aid tended to be better integrated into broader strategic and tactical goals. The food justice movement likewise promises to combine political education and strategic action in the spirit of mutual aid through its focus on ecologically sustainable production and distribution of nutritious food to local underserved communities. The long-term commitment of food sovereignty and food justice movements to start and maintain small farms and gardens roots political activism in literal and figurative soils for change. Mutual aid efforts like those that arose in Flatbush-PLG and many other communities during the pandemic are harder to sustain due to lack of resources, structure, and strategic vision to meet the overwhelming human need the state perpetuates in its protection of ruling class interests and systemic injustices produced by capitalism.[2] Cultural projects like Flatbush Eats are also hard to sustain. Less essential than fresh picked vegetables or a home delivery of groceries, the publication of two issues of the VoL journal and the collection of some thirty oral history interviews on themes of food and food justice helps make meaning of our collective experience, leaving a record of life histories, essays, and stories by those who live and work in the Flatbush area. That Flatbush Eats, aka Voices of Lefferts, and other neighborhood groups coalesced to start the Parkside Commons is a hopeful sign of growing organizational capacity and commitment to urban sustainability.

However, at the risk of restating the obvious, neither the food justice/sovereignty movement nor mutual aid in themselves will achieve the radical social transformation necessary to avert the global crises humanity faces of hunger, poverty, racial and gender oppression, more pandemics, nuclear war, climate change, and species extinction, perhaps including our own—a true existential threat most of us could not have imagined a decade ago. Nevertheless, these movements can contribute to rebuilding a unified left that can work to confront, contest, and challenge state power and its failures. As Gottlieb and Joshi note, the challenge for the food justice movement is how to translate its increased visibility and activism into "a coherent social movement and force for social change." Accordingly, they situate the movement in the stage of what Gramsci called a "war of position," cautioning that it is only a "war of maneuver" that will transform "the food system itself and the global systems of work, production, supply chains, and power" (Gottlieb and Joshi, 2010, xv). To spell out what they elide: the war of maneuver must replace global capitalism and its perpetual crises of overaccumulation with a socialist system that places human need and respect for labor and nature before profits. Although the food justice movement has grown and deepened in the ten years since the publication of Gottlieb and Joshi's book, solutions to our collective crises, including deadly pathogens, will require us, as Rob Wallace et al. put it, to "walk through the door of a global clash with capital. . . . The way out is nothing short of birthing a world" (Wallace et al. 2020, 11).

Cultural projects like VoL on their own are, of course, powerless to achieve such a sweeping social transformation, but they are catalysts for bringing it about and determining what kind of world we will find when we walk through that door. The Flatbush Eats writing workshop series concluded in mid-May 2021. Dali missed a session because she was "very ill"—news more fraught than ever before.[3] At the first workshop, she elaborated on her resistance to patriarchal explanations, saying they dictated "the type of individual I was supposed to grow up into, so in many respects, not cooking and not finding joy in food has been a method of rebellion for me." But when all the restaurants were closed during the pandemic and she had to start cooking, she found herself "revisiting Nigerian food," which has been "a healing process of a lot of those parts of my identity that I had seen as oppressive but now I'm starting to reevaluate and revision how they're meaningful to me. I think that's the angle from which I'm going to write." Nadia, after expressing deep enthusiasm for the project, emailed me during the third workshop to say that she was dropping out. But after we met briefly on Zoom, she reconsidered. I knew she was anxious about her writing ability when she declared early on, "I'm not a writer. I never wrote but the process, I think, will help me to put my ideas clearly on paper." As encouragement, I suggested that she start with her own powerful words quoted at the beginning of this chapter. She replied: "I

Figure 3.4. Nadia on a bench in Prospect Park near the Greenmarket. Credit: Neil Armstrong.

am always scared to be too rough for people, but it is my nature to provoke, to create a reaction, that will hopefully waken them. That's my hope. This whole year I have worked and evolved in accepting myself for who I am. Thank you, I know where to start now!"

REFERENCES

Breslauer, Gus. 2020, November 27. "Mutual Aid: A Factor of Liberalism." *Regeneration Magazine*. https://regenerationmag.org/mutual-aid-a-factor-of-liberalism/?fbclid=IwAR3i_10YIfrk19VDY8fSHgILEeBZ5-633Gc6kFXHjGNA-MXA6Itd0AdfIwM.

Federici, Silvia. 2009. "Silvia Federici on Capitalism, Colonialism, Women, and Food Politics." An interview with Silvia Federici by Max Haiven. *Politics and Culture*, no. 2. https://politicsandculture.org/2009/11/03/silvia-federici-on-capitalism-colonialism-women-and-food-politics.

Foster, John Bellamy. 2016. "Marx as a Food Theorist." *Monthly Review* 68, no. 7. https://monthlyreview.org/2016/12/01/marx-as-a-food-theorist.

Freytas-Tamura, Kimiko de. 2021, March 3. "How Neighborhood Groups Are Stepping In Where the Neighborhood Didn't." *New York Times*. https://www.nytimes.com/2021/03/03/nyregion/covid-19-mutual-aid-nyc.html.

Gottlieb, Robert, and Anupama Joshi. 2010. *Food Justice*. Cambridge: MIT Press.

Kropotkin, Peter. 1902/2021. *Mutual Aid: An Illuminated Factor of Evolution*. Introduction by David Graeber and Andrej Grubacic. Oakland, CA: PM Press/Kairos.

Lefebvre, Henri. 1996/2000. *Writings on Cities*. Translated by Elenore Kofman and Elizabeth Lebas. Oxford: Blackwell.

Marx, Karl, and Frederick Engels. 1845/1998. *The German Ideology*. Amherst, NY: Prometheus Books.

Morrison, Tony. 1977. *Song of Solomon*. New York: Vintage Press.

Mutnick, Deborah. 2021. "Editorial Perspectives: 'Shut up and Eat': Stories about Food, Culture, Survival, and Love." Special Issue: Flatbush Eats. *Voices of Lefferts: The Flatbush-PLG Community Writing Journal*, no. 7 (Fall): 8–13.

Penniman, Leah. 2018. *Farming While Black: Soul Fire Farm's Practical Guide to Liberation on the Land*. Foreword by Karen Washington. White River Junction, VT: Chelsea Green Publishing.

Romer, Nancy. 2014. "The Radial Potential of the Food Justice Movement." *Radical Teacher* 98: 5–14. http://radicalteacher.library.pitt.edu.

Sitrin, Marina, and Colectiva Sembrar. 2020. *Pandemic Solidarity: Mutual Aid during the Covid-19 Crisis*. London: Pluto Press.

Spade, Dean. 2020. "Solidarity Not Charity: Mutual Aid for Mobilization and Survival." *Social Text* 38, no. 1: 131–51. DOI 10.1215/01642472-7971139.

Treuber, Nancy. 2021. "Flatbush Eats and the Maple Street Community Garden." Special Issue: Flatbush Eats. *Voices of Lefferts: The Flatbush-PLG Community Writing Journal*, issue 7 (Fall): 34–41.

Wallace, Rob, Alex Liebman, Luis Fernando Chavez, and Rodrick Wallace. 2020. "COVID-19 and Circuits of Capital." *Monthly Review* 72, no. 1. https://monthlyreview.org/2020/05/01/covid-19-and-circuits-of-capital.

White, Monica M. 2019. *Freedom Farmers: Agricultural Resistance and the Black Freedom Movement*. Chapel Hill: University of North Carolina Press.

NOTES

1. Though no longer widely used, the term *urban renewal* in the 1960s was vehemently rejected by working-class, Black communities as a form of "Negro removal."

2. It is worth noting that the two community fridges now in operation regularly post social media messages such as: "community fridge update: full of almond and cow milks, lovely oranges and celery, potatoes, and—i think—pawpaws! on midwood & rogers."

3. As I was completing the first draft of this chapter, Dali let me know that she did have COVID-19. Although she had returned to work, she was very tired, needed weekends to rest, and, regrettably, decided to drop out of the workshop. I suggested she consider writing an essay for the special issue anyway, working with her coach, a professional food writer and poet in the neighborhood who had joined the project team. She has not taken up my offer but perhaps someday she will tell us more about her rebellion against patriarchal constraints and how rediscovering Nigerian food the first year of the pandemic was a healing process for her.

Chapter 4

The Smell of the Other and Self-Alienation

A Mani(fold)festo of Race, Ethnicity, and Rhetorical (In)Accessibility to Food

Bibhushana Poudyal and Mala Rai

Figure 4.1. An image of red-hot chili peppers spread to be sun-dried on a *nanglo* (flat round woven tray made up of bamboo) placed on a *muda* (Nepali traditional chair). Credit: Photo taken in Nepal by Bibhushana Poudyal.

How many of us know how a small piece of madeleine triggers Marcel Proust's memories of childhood and he goes in search of a lost time? And isn't it just amazing that not only Proust but the rest of the globe (not the planet)[1] go along with him? And those of us, the non-Western others, who have read those volumes by Marcel Proust and the scholarships that followed, might have never tasted or let alone smelled that madeleine but are tempted to believe that it must taste and smell good, really good (regardless of whatever memories were triggered for Proust). So, the question is, Why? Why, without ever having a material experience of its smell, we are already convinced it must smell good? Same with the Netflix series *Bridgerton*. We are just wooed by the show's color palette, its rhetoric, the way of imaginary postracial yet whitist-ish British life, and its vividly colorful food. The onscreen situated aesthetics of this whitewashed, upper-class, "racially ideal" society becomes globally accepted, desired, and pined for. However, the Other visual and olfactory aesthetics situated in diverse contexts become something else. This chapter is about that "something else."

Food justice scholars and activists have resisted the unjust food system by recognizing the entangled relationship between the materiality and the discursivity of food (Barad 2003, 822) and the relationship among food, discourse, materiality, and power (Frye and Bruner 2012). Food justice cannot be envisioned and materialized by disconnecting it from the larger issue of systematic and systemic oppression and social and racial justice (LeGreco and Douglas 2021; Garth and Reese 2020; Penniman 2018). If food justice is "a work in progress, residing at the edges of an emerging alternative food movement" (Gottlieb and Joshi 2013, 6), this chapter joins this movement by proposing an anticolonial, antiracist, anticasteist, and feminist rhetorical framework that we call, *the smell of the Other*. This chapter is not only about material accessibility and right to food but also about a rhetorical one. Even if all the ingredients are accessible to prepare our food—which, as we all might know, is not always the case—they can be rhetorically removed from accessibility by the dominant structure. This rhetorical framework of "the smell of the Other" will help us see the vicious relationship between rhetorical conditions and material conditions that forces the Others to self-alienate ourselves from the food that connects us to our communities, our homes, and us.

To the field of food justice, we propose "the smell of the Other" and "rhetorical accessibility" as analytical frameworks that allow activists and scholars to investigate the issue of food sovereignty, accessibility, and dignity from a rhetorical-olfactory perspective by critically contemplating upon our situatedness in terms of caste, ethnicity, and race and their dynamic relationship with larger rhetorical-material structures. Through an autoethnography approach to caste, ethnicity, and race, we show the vicious relationship between rhetorical conditions and material conditions that force the Others to self-alienate ourselves from the food that connects us to our communities, our homes, and ourselves. Hence, this chapter instrumentalizes "the smell of the Other" as an analytical framework and offers a look at how autoethnographicmethods can be utilized to bring voices which are yet to be listened to and learned from to make food activism scholarship and praxis more inclusive.

Now, we introduce the rhetorical framework of "the smell of the Other" through an analysis of the following statement uttered by a person from an Asian community: "Asians smell of food. It is funny, but we Asians really smell of what we eat. We walk around and our kitchens stay with us. You know, Koreans smell of garlic, Indians smell of curry, Filipinos smell of vinegar . . . and so on. Caucasians—a lot of them just smell bad" (Manalasian 2006, 45). The quote entails that *a lot of* Caucasians *can* smell bad, but *all* Asians *do* smell of our food without any escape, and that smell is often perceived as "bad" by non-Others. The smell of Asians' food lingers and follows us around without our knowledge, making us fearful about our smelliness, and becomes a haunting part of our rhetorical and material existence. We just cannot get rid of it. That smell is a ghost that haunts and taunts us. It lingers in our clothes, apartments, and hermetically seals us into stereotypes that make us the subject of ridicule, disgust, and discrimination.

Do we Asians really smell of our food? Why do we smell of our food? Do we smell of our food at home where we are not the Other? Does the Other still smell at our home, their home, or somewhere else? In this chapter, we argue that it is not about what Asians smell of but about the othering of the smell and food that is different from dominant groups. Therefore, it is not that Asians smell of their food but that the smell of Asian food situates them as The Other in the context of both global and regional racialized and ethnicized structures. According to those structures, these Others "reek so bad" that it makes them fear the smell of their own food. Hence, it is not the Asians who smell of food, it is the Others who smell of their food. Written by two of these Others—a Nepali female PhD student in the United States (Author One) and an indigenous Nepali educator in Nepal (Author Two), this chapter is a consequence of our embodied experiences and knowledge analyzing the relationship between our food and its "racialized" and "ethnicized" situatedness in the contexts of white supremacy in the United States and Brahminism in Nepal (Free for Life 2020).

As Frye and Bruner encapsulate, "[Food] is a requirement for survival, but also functions as a defining element of human culture and identity" (Frye and Bruner 2012, 1). Along a similar line, Alkon and Agyeman write, "Food informs individuals' identities, including their racial identities, in ways that other environmental justice and sustainability issues—energy, water, garbage and so on—do not" (Alkon and Agyeman 2011, 10). We approach it more as not how food informs our identity but how we interact with this life through our food and how our food is ab/used to discriminatorily identify us racially and ethnically: The Others are not only othered by their food, but forced into self-othering. This chapter is built upon the feminist dictum that the personal is political, and the personal experiences that we share here are, perhaps, not "the end point," but definitely "the beginning of an exploration of the relationship between the personal and the social and therefore the political" (Agnew 2007, 6). Even if there are many similarities between the experiences of the two of us, our relationship with the Brahminic Nepali society is not the same. We are not the Other in that society in the same way. This chapter attempts to illustrate these arguments through our individual segments.

MALA RAI: NOT-SO-DIVERSE DIVERSITY AND THE SMELL OF INDIGENOUS FOOD IN NEPALI BRAHMANICAL STRUCTURE

What happens when indigenous peoples dare to enjoy their cuisine closest to their community in a society gagged by Brahmanism? Let me begin to address this question by introducing *Kinema*. *Kinema* is one of the indigenous cuisines and popular among the "Rai" and "Limbu" indigenous communities in the eastern part of Nepal. Basically, it is eaten as curry with rice or as a pickle mixed with chili, lemon, and tomatoes. It "is a nonsalted and solid-state alkaline fermented soybean food product of the eastern hills of Nepal" (Khadka and Lama 2020, 172). Though it is largely popular among the members of these two indigenous communities, some people from other indigenous and non-indigenous communities who are accustomed to it (and its smell) are also fond of it. *Kinema* is said to have a very strong and "peculiar" smell, but for us, it is an aroma that makes us can't-wait-to-eat-it hungry. Unfortunately, this is the smell of the Other in the Brahmanical social order, and therefore, it is not only detested by the non-indigenous communities but also feared and detested, phobically, by many indigenous peoples. This is a hatred caused by the fear of being further othered in a structure where we are already the Other. I will share a personal anecdote to illustrate this fear.

A few years back, I was cooking *Kinema* for lunch in my apartment in Kathmandu. Or let's put it this way: I finally "dared" to cook Kinema one day because the non-indigenous peoples who used to live on another floor were not home. That day, I felt like the house also belonged to us (me and my family). After giving it a couple of thoughts, I finally cooked kinema by closing the kitchen door so that the smell was locked in the kitchen and did not leak into the world outside where we were the Other. But, to our horror, the young non-indigenous landlord appeared in the house the same day with a bunch of his non-indigenous friends. We could clearly hear their response to the smell the moment they entered the house. The friends started shouting, "Oh shit! What's this smell? It stinks like socks. Something must be rotting somewhere in your house." We heard the landlord's reply, "This foul smell must be coming from the toilet. Plumbing issues again. Ugh!" And the sneers and laughter accompanied by expressions of disgust continued for a while.

I think, at first, they didn't realize that the smell wasn't caused by something rotting somewhere or plumbing issues. However, I am pretty sure, they might have later conjectured that the smell must be the smell of our food. By then, we were already mortified and anxious, thinking, "What they might have thought about us? Savage, uneducated, uncivilized, repellent! How they might treat us now!" The way they were reacting to that smell was also their reaction to our presence and how we are identified. Now I wonder why I could not take pride in my food, in the smell of my food, our food. How did they dare to laugh and insult our food? But it is easier said than done, isn't it? After all, I was not only angry at them, but I was angrier at myself for cooking the food that embarrassed us so dreadfully. Worse still, I was angry that when the rest of the world has so many varieties of food, we had *kinema*. The way we were reacting to the embarrassment caused by that smell was also our reaction to our presence in this society.

Kinema is a legume-based fermented food. Therefore, we might say that it is a fermentation that causes a haunting smell for them and a delectable aroma for us. Still, this indigenous food is not the only fermented food that Nepalis eat. Various ethnic groups, castes, and economic backgrounds have food cultures that involve fermented food. For instance,

> Traditional fermented foods can be basically divided based upon the major substrate used for fermentation such as cereal-based fermented foods (*selroti, jand, tongba, nigar*), legume-based fermented foods (*kinema, masyaura*), fruits and vegetable-based fermented foods (*gundruk, sinki, khalpi, mesu*), milk-based fermented foods (*dahi, mohi, gheu, solar, somar*), and meat- and fish-based fermented foods (*sidra, sukaako machha, sukuti, masular*). (Khadka and Lama 2020, 170)

But not the smell of all fermented foods has equal effects on the ones who produce and consume them. It does not cause the same level of embarrassment that *kinema* happened to cause us. Later, the landlord did not say anything to us, nor did he change his behavior toward us. Yet, we can imagine how they might have talked about us and our food behind our backs. This haunting fear is real. Because our country, the Federal Democratic Republic of Nepal, does not offer the same level of dignity and sense of belonging to everyone living here or the ones identifying themselves as Nepalis. Some Nepalis are more equal than the Others even if there are many patriotic songs written and sung as the celebration of a multicultural, multilingual, multiracial, multiethnic, and multireligious country. Our national song, *Sayaun Thunga Phool Ka Hami* (rough translation: We Are Made of Hundreds of Flowers), itself is a celebration of that diversity. It was even ranked third in the BBC's list of "Rio 2016: The Most Amazing National Anthems." But does that translate into our lived experience? No, because the character, attitudes, policymaking, working style of the government and state is only favorable to one caste and ethnicity, that is, Hill Brahmin (preferably male), and thus, discriminatory toward other marginalized and oppressed groups such as Indigenous peoples, Madheshi, Dalit, Muslim, and Women. The hill Brahmin/ism is still very much a default way of living. That's why the smell of all fermented foods does not get the same response or affect the consumers the same way.

Many of my Brahmin friends' households oftentimes used to have the smell of milk, curd, ghee. I find it intolerable, especially the smell of *nauni-gheu*,[2] *dahi-mohi*.[3] No matter what, the haunting smell was always there. After all, the smell of their food was as intolerable to me as the smell of our food was to them. Isn't it always the minoritized and marginalized people who have to remain in a state of fear? My privileged friends never had to worry or experience shame while eating the food that smells because that food is not the smell of the Other.

It is not only on the societal level that we face discrimination, but on the state level as well. State laws and policies are discriminatory and unjust towards the marginalized communities and the food they consume. For example, Hindus consider a cow as a sacred symbol of life. Even after Nepal became a secular state under the Constitution of Nepal 2015, a cow is still continued a national animal. Cow-killing is banned. Its effect on non-Brahmins, especially Dalits, Muslims, and Indigenous peoples, who could be falsely accused of cow slaughter is terrible. Nepal and India have abundant instances of the criminalization of cow-slaughter being used as a tool of caste terror. While "Nepal Police often does not fully investigate crimes such as rape and untouchability. . . . Cow-slaughter is an altogether different matter" (Gyawali 2019). Richard Quinney has rightly pointed out that the weight of a crime is how its meaning is constructed in its societal context (Quinney 1970). This example suggests that it is more about which symbol is associated with whom, the circulating discourse of that symbol, and the affects of such rhetorics on the everyday lives of the Others. In Nepal, the laws and constitution reinforce the dominant culture by nurturing the cultural politics of the rulers.

BIBHUSHANA POUDYAL: ETERNALLY CURRY-REEKING EXISTENCE AND A NEPALI ACADEMIC'S DEFERRED HEALING PROCESS IN THE UNITED STATES

It was October 2020. After so many months of lockdown and cancellation of all flights from Nepal due to the COVID-19, my partner—a food enthusiast—was finally able to visit me in the United States. For this during-pandemic fourth-year International PhD student dealing with toxic academic colonization in the field—a subject for another day—my partner's arrival was something beyond any words can ever express. He had also brought many spices that he had been preparing and packing for months so that we could enjoy his cooking together and the aroma of spices from Nepal, from home. Coincidentally, it was Dashain, which is considered the biggest Nepali festival celebrated mostly by Hindus. My partner and I celebrate it more culinarily than religiously. It was a wonderful Dashain morning in El Paso. I had just gotten up and was enjoying Nepali-styled *masala chiya*/tea while working on my computer. My partner was cooking Dashain special varieties of food. Our apartment was filled with the festive aroma of home. What a moment that was! Perhaps that is how the rare moments of healing feel.

Just then, the Mexican American[4] manager and the owner of the complex arrived to inspect our unit, which was filled with the mouthwatering aroma of our homeland. The moment I saw them, I was already stressed. After all, I had directly and indirectly heard a lot about the smell of our food. While leaving, one of them made a "Whew!" sound. I still do not know why that sound was made. I was hurt. I was angry. I was ashamed. I was angry that I was ashamed. I did not say any of this to my partner. I did not want to disrupt that beautiful moment for him. But that "whew" sound haunted me for a long time. I can still feel the specter of that sound in our apartment sometimes.

That "whew" is not an isolated incident. There is a structural exclusion that makes this "whew" sound haunting. The following question was asked on Reddit:

> Landlords, how do you deal with curry smells left by tenants?
> My parents are attempting to rent out their house and they're adamantly against renting to Indian families[5] because they're afraid Indian cooking will cause the house to smell. . . . The smell lingers on the walls, in the carpets, cabinets, and is extremely difficult to get rid of without months of effort. Can they write food odors into their rental agreement somehow? What do you landlords out there do with regards to this possible problem?[6]

One of the answers reads: "It's totally true and a little known secret of Indian cooking. . . . Otherwise, you'll spend $$$$ cleaning up the smell from your property. Not to mention the air quality of the neighborhood.:(:(" Another responder writes, "I work in property management and this is a common issue. This is why you hold a damage deposit." Here is another one: "Rent to Indians. House Smells like curry. Indians move out. Advertise listing as '.T. / Software Engineer Special: Spicy atmosphere, just like Mom's house.' Rent to Indians again, they'll feel right at home. Profit."

In 2017, *The Sun* reports that Fergus Wilson, UK's biggest buy-to-let millionaire "secretly" bans his agents in an email leaked to *The Sun* from letting properties to "colored people" because "of the curry smell at the end of the tenancy" (Royston 2017). Wilson clarified that he did not mean all "colored people" have this "problem" but only "certain types of coloured people—those who consume curry—it sticks to the carpet" (Royston 2017). He refused to apologize after public backlash over his decision to ban "colored people." Why would he? After all, Wilson's problem is understandably colossal: "You have to get some chemical thing that takes the smell out. In extreme cases you have to replace the carpet" (Royston 2017). He bans the curry-smelling "colored people" instead of throwing out the carpet. Wilson continued standing by his directives. He claimed that he is not racist but only making a sound economic decision. How can he be racist when he is happy to rent to black people[7] as their food does not generate a curry smell at the end of the tenancy. And he adds, "If you want to sell your house to a market mainly composed of white British purchasers, then you considerably reduce your chances of selling by having a house that smells of curry" (Bulman 2017).

In 2019, a hijab-clad woman launched a racist attack on an Indian co-passenger after the former's mother had clashed with the bus driver over overcrowding in the bus and the latter came to the bus driver's defense. The woman told him, "You smell of curry, dumb b**tard. Go back to your f**king Southall slum" ("'You Smell of Curry'" 2019). In another episode, Sharanya Deepak is fired from a job because she is told she smelled like curry. As a response to it, she blogged,

> When you grow up in India, curry isn't really a smell. It isn't even a word. But on one day in April 2015, at my bartending job in Brussels, I was told I smelled like curry. And became, in one instant, reduced to a dish. . . .
>
> "Okay, alright, then, you're fired," he said. More short sentences. "I am?" I asked.
>
> "Yes." He answered. "You smell like curry, we don't want the customers to complain."

I just stood there—deep in thought, wondering, how could someone smell like curry? My thought process switched. What does curry even smell like? Which specific spice? (Deepak 2018)

Perhaps Deepak's food was not that of Others in India like mine was not in Nepal (I recommend readers watching the movie *Axone*). That's why Deepak and I were ignorant of this discrimination until we landed in the West. After I came to the United States, it did not take too long for me to realize that we (Nepalis/South Asians) are not supposed to enjoy our cuisine without fearing its smell. I didn't know the smell of my food was so undesirable. After all, in terms of food and its smell, I am not the Other where I come from. Though I don't identify myself as Brahmin, I come from a Hill Brahmin family, and I still have the privilege of being identified as Brahmin. Therefore, my food never smelled undesirable. Even if it did smell to Others, it didn't change the way I felt about my food and its smell (as my co-author Mala has already discussed). When I came to the United States, I couldn't understand why Nepalis are so petrified by the smell of our own food. It took a while to realize I had transitioned from the privileged Brahmin Self to the "curry-reeking" South Asian Other. Suddenly, the aroma of our food started turning into a peculiar smell that reeks of haunting cooking odors. Desperately, we would close the door of our wardrobes, spray "cherry" air fresheners in our apartments, burn scented candles (the more assimilatory fragrance, the better), check if kitchen exhaust fans are working. If we live in our own house, we would select the materials of our furniture (like the fabric of a couch) that do not absorb the smell of our cooking. We constantly struggle to keep ourselves from becoming one of the five smelliest neighbors "across the globe" (Kirk 2017).

I wrap up this section with one more experience of the ways that material and rhetorical conditions are intertwined.[8] A few years prior to my move to the United States, my mother and I were combing through Kathmandu's streets for grocery shopping. Suddenly, my nose picked up a smell I found repulsive. I complained, "Why do people just throw trash on the streets? It smells horrible." My mother laughed and pointed me toward one roadside shop. I figured out that it was the smell of *tama* (fermented bamboo shoot). I laughed along. Because it is the food that is desired by my entire family and a regular food item in our household, it was suddenly no longer repulsive or horrible. *Tama*'s smell was still the same, but my relationship with that specific materiality shifted because it was no longer the smell of the Other. I relayed this instance to invite scholars, educators, and activists working at the intersection of rhetorics, writing studies, and food justice to pay attention to the following observation: We often think we experience materiality for what it is. We take it for granted. Sadly, we often fail to recognize that the way we experience materiality has a lot to do with our rhetorical situatedness and our privileges and marginalization in the global and local socio-symbolic structure. It is not to suggest that we are entirely conditioned by our rhetorical situatedness. Recognizing how we are conditioned by it is the only way to liberate ourselves from that unjust control and move toward more just rhetorical-material conditions. The framework of the smell of the Other that we are proposing in this chapter is a call for that move.

RECLAIMING FOOD, RECLAIMING SMELL, AND RECLAIMING DIGNITY

If "making visible how intrinsic food is to our sense of being, self-identity, self-expression, pleasure, well-being and connection is an act of making oneself visible" (Andrews, Smith, and Morena 2019, 14), what do our experiences say about our in/visibility and in/dignity? Isn't it another form of denial of the right to food? And is not it high time we start incorporating these embodied experiences, knowledge, and rhetorics in our scholarship and food justice activism through the framework of the smell of the Other? Though this chapter is written from two different subject positions in two different contexts, the exclusionary rhetorics and practices against the smell of the Other and our experiences with it are strikingly similar. As we are yet to raise our voices to combat these rhetorics and practices loudly, actively, and assertively in academia and beyond, many of us are suffering discrimination silently. We are losing jobs and being banned from housing. We suffer embarrassment, insult, shame, and self-alienation. Our connection to our home, community, and ourselves is forcibly disrupted. Hence, aligning with this edited collection's call for begetting new ways to continue to fight injustices in the food system on both a local and global level, the raison d'etre of this chapter is to invite food justice activists, educators, researchers, and the members of diverse minoritized and oppressed communities to join this "smelly" movement toward reclaiming food, smell, and dignity by bringing in structually silenced experiences and voices to fight rhetorical inaccessibility to food.

REFERENCES

Agnew, Vijay. 2007. *Interrogating Race and Racism.* Toronto: University of Toronto Press.
Alkon, Alison Hope, and Julian Agyeman. 2011. *Cultivating Food: Justice Race, Class, and Sustainability.* Cambridge: MIT Press.
Andrews, Donna, Kiah Smith, and M. Alejandra Morena. 2019. "Enraged: Women and Nature." In *Right to Food and Nutrition Watch*, 6–15. Brot für die Welt and

FIAN International, no. 11. https://www.righttofoodandnutrition.org/files/rtfn-watch11-2019_eng.pdf.
Barad, Karen. 2003. "Posthumanist Performativity: Toward an Understanding of How Matter Comes to Matter." *Signs: Journal of Women in Culture and Society*, no. 28.
Bulman, May. 2017, March 30. "Landlord Who Banned 'Coloured' People 'Because of Curry Smell' Insists He's Not Racist and Is Happy to Rent to 'Negroes.'." https://www.independent.co.uk/news/uk/home-news/landlord-who-banned-coloured-people-because-curry-smell-says-he-s-not-racist-a7657231.html.
Deepak, Sharanya. 2018, May 10. "'You Smell Like Curry, You're Fired.'" https://www.buzzfeed.com/sharanyadeepak/you-smell-like-curry-youre-fired.
Free for Life. 2020. "A Culture of Oppression: The Hindu Caste System." https://freeforlifeintl.org/2020/08/21/a-culture-of-oppression-the-hindu-caste-system.
Frye, Joshua J., and Michael S. Bruner. 2012. "Introduction." In *The Rhetoric of Food Discourse, Materiality, and Power*, edited by Joshua J. Frye and Michael S. Bruner, 1–6. New York: Routledge.
Garth, Hanna, and Ashanté M. Reese. 2020. *Black Food Matters Racial Justice in the Wake of Food Justice*. Minneapolis: University of Minnesota Press.
Gottlieb, Robert, and Anupama Joshi. 2013. *Food Justice*. Cambridge: MIT Press.
Gyawali, Shiva Hari. 2019, June 14. "Criminalization of Cow-Slaughter Is a Tool of Caste Terror." https://www.recordnepal.com/criminalization-of-cow-slaughter-is-a-tool-of-caste-terror.
Khadka, Dambar Bahadur, and Jiwan Prava Lama. 2020. "Traditional Fermented Food of Nepal and Their Nutritional and Nutraceutical Potential." In *Nutritional and Health Aspects of Food in South Asian Countries*, edited by Jamuna Prakash, Viduranga Waisundara, and Vishweshwaraiah Prakash, 165–94. London: Academic Press.
Kirk, Mimi. 2017, June 29. "When Neighbors Raise a Stink." https://www.bloomberg.com/news/articles/2017-06-29/five-of-the-world-s-smelliest-neighbors.
LeGreco, Marianne, and Niesha Douglas. 2021. *Everybody Eats: Communication and the Paths to Food Justice*. Berkeley: University of California Press.
Manalansan IV, Martin F. 2006. "Immigrant Lives and the Politics of Olfaction in the Global City." In *The Smell Culture Reader*, edited by Jim Drobnick, 41–52. New York: Routledge.
Penniman, Leah. 2018. *Farming while Black: Soul Fire Farm's Practical Guide to Liberation on the Land*. Hartford: Chelsea Green.
Quinney, Richard. 1970. *The Social Reality of Crime*. New York: Little, Brown and Company.
Royston, Jack. 2017, March 29. "'No More Coloureds or Curries': Fury as Britain's Biggest Buy-to-Let Landlord Bans 'Coloured' People in Racist Rant Because They Make His Properties 'Smell of Curry.'" https://www.thesun.co.uk/news/3192423/fury-as-britains-biggest-buy-to-let-landlord-bans-coloured-people-in-racist-rant-because-they-make-his-properties-smell-of-curry/?CMP=Spklr-_-Editorial-_-TheSun-_-News-_-TwImageandlink-_-Statement-_-TWITTER.
"'You Smell of Curry': Hijab-Clad Woman Launches Racist Attack on Indian Passenger in London." 2019, September 18. *DNA* online. https://www.dnaindia

.com/world/report-you-smell-of-curry-hijab-clad-woman-launches-racist-attack-on-indian-passenger-in-london-2790784.

NOTES

1. We invite audiences to contemplate the differences between global and planetary.
2. A butter-like product achieved by churning yogurt.
3. *Dahi* is yogurt and *mohi* is yogurt made by churning milk.
4. Notice the intersectionality and multiple layers of other(ed)ness among Others themselves.
5. Due to the underrepresentation of Nepalis in the United States, we become invisible behind the name Indian. Again, that is another subject for another time.
6. Though these conversations are on a public platform, the individuals engaged in this conversation might not have intended it for public consumption. Hence, for ethical reasons, we are not citing the source.
7. Wilson uses the N-word here.
8. Not to mention the time when one of my non-Western colleagues made a remark one day that I smelled of the incense Indian folks burn when I was actually wearing Versace perfume. I wonder if that perfume would still smell of incense if, for instance, I were a white person.

PART II

Chapter 5

Seeds of the Diaspora

Using Creative and Collaborative Writing to Explore Critical Food Literacies with Black Youth

OreOluwa Badaki

FOOD LITERACY ON THE FARM

"Some people just be slappin' 'organic' on everything, at least these potato chips keep it real." Kembi[1] (2020) announces this to the group as she proudly munches on her crispy, bright yellow snack. I laugh alongside the fifteen other high schoolers in the circle. We are at a community farm, and these high schoolers are part of a youth internship program that teaches them about African Diasporic foodways and engages them in food justice and sovereignty initiatives in their community. Kembi is a youth leader in this program. She speaks her mind, and in her mind, she can be *both* a food justice advocate *and* an occasional fan of greasy potato chips. She can be critical of "greenwashing" (Dahl 2010) *and* acknowledge what she considers honest food messaging, even when it shows up in unexpected places. Kembi brings together diverse perspectives and preferences as she assesses for herself what it means to be a conscious consumer of food.

This chapter explores how youth of color, like Kembi, engage aspects of *critical food literacies*. I center stories from three youth of color—two of whom exist in our reality, one of whom exists in an imagined reality—as I inquire into the ways in which creative storytelling and collaborative writing can offer unique opportunities to engage critical food literacies. First, I articulate the conceptual framing around critical food literacies. Second, I describe the study design and explain the inspiration, rationale, and process of using creative storytelling and collaborative writing to better understand critical food literacies. Third, I discuss an example of what exploring critical food literacies through creative storytelling and collaborative writing with youth of color can look like. Fourth, and finally, I reflect on the implications of this inquiry for research, teaching and learning interested in supporting young people as they work toward healthier, more just, and more sustainable futures.

Critical Food Literacies

As a literacy researcher and educator interested in community health and environmental justice, I focus on what a critical engagement with food "before and beyond the plate" (Widener and Karides 2014) can do for our understanding of how we read the word, how we read the world, and how we read ourselves (Friere and Macedo 2005). I am drawn to the power of words as both reflective and agentive tools. This inquiry, therefore, defines literacy not just as the process by which individuals receive and share information through texts, but also as the process by which "values, attitudes, feelings and social relationships" (Street 1993, 12) inform interactions with text. This definition stems from critical literacy studies, which goes beyond a skills-based orientation toward literacy that focuses on acquiring observable and neutral competencies (Freebody and Luke 1990). Critical literacy highlights the social, historical, and political levers that influence what gets defined as "literacy" and who gets to be deemed "literate." It also acknowledges that there are multiple literacies associated with multiple contexts, and that different modalities (written, visual, auditory, performed, etc.) should also be considered in the study of literacy (Campano, Nichols, and Player 2020; Janks 2009; Cope and Kalantzis 2000).

A multimodal and critical understanding of literacy is important in the context of food literacy, especially since common conceptualizations of food literacy have been critiqued for being myopic and limited in scope. Sumner (2015) challenges the narrow focus on the individual in food literacy research, arguing for food literacy definitions to "encompass more than individual responsibility" and to confront issues of power, privilege, and hegemony. She points to the harmful influences of neoliberal ideologies that thrive on inequity and that promote pathologizing and reductive notions of health and wellness. Vidgen and Gallegos (2014) note that most common metrics of food literacy are based on conceptualizations developed by individual researchers with little to no input from, nor understanding of, the communities that these metrics target.

Despite its shortcomings, food literacy research can help to galvanize and synthesize work on food justice and food sovereignty, especially when critical lenses are employed. Winslow defines critical food literacy as a "politicized knowledge about food" that enables one to critically engage with arguments, resources, and information on issues of food and food production (2012, 6). Yamashita and Robinson (2016) build on this conceptualization, focusing more explicitly on marginalized populations who are often rendered invisible by the very food systems that are wholly dependent on them. They define critical food literacy as the ability to examine and grapple with the myriad values and perspectives that inform food choices and processes, to engage with the larger socio-political phenomena that influence food systems, and to address issues of food justice and sovereignty with decisive action.

To these important foundations, I contribute a concept from the field of health literacy. Food literacy is often considered a type of health literacy (Renwick and Powell 2019; Velardo 2015). Like food literacy scholarship, health literacy scholarship has not yet been unified under a common definition, however Nutbeam's (2000) health literacy model is widely accepted as a starting point. In developing his health literacy model, Nutbeam draws from Freebody and Luke's (1990) emphasis on thinking about literacy not just in terms of lists of universal skills and assessments, but rather in terms of the contexts and processes literacy enables individuals to engage in: *functional health literacy* refers to the basic reading and writing skills that enable individuals to navigate health situations, *interactive health literacy* refers to the skills that enable individuals to actively participate in health institutions and to adapt to changing circumstances, and *critical health literacy* refers to the skills that enable individuals to critically interrogate information and use it in empowering and conscientious ways. More recent health literacy scholarship has further emphasized the importance of context and process; going beyond a focus on creating health literate individuals and emphasizing the need for more *health literate systems and institutions* (Kindig, Panzer, and Nielsen-Bohlman 2004; Begoray, Gillis, and Rowlands 2012; Sørensen et al. 2021). Kindig, Panzer, and Nielsen-Bohlman (2004) posit that the challenges in health literacy promotion may be a result of the mismatch between the assumptions, values and goals prioritized by those in charge of health care systems and those of the communities they claim to serve. Therefore, we need leaders of health literate systems who "are able to recognize and break down barriers that prevent people from accessing and understanding information and services provided to support health (Begoray, Gillis, and Rowlands 2012, 4).

Harking back to Sumner's critique of hyperindividualized food literacy conceptualizations, I consider what it might mean to go beyond individualized notions of critical food literacy and push for *food literate systems* that are more responsive to the realities of the communities they are meant to serve. Sumner goes on to argue for "food systems transformation" (2015), and other food literacy scholars have called for more "radical food literacy" that "moves away from the idea of focusing on nutrition or cooking skills to instead argue that the system itself . . . should be challenged—and changed" (Truman, Lane, and Elliott 2017, 212). In the following inquiry, I focus on how engaging *critical food literacies* with youth of color, through creative storytelling and collaborative writing, can support efforts toward more *food literate systems*.

CENTERING CREATIVITY, COLLABORATION, AND POSITIONALITY

This chapter explores the question, *What happens when youth of color are invited to engage in creative storytelling and collaborative writing around issues of food and environmental justice?* This question was part of my larger dissertation study on the creative, critical, and citizenship practices of youth of color working in urban agriculture. I conducted my research over three years with twenty high school and college-aged youth of color working at Diaspora Farm; an urban farm that centers African diasporic foodways and that supports young people and their communities in becoming leaders in community health, urban agriculture, and food sovereignty.

During my last year of fieldwork, I facilitated a creative writing group with seven Black youth participants who wanted to explore the intersections between their creative interests and their food justice work. In addition to traditional ethnographic data collection and analysis methods used for my larger study, I drew from research in practitioner inquiry (Appadurai 2006; Carr and Kemis 1986; Schön 1995) to analyze both the writing group as well as my practice as a member and facilitator of the writing group. I engaged Gallagher, Wessels and Ntelioglou's notion of a "metho-pedagogy," in which "using arts-based or participatory methods, asks the researchers to adapt fluidly to important affective moments as they arise in research sites and reshape the social relations within them" (2012, 239). In inquiring into the pedagogical and methodological possibilities of collaborative storytelling and creative writing, I build on decades of scholarship that highlights the ways in which the creative arts can engage young people in discussions about positionality, power, and political conscientization.

Creative Storytelling

Researchers have shown the ways in which creative and imaginative storytelling can help young people "author themselves" (Vasudevan, Schultz, and Bateman 2010), explore and convey strong advocacy messaging (Blanks Jones 2015), and promote dialogue across differences (Whitelaw 2012). In this inquiry, I center what Gallagher, Rodricks, and Jacobson (2020) call "civic storytelling," or the practice of merging creativity and criticality to add diverse voices to social justice movements. They argue that a focus on creative and dramatic construction offers "a unique way to access the imagined as well as the real in youth research" (6), opening pathways toward a "creative resilience" that "permits both critical thinking and co-creation of possibilities for action and care" (11). This "creative resilience" is especially important for youth of color working for food justice and sovereignty. They often come from communities that are both afflicted and silenced by sociopolitical injustices in the food system.

In her exploratory study, Naya Jones (2019a) uses creative modalities to "bear witness to testimonies of racial surveillance" in Black food geographies. By unpacking "verbal and non-verbal storytelling" of the racial profiling, targeting, and hypervisibility experienced by Black and Latinx research participants, Jones complicates Nixon's (2011) popular conceptualization of "slow violence" as being "out of sight." For some communities, Jones argues, the violence of predatory environmental and food systems is all too visible and visceral. Jones urges us to sustain an acute awareness of this violence and to consider "affective approaches" to addressing it. One way Jones does this is by infusing her creative storytelling with what McKittrick (2006), drawing from Glissant (1997), calls "geographic expressions." These expressions can include "writing and imagining space and place" (xxi).

The youth writers who joined the creative writing group imagined and wrote into existence spaces and places that no longer preyed on the bodies, minds, and spirits of youth of color and their communities. The goal was to combat the "narratives of nothingness" (Reese, 2019) often surrounding youth and communities of color working for food justice, as well as the rising rates of "climate anxiety" (Majeed and Lee 2017; Wu, Snell, and Samji 2020) and emotional despair among young people who are worried about the future of the planet. The writing group invited youth interns at Diaspora to activate their imaginations as they worked to become more conscious consumers and producers of food, and to build more just and sustainable food systems in the real world. This chapter explores how these young people engaged various kinds of critical food literacies, and practiced civic storytelling, through creative and collaborative writing.

Collaborative Writing

The creative writing group at Diaspora offered young people the opportunity to interweave their experiences with the converging and diverging experiences of their peers, families, educators, and community members, across time and space. While an explicit focus on collaborative writing was important, the term "collaborative writing" may, in fact, be redundant. Researchers have argued that all writing can be considered "collaborative" in one way or another. Yagelski posits that "writing is inherently an act of connection. What emerges as we write in the moment is a multifaceted sense of self that is connected, through language, to other selves and to the world we share" (2012, 193). Arola's notion of "composing as culturing" decenters the myth of "a lone genius who generates original ideas on her own" (2017, 278). Hyland (2003) attributes this sort of myth to an "ideology of individualism" that sees the "writer as an isolated individual struggling to express personal meanings" (p. 18). Rooted in Native American philosophies and rhetoric, Arola's "composing as culturing" approach rejects the image of a "lone author, or lone remixer" and argues that composing is a relational and iterative action done in the pursuit of furthering the work of a community (or "culturing"). Rather than asking *whether or not* writing is collaborative, a more useful question is *in what way*s is writing collaborative and how does it sustain community?

The scene I explore in this chapter was inspired by a story told by Shauna during my second year of fieldwork. Shauna is Kembi's younger sister and was a newer intern at Diaspora at the time. Her story sparked ideas in me, which in turn sparked ideas in others and created the foundation for the creative writing group. I discuss this process later in the chapter to illustrate how the creative writing group was a way to take a deeper dive into the collaborative nature of idea generation and expression through writing. As discussed earlier, even when the term "collaborative" is not used to describe writing, the practice of writing is still inherently relational and interactional. Writing is part of a process of continuous giving and taking; it is part of a pervasive mutuality that informs the process and the product whether that mutuality is acknowledged or not.

To bring the characters, worlds, questions, and themes in our imaginations to life, the writing group decided to write a screenplay. Writing for performance, either for the theater or for the screen, can be a generative exercise for exploring the multiple dimensions of social issues in general (Gallagher et al. 2022, 2020, 2012; Medina and Campano 2006; Whitelaw 2019; Vasudevan et al. 2010) as well as issues of climate and environmental justice more specifically (Doyle 2020; Osnes 2018, 2017). Whitelaw found that giving young people the opportunity to explore differing perspectives and opinions through script writing helped them navigate the various contradictions and interpretations that make up real-world social interactions. In some cases, an emphasis on polyvocality, rather than on representations of good and evil, also helped to make "visible an aspect of power that might have remained hidden in more conventional approaches to the subject" (2019, 139). In addition, exploring a "polyphony of voices" can support "representations of culture [that] are not essentialized portrayals of generic ethnic prescriptions. Rather, they employ and craft literacy practices to adapt to their respective situations" (Medina & Campano 2006, 340).

This inquiry focuses on what writing collaboratively for performance, whether for the screen or for the stage, can do for our collective imagination. While scriptwriting is a foundational pillar of theater methodologies, I focus on scriptwriting not as a means to an end (or to a performance), but as a writing genre in and of itself. As Hyland notes, "Writing is a basic resource for constructing our relationships with others and for understanding our experience of the world, and as such genre is centrally involved in the ways we negotiate, construct, and change our understanding of our societies and ourselves" (2003, 27). I am interested in how scriptwriting as a genre of writing, which brings with it considerations around set design, action lines, transitions, camera movement, parentheticals, and dialogue, might inform the ways we use our imaginative capacities to negotiate the world around us. Gallagher, Rodricks, and Jacobson (2020) posit that writing for performance, and performance in and of itself, can be a "lens that illuminates the constructed, creative, contingent, collaborative dimensions of human communication" (108). Writing dialogue and action lines, for example, encourages a certain meta-awareness of the ways in which people use verbal and body language to communicate (sometimes conflicting, sometimes subconscious) messages.

Some of the young people in my study claimed they "do not like reading," yet the script format opens doors for different types of engagement with text (e.g., focusing more on spatial structure and design, verbal speech and communication, or embodied movement and direction). Script writing offered youth writers an opportunity to think purposefully about space, place, and the human body as they constructed and populated the imagined world of their screenplay. While I do not delve too deeply into the genre-specific elements of scriptwriting in this chapter, I consider how young people engaged critical food literacies through collaborative writing within this genre.

Positionality and Power

As discussed above, I was intentional about exploring the collaborative nature of writing in this inquiry. However, I also recognize that collaboration does not automatically lead to democratic processes or equitable outcomes. It is important for researchers and practitioners to consider their power and positionality within any writing collaboration. Cochran-Smith and Lytle (2015) ask, "How do various collaborators participate in conceptualizing, drafting, revising and editing and what does collaboration really mean, when sometimes, in the final product, we retain for ourselves the 'last word' or the shape of the 'final draft'?" (103). In this chapter, I retain the final word. This chapter, while written in communication with young people, was not written by young people. It is still through my lens that their stories are told. This is an important consideration in any research, even when (or perhaps, especially when) there are efforts to be more participatory or collaborative.

In her participatory ethnography, Laurie Thorp (2006) centered the stories of her research participants "not as low hanging fruit simply to be plucked during an interview" (120), but as opportunities to listen deeply to the various possibilities for collective meaning-making and understanding offered by these interactions. She posits that in listening to and telling stories, "we are able to sequence events into unified episodes; this develops into plot and, by being in plot . . . there is a 'temporal thickness' . . . [that] suggest a causal or thematic relation among events beyond temporal order" (123). In leaning into this "temporal thickness" as I considered imaginative possibilities for story and plot, I aimed to decenter my immediate reactions and ideas of experiences in hopes of slowing down my own meaning-making processes and making room for the imaginative contributions of others. During the creative writing group sessions, in order to generate ideas for the story, I called back into the space insights and questions interns had introduced during past interviews or observations. This offered me the opportunity to get second, third, and sometimes even fourth interpretations of things the interns had previously said and done, both from the interns who had said and done them as well as from their peers. Sometimes the temporal accuracy of the actual sequence of events was important in these recollections, and sometimes it was not. Writing our story, therefore, was not only a way to explore a collective imagined reality, but also a way to center a "temporal thickness" that allowed us to revisit, remix, and re-examine aspects of our own lived realities.

TELLING THE *STORY OF ADA*

Below are drafts of the synopsis and first scene of the screenplay the creative writing group is working on, temporarily titled *Story of Ada*. In the sections that follow, I dissect the early stages of the collaborative and creative storytelling process that led to the creation of these drafts.

SYNOPSIS:

Ada is part of a group of orphans sent to become food cultivators on a new planet. Along the journey, she finds that she can time travel in her dreams and that her destiny is tied to the powerful okra seed. With the help of her friends, Ada has to unlock the mystery of her past, in order to reveal a hidden conspiracy that threatens all of their futures. This is her story.

SCENE 1. INT—NIGHT

ADA (16) sits on the floor of a modest living room and watches the NEWS. MAMA (40s) hums a song while braiding Ada's hair.

MAMA

Make sure you don't let anyone touch your hair. I worked hard on this and I don't want anyone to mess it up.

ADA

(distracted by the news)

Uh huh.

MAMA

Remember to keep it moisturized. The shea butter . . .

ADA

Right . . .

MAMA

Cover it when you can, especially before going to sleep.

ADA

(annoyed)

Mama, I know all this. Why're you making such a big deal?

MAMA

(sighs)

I just . . . it's important.

ADA

It's just hair Mama.

Mama moves so she is in front of Ada. She holds Ada's shoulders and looks her in the eyes.

MAMA

It's NOT just hair. You need to understand that.

ADA

(weirded out)

Ok . . . sorry.

Mama goes back to Ada's cornrows. She resumes her humming. Ada feels her mom place something into her hair as she braids.

ADA

What're you putting in my hair?

Mama hesitates, then a loud CRASH as the door gets knocked. Two uniformed men with weapons burst into the room. They move straight for Mama. Before they reach her, Mama grabs Ada's braids and brings their heads close. Mama gives Ada a look filled with hope and fear.

MAMA

Survive. You must survive.

The men grab Mama and force her out of the room. Mama YELLS and SCREAMS and reaches for Ada, Ada does the same. The men don't seem to notice Ada. She yells but no sound comes out.

The sound of Mama's YELLS become muffled. The scene begins to fade. We hear DJEMBE DRUMS beating softly at first, then the sound gets louder as the scene fades to black.

Cut to:

Ada wakes up with a jolt. Her ALARM is going off. She feels around and realizes that she is back in her bed. The sound of the DJEMBE turns into a low HUM of a ship.

Ada looks outside of her window and sees nothing but space, as in outer space. She is on a spaceship. She gets up and stumbles into the bathroom. She turns on the light and stares at the mirror.

ADA

(shocked)

What the . . . ?

Ada gulps and takes a breath; she touches the hair that is now in cornrows. These were not there when she went to sleep last night.

Ada slowly takes out one of the braids, the smallest one next to her left ear. Three small seeds fall out. They are okra seeds.

Ada's Origin: Inviting Imaginative and Speculative Thinking

Ada's story begins long before we meet her sitting at her mother's feet in this first scene. As mentioned earlier, Ada's story was inspired by a story that Shauna told in response to a reflective prompt youth interns were given by Diaspora educators. Diaspora interns were often offered reflective writing prompts to help them review lessons, yet on this occasion they were asked to come up with an Afrofuturist story inspired by food of the African Diaspora.

This prompt was rare in that it invited interns to engage their speculative and imaginative thinking. Given that my work in literacy education is informed by my interest in the creative arts, I was particularly intrigued by this prompt as well as by the stories the interns came up with.

Though the activity was short-lived, the excitement some of the interns expressed around the prompt suggested to me that there was more room for this sort of thinking and engagement. While some interns gave intriguing, yet short, one-line summaries of the plots of their stories, interns like Shauna went into vivid detail. Shauna waved her hands excitedly as she painted for us a picture of the world unfolding in her imagination. Hers would be an epic space odyssey about the sweet potato, a food that although not indigenous to Africa, has played a major role in African Diasporic cuisine. In Shauna's story, a young African American girl in the distant future is kept against her will on a spaceship headed to an unknown planet. All she has with her are the sweet potato seeds her mother snuck into her thick afro just before she was captured. She however, does not remember this because her memory, as well as the memories of all the captives on board, has been wiped clean.

Clearly, there are resonances of Shauna's original story in the *Story of Ada*, and clearly there are resonances of other Afrofuturist stories in Shauna's story. Toliver (2021) and Holbert, Dando, and Correa (2020) show that remixing and reconstructing are important aspects of crafting Afrofuturist stories, as exploring new avenues of possibility within existing narratives are crucial components of this genre. Afrofuturism is often considered a subgenre of speculative fiction, a genre that specializes in narrativizing new potentialities as well as processes for reaching new possibilities. This sort of storytelling is especially beneficial for youth and for research concerning youth. Gallagher, Rodricks, and Jacobson (2020) posit, "Whether researchers of the social world can study what might be, not simply what is. This question seems altogether critical for youth studies, given the human becomings or beings-in-process that young people are often imagined to be" (84). Young people are often inundated with messages about the potentialities and possibilities that lie in their futures. Sometimes these messages are hopeful and sometimes they bring fear and anxiety, especially when it comes to global warming and environmental degradation.

Haraway (2016) asserts that "being with the students, or 'becoming-with'" (12) is a crucial part of the creative and collaborative process. I became curious about the pedagogical possibilities of engaging more deeply with the imagined realities that are central to the stories young people tell about the future. As a creative writer, myself, I welcomed the opportunity to build on the imaginative contributions of the youth I work with, and therefore I used the original Afrofuturist prompt described above as a jumping off point for the writing group. The stories that came from this prompt highlighted themes, questions, and insights that shed light on the ways that young people at Diaspora were activating different aspects of critical food literacies and grappling with questions about the future of food, climate, and environmental justice.

Inspired by the work of Vasudevan and Riina-Ferrie (2019) and others who iteratively compose creative artifacts from data, and subsequently use these artifacts to elicit more data, I wrote a short scene using the same prompt youth interns were given. I used observations I had made during my first two years of fieldwork to write the scene, and subsequently used this scene as an anchoring text for the creative writing group. In our initial meetings, the group discussed if, where, and how they saw themselves in the story, as well as how they wanted to take the story forward. In the following two sections, I focus on contributions from Shauna and Hashi, two young women who were particularly instrumental in building the *Story of Ada*. I discuss how they helped to inform the first scene of Ada's story (shown above) and draw attention to the ways in which they engaged aspects of critical food literacies to bring Ada's story to life.

"SURVIVE. YOU MUST SURVIVE": SHAUNA FOREGROUNDS MEMORY AND AGENCY

Afrofuturist stories often project images of Black futures rooted in African Diasporic histories and experiences. Therefore, they connect past, present, and future narratives in imaginative and innovative ways. Memory is a key ingredient in this process and in her original sweet potato story, Shauna foregrounds memory as a primary axis upon which the story rotates. The *Story of Ada*, similarly, centers memory, or the lack thereof, as a point of departure.

Activating memory as a vehicle for action is a core aspect of a critical food literacy cognizant of the sociohistorical aspects of food. Ashanté Reese (2019) highlights the spatial component of nostalgic imaginaries related to food and land for African Americans. These imaginaries involve experiences with "enslavement, Jim Crow, residential segregation" and "are produced through the ways Black people negotiate power, space, and confinement to create places of care and celebration" (70–71). These imaginaries show up in Shauna's original story as well as in the *Story of Ada*; stories for which the spatial and temporal context are even further removed from the experiences that inspired them. During a brainstorming session, Shauna shared a suggestion for Ada's storyline, "When they make it to the new planet . . . [Ada] goes and she finds a place to grow the seeds in the forest and she starts to gather dreams from her past and her ancestors. . . . [Ada] tells more kids about the truth about the government and they make their own in the forest" (Shauna,

2021). Here, Shauna projects a hopeful future for Ada, a future rooted in a deep knowledge of food and ancestry as well as in a commitment to liberation from oppressive regimes. These were themes that Shauna was grappling with in her own life. The first time I met Shauna, a couple months before she planted the seeds for Ada's story, I asked her about why she wanted to learn how to grow food at Diaspora. She responded with the following,

> It's a lot of bad things, like, messing up the world, like global warming. . . . I was having thoughts that the world is going to end and all that stuff. So then, I was like, but what can I do? . . . I was just scared; I was scared for myself, and like, my family. I was like, if we were in a situation, I can't. . . . I wouldn't even be able to help them. Now I feel like if the world was to end, I'd be able to survive for a while with them. (Shauna, 2019)

In this reflection, Shauna expresses trepidation about her future given the dire consequences of global warming.

Shauna, like many of the other youth interns at Diaspora, wanted to learn more about problems as well as potential solutions associated with human-made climate change. Yet simply learning more about climate change does not necessarily result in action (Hestness, McGinnis, and Breslyn 2019; Lehtonen 2012) and in some cases, more knowledge can even lead to greater fear and hopelessness (Doyle 2019; Ojala 2013). Shauna asks in her reflection, "but what can I do?" Exploring themes of memory and agency through the *Story of Ada* is one way Shauna and her peers could address questions about what can be done about their futures. Facer (2019) emphasizes that "supporting students to make, tell and listen to stories has a critical role to play in enabling students to identify and articulate desires, hopes, fears and dreams for the future and to engage with the rich complexities of the present" (3). Making space for creative, speculative, and imaginative reading, writing, and discussion about global warming is crucial for improving young people's self-efficacy and for turning knowledge into action (Doyle 2019; Facer 2019; Gallagher et al. 2022; Haraway 2016; Osnes 2018, 2017).

In the first scene of Ada's story, the last thing Ada's mother says to her before she is abducted is "survive, you must survive." A question at the core of Ada's story is how she will use memory and the cultural resources available to her to do that which her mother has commanded of her. Like the fictional Ada, Shauna and many young people all over the world have serious questions about their capacity to endure what lies ahead. Shauna suggests that in the story, Ada's power comes from her knowledge of and connection to okra seeds and that it is this power that Ada uses to spread truth and challenge the status quo. There are important connections here between Shauna's real-life concerns about the future, and the future she imagines for Ada. If Shauna can imagine a brighter future for Ada, one that foregrounds the importance of memory and agency in the ways we engage with food and land systems, maybe she can imagine a brighter future for herself as well.

Shauna also hints at the need to topple oppressive power structures when she suggests that Ada "tells more kids about the truth about the government and they make their own in the forest." Here again, Shauna invokes real-world phenomena given that communities like hers are often exploited and silenced by the unjust food and land systems that have contributed to global warming. Creative and imaginative storytelling, like the type Shauna and the writing group are engaging in with the *Story of Ada*, has long been considered an important way to speak truth to unjust systems. Boal (1979) argues that theater was originally "free people singing in the open air," before "ruling classes took possession of the theater and built their dividing walls" (1979, 19). These "ruling classes" separated spectators from actors and restricted the protagonist to someone who could only exist on stage, rather than someone who could exist among the masses. A theater, or poetics, of the oppressed, Boal argues, goes beyond the catharsis centered in Aristotelian conceptions of theater and beyond the critical consciousness centered in Brechtian notions. A theater of the oppressed invites the spectator themselves to "assume the protagonic role," the spectator "changes the dramatic action, tries out solutions, discusses plans for change—in short, trains himself for real action" (122). By using the *Story of Ada* to challenge and talk back to some of the oppressive structures they and their communities have been subjected to, youth writers at Diaspora were able to "assume the protagonic role" within the narratives of their lives.

The Legacy of the Seeds: Hashi Centers Intergenerational Experiences

Youth writers at Diaspora engaged critical food literacies in their civic storytelling as they pursued questions about how to use memory and agency to combat hegemonic structures within food systems. In so doing, they "grapple with, deliberate across, and work through diverse views and conflicting values to make informed, nuanced decisions" about what it means to bring about "just, sustainable food systems" (Yamashita and Robinson 2016, 277). Like Shauna, Hashi was a newer intern at Diaspora and wanted to center justice and equity in the *Story of Ada*. Building on Shauna's contributions to Ada's storyline above, Hashi proposed that Ada should become a "silent revolutionary" who uses the powers that she gains through the seeds to challenge the adults who have control over her and her friends. Hashi suggested that Ada and her friends should use their knowledge of food to right the wrongdoing committed by older generations who were led astray.

Hashi thought a lot about the experiences that connect different generations. Ada's interaction with her mother in the opening scene was inspired by Hashi, who wanted to start the story with a nod to a historical account that had captured many of the interns' imagination. Diaspora interns heard the story of enslaved West African ancestors sowing seeds into the hair of their children before being captured and sent across the Atlantic. The stories suggest that these ancestors hoped that the seeds would ensure sustenance and survival for their progeny in the midst of the terrors that lay ahead. Though there are anecdotal accounts that suggest okra might have come to the Americas this way (Penniman 2018), there are no official historical records that suggest that this is how okra arrived. Michael Twitty (2019) argues that seeds were not literally sewn into hair and that this image instead serves as a metaphor for the agricultural wisdom brought over by enslaved Africans, "the seeds were in their minds and symbolically in their hearts." Judith Carney and Nicholas Rosomoff (2009) do give historical accounts of okra coming to the Americas from Africa during the Slave Trade. Carney (2004) also traces the history of oral tradition that tells the story of a West African variety of rice (Oryza glaberrima) arriving in the Americas in the sixteenth or seventeenth centuries thanks to the efforts of an African woman, likely coming from rice-growing regions of the Upper Guinea Coast, who is thought to have hidden rice grains in her children's hair before they were captured. From there, the grains supposedly found their way to the Americas by way of Suriname, Cayenne, Brazil, and eventually South Carolina. Notably, Carney argues that this story of how rice came to the Americas complicates traditional Western narratives that credit "European navigators, colonists, and men of science" (2004, 1) as the primary cultivators and distributors of agricultural knowledge in early America. These stories and accounts reposition enslaved African ancestors, especially women ancestors, as agentive and strategic in the face of tremendous strife.

This is what Hashi (2019) was drawing from when she suggested that our story open with a scene of a mother braiding seeds into her daughter's hair. Hashi informed us that she liked "realistic stories" and therefore suggested starting the story with a nod to the anecdotal and historical accounts described above. Here again, we see the importance of retrieving one's memory and reclaiming one's narrative, with seeds as a metaphor for both. In her ethnography of Black food geographies in Washington DC, anthropologist Ashanté Reese (2019) shows that "the ways residents remembered, imagined, and engaged the past were important, because they measured (or critiqued) food access and consumption in the present based on the nostalgic food imaginaries they created" (89). The residents in Reese's study found ways to exert agency even amidst macrosociological and geopolitical forces that inhibited equitable food access, quality, and security in their town. Reese's findings, like Hashi's invocation of the legacies of African seeds, highlight the role that memory and imagination can play in helping people navigate the structural constraints that affect their personal and collective food landscapes. Recognizing how knowledge can be passed down, both materially and metaphorically, through embodied actions like braiding hair or saving seeds, is an important aspect of critical food literacies and food pedagogies rooted in an understanding of power, oppression, and resilience (Badaki 2020; Jones 2019b).

In addition to knowledge and resources however, trauma and injustice can also be passed down from generation to generation. Both as part of her contributions to Ada's story as well as part of her own personal reflections, Hashi recognized how intergenerational ties can influence health and wellbeing. A year prior to the brainstorming session described above, during her first season on the farm, I had an interview with Hashi in which I asked her to choose a word that she felt best described the relationship between food and wellness. She picked the word "balance" and said the following,

> It's like, some people can afford to have balance. Like, your mom might have it but somebody else's mom might not have it so they get their food from the corner store, which is not really a good balance . . . [it can] cause their health bills to be higher in costs. Because they're not eating the best. But somebody who has like, a mom and dad or grandparents or whoever takes care of you, you can afford to have balance. You can afford [to go to] the best places for your food and farmers market all the time. (Hashi, 2019)

Here, Hashi suggests that poverty is a major factor in a person's ability to choose the foods they eat, connecting back to the earlier discussion on agency and memory. For Hashi, even the ability to have "balance" in one's choices is not equally accessible to all. Hashi therefore does not buy into an "ideology of healthism" (Crawford 1980) that prioritizes enforcing healthy "balanced" diet mandates over addressing systemic and endemic fractures in the food system. For her, "balance" is a resource that is only accessible to those who can "afford" it.

Hashi also suggests that these inequities have ripple effects for future generations. Access to choice and balance is largely influenced by whether someone has a "mom and dad or grandparents or whoever takes care of you" who can afford to provide resources. Jones (2019b) notes that the food practices and choices of youth of color cannot be understood in isolation, as they are heavily dependent on the adults in their lives. She argues that "food pedagogies largely maintain focus on individuals: in other words, it is up to the individual guardian or family member to provide proper meals" (2019b, 919). These pedagogies do not sufficiently take into account the intergenerational dynamics at play and the ways that social, economic, political, and historical forces affect these relationships. Jones argues for "a critical and embodied perspective that reframes relationships as a platform for (re)building how food is accessed (and enjoyed)" (919). In this orientation, there is an acknowledgment of persistent and residual injustices (such as intergenerational poverty or trauma associated with land work), as well as an invitation to chart new territories with food in healthful and holistic ways.

When Ada's mother gets abducted in the first scene of the screenplay, she looks to Ada "with hope and fear." While she is cognizant of the pain and suffering that has afflicted her people for generations, and that likely lies ahead for both her and her daughter, she is hopeful for a future of healing and thriving. Part of her hope comes from her confidence in the legacy and power of the okra seeds she has braided into Ada's hair. As youth writers like Hashi develop Ada's story, they can continue to explore the complexities of intergenerational experiences around food in both the imagined world of Ada as well as in their own lived realities.

MAKING ROOM FOR CREATIVE AND COLLABORATIVE WRITING

A key goal of this study was to address the "narratives of nothingness" that pervade the national conversation concerning Black people and accessing food" (Reese 2019, 46). This study shows how Black youth at Diaspora combatted these narratives by creating new narratives that were more agentive, hopeful, and honest. In this chapter, I explored the ways in which creative storytelling through the *Story of Ada* offered a unique opportunity for young people to engage the critical food literacies they use to make sense of the food landscapes around them.

Although the *Story of Ada* is not yet complete, this inquiry into how this story came to be examines the ways in which critical food literacies can emerge as young people integrate aspects of their lived realities into imagined realities. Opening space to collectively create and imagine stories of *food literate systems* that go beyond individualized notions of food literacy and that are more responsive to the communities they serve, is an important step toward bringing these stories to life in our shared, lived realities. During this process, young people like Shauna and Hashi engaged various aspects of critical food literacies: analyzing food throughout its life cycle, examining the historical and cultural significance of food, paying attention to the embodied and affective dimensions of food, unpacking the intergenerational processes necessary for sustaining food knowledge, and challenging unjust power structures associated with food.

In alignment with Keri Facer's proposition "that a central purpose of education in this period is to support students to imagine and make liveable futures on their own terms" (2019, 3), the creative writing group offered young people the opportunity to imagine, on their own terms, a future rooted in food and environmental justice. As they imagined new worlds and possibilities, they unpacked lessons about food and environmental justice, processed fears and concerns, spoke back to unjust structures, and designed solutions for the future. The chapter argues that in constructing a fictional world rooted in the everyday realities that they experienced, youth interns wrote themselves into a narrative that helped them prepare for the world they will one day lead.

It is important to note that this inquiry was conducted in an out-of-school context, and therefore I was not subject to the same structures and challenges that school-based researchers and educators face. Food in schools can be highly politicized, and it often falls under discussions of health disparities, biopedagogies, surveillance, political will, or health standards (Leahy and Write, 2016). The current state of public education in this country makes it so that teachers often have various mandates, responsibilities, challenges, restrictions, and resource insufficiencies that stand in the way of them engaging some of these topics even if they wanted to. Still, there are different entry points into this work. In their account of teaching food literacy in and beyond the classroom, Jo Fanzen and Brent Peters (2019) note that "if we can read a garden, then we can read a cafeteria . . . the farmer's market and the grocery store, the concession stand, and the vending machines" (4). They describe various activities, lessons, and topics they engaged in their Food Literature course. Activities such as "food maps," food narratives, and food and text pairings, they suggest, helped them to support their students "critically engage with every text around them through using food as a contextual theme to understand, explore, engage, and evaluate the world for themselves" (5). Creativity is a crucial part of this sort of critical engagement. As Gadsden notes, conscientious engagement with creativity in educational spaces can present opportunities to challenge notions of "what counts as knowledge . . . the arts act as a venue for social justice and a platform for those often invisible in traditional classroom settings" (2008, 32).

In this chapter, I explored the ways in which creative storytelling and collaborative writing can offer unique opportunities for young people, in any context, to engage critical food literacies as they make sense of the world around them. Upon reflection, three main topics emerged when considering implications for teaching, learning, and research concerning youth agency and food justice:

1. *Creative and flexible designs*: For this inquiry, I used data I had collected to devise Scene 1 of Ada's story, I then used this artifact to

inform a creative writing inquiry group that built on Scene 1 of Ada's story. Though I did not originally set out to format this inquiry in this way, taking seriously the creative contributions of the youth interns in my study and leaning into my own creative impulses afforded me the opportunity to pursue creative structures that privileged "temporal thickness" (Thorp 2006), that gave shape to the sometimes ephemeral or improvisational nature of knowledge production, and that made room for the iterative nature of narrative construction. Embracing creative designs and structures for storytelling around food can help support the inclusion of diverse perspectives needed to ensure more just food futures.

2. *Visible connections*: As indicated earlier in this chapter, Ada's story is a result of multiple voices and experiences. While engaging various perspectives is an essential part of collective storytelling, it was sometimes a challenge to ensure that these voices worked harmoniously to tell a unified story around issues of food justice. Taking time to explicitly draw and track connections between different perspectives and show how or why they do or do not cohere can help promote a group meta-awareness around idea generation and narrative construction. Visual displays that prompt collective brainstorming, discourse cues or sentence starters that draw attention to how ideas work their way through conversations, and/or opportunities for group members to interview and check-in with each other about the process, are some ways the creative writing group worked to make connections more visible and actionable.

3. *Audience and advocacy*: During this phase of the study, there was no specific, desired audience for the *Story of Ada*. The primary goal of the writing inquiry group was to first understand what the process of creative, collaborative storytelling could look like for youth participants and what they could learn about themselves and their communities in relation to their food justice work. However, the desire for this story to eventually be produced and performed for a wider audience, and to spark the changes within the food system that youth participants hope to see, was always present. Questions about which communities the interns wanted the story to reach, and which communities they hoped would see themselves *in* the story, worked their way into many discussions. As the *Story of Ada* develops and advances, I look forward to delving deeper into these conversations and exploring the affordance and limitations of performance more specifically.

To the impressive body of ongoing work on engaging critical food literacies with young people and their communities, I contribute this inquiry into the methodological and pedagogical possibilities of creative storytelling and collaborative writing. The hope is that the insights and experiences shared here can help support a more nuanced understanding of critical food literacies and more creative and responsive approaches for catalyzing further learning and necessary change.

REFERENCES

Appadurai, Arjun. 2006. "The Right to Research." *Globalisation, Societies and Education* 4, no. 2: 167–77.

Arola, Kristin L. 2017. "Composing as Culturing: An American Indian Approach to Digital Ethics." In *Handbook of Writing, Literacies, and Education in Digital Cultures*, 275–84. New York: Routledge.

Badaki, OreOluwa. 2020. "Embodied Learning and Community Resilience." *Penn GSE Perspectives on Urban Education* 18, no. 1: n1.

Begoray, Deborah, Doris Gillis, and Gillian Rowlands. 2012. *Health Literacy in Context: International Perspectives*. Nova Science.

Blanks Jones, Jasmine L. 2015. "Staging and Streaming: Murder in the Cassava Patch Performed 'Live' in Its 50th Year." *Liberian Studies Journal* 40.

Boal, Augusto. 1979/1985. "Theatre of the Oppressed. [1974]. Translated by Charles A. and Maria-Odilia Leal McBride. New York: Theatre Communications Group.

Campano, Gerald, María Paula Ghiso, OreOluwa Badaki, and Chloe Kannan. 2020. "Agency as Collectivity: Community-Based Research for Educational Equity." *Theory Into Practice* 59, no. 2: 223–33.

Campano, Gerald, T. Philip Nichols, and Grace D. Player. 2020. "Multimodal Critical Inquiry: Nurturing Decolonial Imaginaries." In *Handbook of Reading Research, Volume V*, 137–52. London: Routledge.

Carney, Judith A. 2004. "'With Grains in Her Hair': Rice in Colonial Brazil." *Slavery & Abolition* 25, no. 1: 1–27.

Carney, Judith, and Richard Nicholas Rosomoff. 2009. *In the Shadow of Slavery: Africa's Botanical Legacy in the Atlantic World*. Berkeley: University of California Press.

Carr, Wilfred, and Stephen Kemmis. 2003. *Becoming Critical: Education Knowledge and Action Research*. London: Routledge.

Cochran-Smith, Marilyn, and Susan L. Lytle. 2015. *Inquiry as Stance: Practitioner Research for the Next Generation*. New York: Teachers College Press.

Cope, Bill, and Mary Kalantzis, eds. 2000. *Multiliteracies: Literacy learning and the design of social futures*. London: Routledge.

Crawford, Robert. 1980. "Healthism and the Medicalization of Everyday Life." *International Journal of Health Services* 10, no. 3: 365–88.

Dahl, Richard. 2010. "Green Washing: Do You Know What You're Buying?" A246–52.

Doyle, Julie. 2020. "Creative Communication Approaches to Youth Climate Engagement: Using Speculative Fiction and Participatory Play to Facilitate Young

People's Multidimensional Engagement with Climate Change." *International Journal of Communication* 14: 24.

Facer, Keri. 2019. "Storytelling in Troubled Times: What Is the Role for Educators in the Deep Crises of the 21st Century?" *Literacy* 53, no. 1: 3–13.

Franzen, Joseph, and Brent Peters. 2019. *Say Yes to Pears: Food Literacy In and Beyond the English Classroom*. Urbana, IL: National Council of Teachers of English.

Freebody, Peter, and Allan Luke. 1990. "Literacies Programs: Debates and Demands in Cultural Context." *Prospect: An Australian Journal of TESOL* 5, no. 3: 7–16.

Freire, Paulo, and Donaldo Macedo. 2005. *Literacy: Reading the Word and the World*. London: Routledge.

Gadsden, Vivian L. 2008. "The Arts and Education: Knowledge Generation, Pedagogy, and the Discourse of Learning." *Review of Research in Education* 32, no. 1: 29–61.

Gallagher, Kathleen, Nancy Cardwell, Danielle Denichaud, and Lindsay Valve. 2022. "The Ecology of Global, Collaborative Ethnography: Metho-Pedagogical Moves in Research on Climate Change with Youth in Pandemic Times." *Ethnography and Education*: 1–16.

Gallagher, Kathleen, Dirk J. Rodricks, and Kelsey Jacobson. 2020. *Global Youth Citizenry and Radical Hope*. Singapore: Springer.

Gallagher, Kathleen, Anne Wessels, and Burcu Wayman Ntelioglou. 2012. "Verbatim Theatre and Social Research: Turning toward the Stories of Others." *Theatre Research in Canada* 33, no. 1: 24–43.

Glissant, Édouard. 1997. *Poetics of Relation*. Ann Arbor: University of Michigan Press.

Hashi. 2019, July 16. Personal communication.

Haraway, Donna J. 2016. *Staying with the Trouble: Making Kin in the Chthulucene*. Durham, NC: Duke University Press.

Hyland, Ken. 2003. "Genre-Based Pedagogies: A Social Response to Process." *Journal of Second Language Writing* 12, no. 1: 17–29.

Hestness, Emily, J. Randy McGinnis, and Wayne Breslyn. 2019. "Examining the Relationship between Middle School Students' Sociocultural Participation and Their Ideas about climate Change." *Environmental Education Research* 25, no. 6: 912–24.

Holbert, Nathan, Michael Dando, and Isabel Correa. 2020. "Afrofuturism as Critical Constructionist Design: Building Futures from the Past and Present." *Learning, Media and Technology* 45, no. 4: 328–44.

Janks, Hilary. 2009. *Literacy and power*. London: Routledge.

Jones, Naya. 2019a. "Dying to Eat? Black Food Geographies of Slow Violence and Resilience." *ACME: An International Journal for Critical Geographies* 18, no. 5: 1076–99.

Jones, Naya. 2019b. "It Tastes Like Heaven": Critical and Embodied Food Pedagogy with Black Youth in the Anthropocene." *Policy Futures in Education* 17, no. 7: 905–23.

Kembi. 2020, February 13. Personal communication.

Kindig, David A., Allison M. Panzer, and Lynn Nielsen-Bohlman, eds. 2004. *Health Literacy: A Prescription to End Confusion.* Washington, DC: National Academies Press.

Leahy, Deana, and Jan Wright. 2016. "Governing Food Choices: A Critical Analysis of School Food Pedagogies and Young People's Responses in Contemporary Times." *Cambridge Journal of Education* 46, no. 2: 233–46.

Lehtonen, Anna. 2012. "Future Thinking and Learning in Improvisation and a Collaborative Devised Theatre Project within Primary School Students." *Procedia-Social and Behavioral Sciences* 45: 104–13.

Majeed, Haris, and Jonathan Lee. 2017. "The Impact of Climate Change on Youth Depression and Mental Health." *The Lancet Planetary Health* 1, no. 3: e94–95.

McKittrick, Katherine. 2006. *Demonic Grounds: Black Women and the Cartographies of Struggle.* Minneapolis: University of Minnesota Press.

Medina, Carmen L., and Gerald Campano. 2006, March. "Performing identities through drama and teatro practices in multilingual classrooms." *Language Arts* 83, no. 4: 332–41.

Nixon, Rob. 2011. *Slow Violence and the Environmentalism of the Poor.* Cambridge: Harvard University Press.

Nutbeam, Don. 2000. "Health Literacy as a Public Health Goal: A Challenge for Contemporary Health Education and Communication Strategies into the 21st Century." *Health Promotion International* 15, no. 3: 259–67.

Ojala, Maria. 2013. "Coping with Climate Change among Adolescents: Implications for Subjective Well-Being and Environmental Engagement." *Sustainability* 5, no. 5: 2191–2209.

Osnes, Beth. 2017. *Performance for Resilience: Engaging Youth on Energy and Climate through Music, Movement, and Theatre.* Cham, Switzerland: Springer.

Osnes, Beth. 2018. "Youth Shine in Performance for Resilience." *Theatre Topics* 28, no. 3: 191–202.

Reese, Ashanté M. 2019. *Black Food Geographies: Race, Self-Reliance, and Food Access in Washington, DC.* Chapel Hill: University of North Carolina Press.

Renwick, Kerry, and Lisa Jordan Powell. 2019. "Focusing on the Literacy in Food Literacy: Practice, Community, and Food Sovereignty." *Journal of Family & Consumer Sciences* 111, no. 1.

Thorp, Laurie. 2006. *The Pull of the Earth: Participatory Ethnography in the School Garden.* Vol. 7. Lanham, MD: Altamira Press.

Toliver, S. R. 2021. *Recovering Black Storytelling in Qualitative Research: Endarkened Storywork.* London: Routledge.

Truman, Emily, Daniel Lane, and Charlene Elliott. 2017. "Defining Food Literacy: A Scoping Review." *Appetite* 116: 365–71.

Shauna. 2019, July 17. Personal communication.

Shauna. 2021, March 9. Personal communication.

Schön, Donald A. 2017. *The Reflective Practitioner: How Professionals Think in Action.* London: Routledge.

Sørensen, Kristine, Diane Levin-Zamir, Tuyen V. Duong, Orkan Okan, Virginia Visconde Brasil, and Don Nutbeam. 2021. "Building Health Literacy System

Capacity: A Framework for Health Literate Systems." *Health Promotion International* 36, no. Supplement_1: i13–23.

Street, Brian V., ed. 1993. *Cross-Cultural Approaches to Literacy.* No. 23. Cambridge: Cambridge University Press.

Sumner, Jennifer. 2015. "Reading the World: Food Literacy and the Potential for Food System Transformation." *Studies in the Education of Adults* 47, no. 2: 128–41.

Twitty, Michael W. 2019, October 9. "The Cowpea: A Recipe for Resilience." *Emergence Magazine.* https://emergencemagazine.org/essay/the-cowpea-a-recipe-for-resilience.

Vasudevan, Lalitha, and Joseph Riina-Ferrie. 2019. "Collaborative Filmmaking and Affective Traces of Belonging." *British Journal of Educational Technology* 50, no. 4: 1560–72.

Vasudevan, Lalitha, Katherine Schultz, and Jennifer Bateman. 2010. "Rethinking Composing in a Digital Age: Authoring Literate Identities through Multimodal Storytelling." *Written Communication* 27, no. 4: 442–68.

Vasudevan, Lalitha, Daniel Stageman, Kristine Rodriguez, Eric Fernandez, and E. Gabriel Dattatreyan. 2010. "Authoring New Narratives with Youth at the Intersection of the Arts and Justice." *Penn GSE Perspectives on Urban Education* 7, no. 1: 54–65.

Velardo, S. 2015. "The Nuances of Health Literacy, Nutrition Literacy, and Food Literacy." *Journal of Nutrition Education and Behavior* 47, no. 4: 385–89.

Vidgen, Helen Anna, and Danielle Gallegos. 2014. "Defining Food Literacy and Its Components." *Appetite* 76: 50–59.

Whitelaw, Jessica. 2012. *Cultivating Aesthetic Practice for 21st Century Learning: Arts-Based Literacy as Critical Inquiry.* PhD dissertation, University of Pennsylvania.

Widener, Patricia, and Marina Karides. 2014. "Food System Literacy: Empowering Citizens and Consumers Beyond Farm-to-Fork Pathways." *Food, Culture & Society* 17, no. 4: 665–87.

Winslow, Dianna. 2012. "Food for Thought: Sustainability, Community-Engaged Teaching and Research, and Critical Food Literacy." PhD dissertation, Syracuse University.

Wu, Judy, Gaelen Snell, and Hasina Samji. 2020. "Climate Anxiety in Young People: A Call to Action." *The Lancet Planetary Health* 4, no. 10: e435–36.

Yagelski, Robert P. 2012. "Writing as Praxis." *English Education* 44, no. 2: 188–204.

Yamashita, Lina, and Diana Robinson. 2016. "Making Visible the People Who Feed Us: Educating for Critical Food Literacy through Multicultural Texts." *Journal of Agriculture, Food Systems, and Community Development* 6, no. 2: 269–81.

Yaszek, Lisa. 2006. "Afrofuturism, Science Fiction, and the History of the Future." *Socialism and Democracy* 20, no. 3: 41–60.

NOTE

1. All names are pseudonyms.

Chapter 6

"Rekindling Hope, Building Resilience"
Critical Agricultural Literacies and Food Justice on the Llano Estacado

Callie F. Kostelich

In *Food Justice*, Gottlieb and Joshi remind us that "if the food system needs changing, the critiques point not just to what's wrong with it, but also to what it ought to be" ("Preface" ix). In this context, food justice work requires critiquing a food system *and* offering a re-envisioning of the system by recognizing injustices and becoming cognizant of what needs to change with equity and inclusion as foundational goals. Similarly, Alison Hope Alkon and Julian Agyeman (2011) note the disparity between the current organic/sustainable food movements and food justice movements, for the former largely fails to recognize that food is "not only linked to ecological sustainability, community, and health but also to racial, economic, and environmental justice" (4).[1] For example, buying all organic foods or visiting a local farmers market is a move toward critiquing neoliberal agricultural systems, yet, there is often a lack of awareness of food systems as sites for injustices with "environmental and social degradation" (4). Importantly, to shift to a polyculture perspective of the food movement and to embark on food justice requires transcending dominant narratives in two ways: a) recognizing and pushing back on food systems dominated by industrial agricultural practices that do not support sustainable, equitable food production and participation and b) resisting solely aligning with counternarratives that promote alternative visions of agricultural participation that do not address larger issues of injustices.

If the quest for food justice is to challenge dominant food systems, advocate for equity for the vulnerable, and connect with other social justice movements, then critical agricultural literacy is a foundational concept. Critical agricultural literacy "allows us to analyze and rethink . . . and *encourages dissenting perspectives*" (Brewster 82, emphasis added). It provides a framework for contemplating agricultural systems and structures that currently contribute to inequities of labor, ownership, participation, and food access and availability, as well as the dominance and lobbying power of multinational agricultural corporations to direct U.S. agricultural policies (Schell 2007). In other words, critical agricultural literacy requires a keen awareness for not only what the agricultural content is but, also, what it reveals about existing power structures, ideological positions, and embedded assumptions about agriculture that must be problematized in the pursuit for fair access, equity, and inclusion. Thus, in alignment with Gottlieb and Joshi's three key areas of action for food justice—restructuring the food system, focusing on equity, and engaging in social justice activism—individuals must develop critical agricultural literacies and ways of seeing the world that actively reject automatic acceptance of *how it's always been* for a justice-oriented *how it could possibly be*.

With this theoretical grounding, I analyze Ogallala Commons, a nonprofit organization based in Nazareth, Texas, as a sponsor of critical agricultural literacy with initiatives to educate the public, support local food production, and reinvigorate regional food systems through their "Rebuilding Local Food Systems" program. I focus my case study on Ogallala Commons as a sponsor of agricultural literacy who, to use Deborah Brandt's (2001) terminology, "deliver[s] the material and ideological possibility for literacy learning" (70) and "leaves their marks on the literacy of the sponsored" (143). The ways in which producers and consumers develop critical agricultural literacies is largely connected with the sponsors of literacy acquisition who promote critical awareness versus perpetuating a way of reading the agricultural world that ultimately benefits dominant narratives and existing power structures which privilege those with access, capital, and power. I look closely at Ogallala Commons' sponsorship of agricultural literacy initiatives through the "Rebuilding Local Food Systems" program, specifically the ways in which the organization creates opportunities for producers and consumers to develop critical agricultural literacies that call into question food production, consumption, and access, as well as justice-focused initiatives, to create more equity and inclusion in the Llano Estacado region.

My driving research questions are: *In what ways does Ogallala Commons sponsor critical agricultural literacies for producers and consumers through the "Rebuilding Local Food Systems" program? And, to what extent does the "Rebuilding Local Food Systems" program promote food justice from its agricultural literacy initiatives?* Sponsorship of critical agricultural literacies is not just a desired component but a foundational concept of food justice initiatives and essential for the recognition of inequities and action on this awareness. I contend that for food justice to gain traction, there must be sponsors of literacy who support critical agricultural literacies that lead to not just critiquing prevailing structures and narratives and providing alternatives but to actively challenging and disrupting food injustices. I locate Ogallala Commons and their "Rebuilding Local Food Systems" program as a sponsor of producers and consumers' critical agricultural literacy acquisition and equitable food systems, and I embark on a mixed-methods approach, including first-hand observation of local programming and textual analysis of the organization's annual reports, web presence, and founding documents. My analysis of their work highlights the importance of this local sponsorship of critical agricultural literacies, while also acknowledging the need for the organization to move further towards food justice initiatives.

THE UNEXPECTED RESEARCH PROJECT

Before I embark on my overview of Ogallala Commons—the next section in the chapter—and analysis of it as a sponsor of critical agricultural literacies and resource for promoting food justice initiatives, I want to be transparent in my position as both a participant within this organization and researcher of it. In 2018, I moved to Lubbock, Texas to join the English department at Texas Tech, and I began attending a faith community, Second Baptist Church. I attended a Wednesday evening session, "Scripture, Culture, and Agriculture," by Dr. Andy Black, at the time the Regional Director of the Texas Hunger Initiative, and Andy shared information about Ogallala Commons and their upcoming Food Summit. Having recently completed an agricultural literacy-focused dissertation and as a member of an agricultural producing family, I was instantly intrigued by this organization, and I signed up to attend the March 2019 Food Summit. It was at this event that I began to learn more about the organization, its guiding principles, and the ways in which it operates across the Ogallala Aquifer. While I will analyze the food summits later in the chapter, I appreciated the intermix of the philosophical framework of rebuilding local foodsheds that served as the organization's guiding principles with the practical information that producers needed: how to reach buyers, how to navigate food laws that privilege large-scale production, how to build networks across vast regions.

Following the Food Summit, I was interested in supporting the organization in a myriad of ways outside of my academic life, such as how I could support local producers with my buying power, advocate for them through my growing network in the community, and use my skills in ways that might be useful to the organization. In 2019, I actively volunteered with the organization and its affiliates to support local programming in the Llano Estacado region. I served on the planning committee for the 2019 Ogallala Commons annual fundraiser "Taste of the Llano," and I advocated for support of the local farmers' markets where many of the affiliates sold their goods. While volunteering, I was inspired by a community-writing workshop that Duane Roen, Sherry Rankins-Robertson, and I planned for CCCC 2020, and I tossed around the idea of a project where I could facilitate opportunities for local producers to write their stories. This idea was still more in line with service to the organization than study of it; however, in 2020, the COVID-19 pandemic halted all my engagement with Ogallala Commons, as I quickly shifted my attention solely to my immediate sphere.

To date, I remain friends with staff, volunteers, and producers who align with Ogallala Commons' mission. I am no longer actively engaged within the organization, but with food access, distribution, and equity at the forefront of my mind, especially with the pandemic, I shifted my focus from volunteering with Ogallala Commons to critically studying it. To my knowledge, Ogallala Commons has not been critically studied in any capacity, and it was kairotic timing for me to explore my driving research questions, to critically analyze the ways in which the organization sponsors critical agricultural literacies and the extent to which it actively promotes food justice initiatives. While my study of the organization is largely indebted to my awareness of its resources, materials, and ways of operation from my time within it, I purposely chose artifacts to study that the organization distributes to general audiences via their website, social media pages, press releases, brochures, and email distribution lists. I am committed to the ethics of transparency for my engagement with the organization and the public artifacts I accessed for my analysis. Nonprofits are key stakeholders in the food justice movement, and as such, I embarked on this project to illuminate and nuance Ogallala Commons' sponsorship of agricultural literacies and food justice initiatives. My purposes are two-fold: a) to contribute an analysis of one nonprofit's approach within the framework of critical agricultural literacies to this edited collection on food justice scholarship, and b) to provide an analysis for Ogallala Commons' consideration that might prompt reflection for how current programming is/is not food justice-focused and opportunities for the organization to become increasingly committed to issues of food equity, inclusion, and justice.

AGRICULTURAL LITERACIES FOR FOOD JUSTICE INITIATIVES ON THE LLANO ESTACADO

Before I go into my examination of Ogallala Commons artifacts and practices, background information about the organization is necessary to contextualize the subject of my analysis. Ogallala Commons is a nonprofit organization that serves the western regions of Texas north to the Dakotas along the lines of the Ogallala Aquifer. Ogallala Commons' mission to "rekindle hope and rebuild resilience," particularly in the rural communities of this region, aligns with their vision of the "12 Key Assets of Commonwealth," a concept created for Ogallala Commons in part by the executive director, Dr. Darryl Birkenfeld, and early founder, Vince Shively. The "12 Key Assets of the Commonwealth" are twelve components within each community that the organization deems essential to the health and well-being of the area and her people.[2] In this holistic view, Ogallala Commons recognizes the value of each component—from education to arts and culture to local foodsheds—and by placing this concept as the foundation or "soil" of their efforts, Ogallala Commons reflects an awareness that hope and resilience are not isolated concepts or quick-fixes that address only one aspect of an area or issue. Rather, Ogallala Commons' mission to rekindle hope and build resilience in this region relies on the nuance and interdependence of the assets and the disruption of a one-size-fix-all model for engagement (Ogallala Commons 2020 Annual Report).

Because Ogallala Commons operates in such a vast territory, its programs are adaptable to the specific needs and parameters of each community. The "Rebuilding Local Food Systems" program is Ogallala Commons' outreach to assist local producers and consumers in two distinct areas: the Arkansas River Valley and the Llano Estacado region, the latter of which is my focus of study. I turn to the Llano Estacado region as a site of exploration for critical agricultural literacy and food justice initiatives, in part because it is where I now call home, but also because it is literally surrounded by food, fiber, and natural resource systems. The Llano Estacado region spans western Texas from Odessa and to Amarillo and covers a slight portion of territory in eastern New Mexico. This vast, arid territory is well-known for its flat plains, dry vegetation, and perpetual wind, not to mention its breathtaking sunsets and fertile ground for crop production, namely cotton and other produce that can be low-water and/or irrigation dependent. This is an area of significant agricultural production that would be "responsible for feeding 9 billion people by 2015" ("Reason No. 8"), and Bayer, formerly Monsanto, recently made Lubbock, Texas its new location for a 16.7-million-dollar Cotton Breeding and Trait Development Station (Steadman 2017). In the areas that surround

Lubbock, cotton growers produce approximately two-thirds of the Texas cotton crop, one-fourth of the U.S. cotton crop, and 4 percent of the global cotton crop ("Ag Facts"). In addition to crop production, the region is well-known for large ranches and beef production, and locals often refer to Amarillo as the "beef capital of the world" for its plethora of feedlots ("Reason No. 8"). As this data demonstrates, the area is literally surrounded by large-scale agricultural production and houses universities—West Texas A&M at Canyon and Texas Tech University—devoted to agricultural research and with buildings named after industrial agricultural corporations (e.g., the Bayer Plant Science Building at TTU). Agriculture significantly impacts the livelihoods of many locals, either through direct production, via the many businesses that support production, and/or through the inescapable sponsorship that corporations and entities have in the area.

Ogallala Commons' "Rebuilding Local Food Systems" program operates in an area that is dominated by big agribusinesses and people and entities that depend on this system of production for survival. Through the "Rebuilding Local Food Systems" program, Ogallala Commons sponsors programming to reinvigorate local areas and the ways in which residents grow, sell, and access foods within the communities. By focusing on dual audiences of producers and consumers, Ogallala Commons harkens to its commitment to the well-being of a community by including those who grow local foods and the consumers within the area who purchase them. The organization's focus on dual audiences within local communities is indicative of their holistic approach to the commonwealth and vision for the organization's role as a sponsor of literacy acquisition.

In "A Region Reforming!: The Philosophy, Definition, and Brief History of Ogallala Commons," Darryl Birkenfeld (2003) writes:

> In terms of economic and social organization, holism moves in the opposite direction of the centralized corporate model that currently holds sway in the U.S. Instead of organizing "from the top down" like the corporate model, a holistic approach turns the pyramid upside down, building reality 'from the bottom up' in the form of a holographic hierarchy. (3)

In this statement, Birkenfeld promotes a vision of disrupting prevailing hierarchies in favor of a structure that is multidimensional with depth, movement, and adaptation based on needs from the bottom up. In other words, the organization's vision to be attuned to local situations, needs, and challenges is in and of itself disruptive to dominant narratives, for it emphasizes the needs of the local over the demands of the sponsoring organization. In this regard, the organization's focus for the "Rebuilding Local Food Systems" program is less about a one-size-fits-all vision for food systems and more in line with the unique needs of each area and the ways in which the organization can support producers and consumers in the creation of healthy and thriving local food systems.

Birkenfeld (2003) further rejects a top-down organizational structure for Ogallala Commons areas, writing that "at its most authentic level, the commons appear as an ongoing conversation, and an invitation to conversion. The commons can be neither established nor maintained by special interest groups, but only by 'common interest' . . . and the fundamental actions in the commons are based on dominion and not domination" (6). The language affirming conversation and dominion and rejecting special interests and domination is unorthodox, particularly for an organization with the intent to sponsor revitalization in local areas. Birkenfeld's vision to support local areas through Ogallala Commons would lead—if following this statement—to the organization operating based on the needs of the local communities, where the Ogallala Commons acts as a sponsor of literacy and as a facilitator of programs, not as a special interest group or entity with agendas for unchecked influence and power.

Ogallala Commons' attention to stewardship and sustainability in the Llano Estacado region is due, in part, to its efforts to align with financial supporters that have a similar vision for cultivating a commonwealth with critical agricultural literacies and food justice initiatives. Financial support for Ogallala Commons comes primarily through grants, local fundraising endeavors, and area foundations that have similar visions. For example, Ogallala Commons received a two-year $200,000 grant from Colorado Health Foundation in 2020 to support the organization's work with the Ark Valley foodshed in Colorado. Additional major partners include High Plains Water District, Amarillo Area Foundation, NWKS Economic Innovations Center, Dixon Water Foundation, and The Tecovas Foundation (Ogallala Commons 2020 Annual Report). The organization also holds yearly fundraisers, such as the Taste of the Llano, in Lubbock, Texas, and I helped organize the event and attended in 2019. While financial inner workings are beyond the scope of this chapter, it is worth noting that the organization's income in 2019 was $449,611.78, and expenses totaled $467,329.95 (Ogallala Commons 2020 Annual Report). Ogallala Commons is overt in their role as a connector and facilitator, as seen in their acknowledgment that the connections they form between communities, themselves, and "external partners" is not a byproduct of their engagement but a direct objective to achieve (Ogallala Commons 2020 Annual Report). Entities that support Ogallala Commons are supporting the organization's mission and programming, which overtly follows a commonwealth model of mutuality and empowerment for local communities, their peoples, and their products. What donors may specifically gain from their support is hypothetical at best. However, given Ogallala Commons' clear and overt mission, we can infer donors support inclusive visions of agricultural production and participation and stand to benefit from more equitable and sustainable food systems.

For my in-depth analysis, I turn to two agricultural literacy initiatives within the "Rebuilding Local Food Systems" program in the Llano Estacado region: the annual food producer summits and the Local Llano digital initiative via the website and social media presence. While both initiatives focus on the Llano Estacado region, I selected these specific initiatives for their distinct foci—the food producer summits appeal primarily to producers, while the Local Llano initiative has a target audience of consumers. The dual audience approach for the "Rebuilding Local Food Systems" program reinforces Ogallala Commons vision for local holism and conversation, to use Birkenfeld's language, as well as connects to Ogallala Commons' anticipated outcomes to increase awareness for local producers, create community knowledge of regional foodsheds, and provide economic opportunities for producers within their regions (Ogallala Commons 2020 Annual Report). It is crucial to contend with how all participants experience—or fail to experience—equitable access and inclusion, be it on the production or consumption side of food systems. Therefore, Ogallala Commons' approach to dual audiences signifies not only its commitment to its foundational principles and core values but also the organization's awareness for the symbiotic relationship between production and consumption on a local scale, which can foster deeper awareness for food systems, equities, and injustices within and beyond a home community.

An Analysis of Food Producer Summits

Each spring, Ogallala Commons sponsors annual food producer summits, either in Lubbock, Texas or Amarillo, Texas or, occasionally, in both locations, and my knowledge of the summits comes from first-hand observation as an attendee in 2019 and from information and materials distributed to past attendees by the organization in 2021. The summits focus specifically on area producers, many who are small-scale producers and/or who operate under cottage laws and rely mainly on farmers' markets to distribute their goods. It is worth noting that while Alkon and Agyeman (2011) push back on the prevalence of dominant narratives that prioritize organic-only purchasing or an anti-GMO agenda, Ogallala Commons similarly resists this narrative by openly welcoming producers within the region, regardless of types of products and/or production. The goal is not to quell the type of products and/or production but to support local, sustainable production in an area of Texas that is predominately big-business, large-scale agriculture. While the latter relies on corporate structures to ultimately stock big chain stores and export their goods across the globe, the former has a much smaller reach within a set radius and relies heavily on word-of-mouth referrals, access to local buyers, and a customer-base that buys their products and supports their local livelihoods. Thus, this is the demographic of producers that Ogallala Commons targets for food summits, and in alignment with their community-focused approach, the organization's support of local food production is about supporting local peoples, goods, economies, and the interconnected assets from the organization's commonwealth structure.

In a press release for the March 4, 2021, summit, Ogallala Commons acknowledges that "while COVID-19 has caused great disruptions and suffering, the need for food that is grown and crafted locally—is more important and impactful than ever" ("Press Release"). When consumers were without regular access to grocery stores and/or when the grocery stores were empty, local, small-scale producers found themselves with a new client-base of people who were looking for alternative methods for accessing foods and for supporting their neighbors. As a component of the "Rebuilding Local Food Systems" program, the local food summits were already established sites for empowering and sponsoring local producers in the Llano Estacado region who envisioned more sustainable, locally centric agricultural participation. Therefore, the 2021 summit featured presentations—Getting Started in Food Production; Small Farm Planning: Tips, Techniques, and Tools; Dealing with Ups & Downs in High Tunnel Production—that were *for* and *by* producers ("Press Release"). In this capacity, Ogallala Commons serves as the sponsor of attendees' agricultural literacies by facilitating the opportunities for producers to gather, share and create knowledge, and learn from and with one another. While Ogallala Commons provided the exigence for this meaning-making, what the producers shared and how they conducted their presentations was bottom-up, not top-down, further aligning with the organization's mission to serve as a trade route for community connection and critical literacy acquisition. By offering a plethora of presentations and opportunities for attendees to crowd-source and share strategies, Ogallala Commons sponsored opportunities for producers—or potential producers—to reject dominant models of agricultural production that prioritize large-scale producers and create spaces for new ideas, methods, and opportunities.

Having attended the 2019 summit, I can attest that the summits are purposefully not sites for open defiance of industrial practices but crucially important opportunities for local producers to recognize an alternative to these practices and to re-envision a type of agricultural production that is locally focused and sustainably driven. For example, attendees, such as Primal Gardens from Seminole, Texas, often have large-scale operations with contracts for mass-produced produce but attend the summits to learn how to cultivate side projects—at least initially envisioned as side projects—to supply local restaurants, farmers' markets, and CSAs. Such attendees would find the 2021 "Inventory Management for Local Food Producers/Marketers" presentation by Waylon Ward, associate director of Texas Manufacturing Assistance Center (TMAC), Inc., particularly helpful as they consider scaling and marketing to smaller niche markets. Moreover, for producers who have specific attention to broadening local food access and availability to folks on food assistance programs, the 2021 "Increasing Access and Growing Markets: Double Up Food Bucks" presentation by Sarah Castro with Double Up Food Bucks of West Texas would be particularly appealing for its focus on the connection between market growth and equitable food access. The food summits are geared at educating local producers in the Llano Estacado region, while providing unique opportunities to find community with fellow farmers and ranchers and to increase awareness of and support for more equitable food systems in these local communities.

From my attendance, as well as the ways in which the sessions are described and marketed, the focus is on empowering producers to engage in smaller, more specialized local markets, with awareness that the larger agricultural context for both producers and consumers in this region is predominately an industrialized agricultural environment. In this regard, the summits serve as sites for literacy acquisition by sponsoring attendees' awareness of how to navigate complex local markets that contain deeply embedded ideologies about agricultural production. If the summits overtly focused on openly defying the predominant agricultural practices of the region and/or attacking those who participate in this manner, Ogallala Commons would risk alienating potential and existing producers who are interested in moving towards more equitable and sustainable agricultural practices but who may be members of agricultural families and communities whose livelihood continues to depend on large-scale industrialized practices. Ogallala Commons' approach is strategic, for the organization's slate of sessions at the summits are purposefully geared at inclusion and knowledge creation, not attack or overt hostile critique. In this large-scale agricultural environment, a more heavy-handed critical stance has the potential to have far more risk of deterring producers than sponsoring movement towards an alternative vision of agricultural production and developing community support for it.

While the panels provide an occasion for attendees' critical agricultural literacy development, Ogallala Commons moves further towards food justice at the summits by including presentations, at least from 2019–2021, by Judith McGeary, JD, founder of the Farm and Ranch Freedom Alliance (FARFA), executive director of the Council for Healthy Food Systems, and member of the USDA Secretary's Advisory Committee on Animal Health ("Staff"). As an avid supporter of and advocate for sustainable agricultural participation and policies, McGeary's portion of the summits moves the conversation from what to do and how to do it in ways that may be outside the norms of standard production, to what is possible and what needs to change from a legal perspective. McGeary's position as a legal advocate is to push for legislation that is inclusive and local, small-scale producer friendly and that values production beyond that which has big-business lobbying power. For example, at the summit in 2019, McGeary overviewed changes to the Texas Cottage Laws that made home food businesses legal and accessible, and this legislative change created more equity and increased opportunities for individuals to make and sell their goods without the expense of commercial-grade facilities and store-front expenses (Masters). In this regard, McGeary's inclusion on the agenda aligns with Alkon and Agyeman's (2011) classification of food justice as "as ensuring that the benefits and risks of where, what, and how food is grown and produced, transported and distributed, and accessed and eaten are shared fairly" (6). McGeary's advocacy for food inclusion and increased availability—both for those producing and consuming—and Ogallala Commons' support of it serves as an example of the connection between an increase in critical agricultural literacies and the necessity to move towards food justice: in other words, once you know what needs to be done, the next step is to advocate for it for the betterment of the food system and to the benefit of those who participate in it.

On the surface, a local summit for smaller-scale producers may seem benign or less than revolutionary for those hoping to read about an organization openly defying, condemning, and/or opposing industrial food production practices. However, in the locational context of West Texas, this attention to local food production, particularly those producers whose business models rely on local contacts, not large-scale contracts, is notable, for it demonstrates the organization's commitment to equitable food systems and the support of local producers who are looking for resources to engage in alternative agricultural practices. Moreover, the inclusion of McGeary's expertise provides attendees with access to crucial information and support from a food justice legal advocate who is devoted to increasing inclusive and equitable food production and access. If we focus solely on what we might think of as big moments of resistance, we miss out on crucial work that is taking place in local communities where organizations, such as Ogallala Commons, are supporting opportunities for producers to re-envision food systems in ways that increase food production access, support, and involvement. In other words, by holding summits for producers to crowd-source their unique ways of production and to contemplate ways to gain a consumer base is and of itself a move that transcends dominant narratives of large-scale industrial agricultural production. The very space of the summit is a move towards equity and inclusion for agricultural producers and a site for critical agricultural literacy acquisition for those seeking resources for an alternative vision for growing, raising, and selling their goods in the Llano Estacado.

An Analysis of the Local Llano Project

In my second example, I turn to another Rebuilding Local Foods Systems initiative in the Llano Estacado: Local Llano project. The Local Llano project is a "toolbox to inform and educate the public regarding locally-grown food in the Llano Estacado region of West Texas and Eastern New Mexico" ("What Is Local Llano"). This "toolbox" consists of a website, blog, and social media components geared primarily to a consumer audience. The website includes a section of recipes for local, seasonal ingredients, a list of local producers that is easy to navigate and organized by types of foods, a list of active farmers markets that includes location and operation information, and a blog that frequently features area producers and inventive methods of production ("Home"). For example, in the May 20, 2021, blog post, "Ogallala Greens," Hattie Robb overviews a new hydroponic farm in Slaton, Texas (Robb, "Ogallala Greens"). While this could seem like just another overview of a producer, Robb draws attention to an alternative version of farming, hydroponic technology, something that is outside the scope of industrialized agricultural production in this region that relies on planted crops with heavy irrigation. In a previous blog post from March 20, 2021, Robb similarly highlights another producer, Alcove Farms, for their stewardship and regenerative farming practices with their poultry enterprise (Robb, "Alcove Farms). Robb's choice of producers and their agricultural practices demonstrates that the website—and specifically the blog—serves as more than just an information sharing avenue. Rather, the specific inclusion of both types of producers and sustainable agricultural practices provide an alternate vision of agricultural production, one that challenges the notion that all agriculture in this area is large-scale and industrial and provides space for readers to learn more about the alternative practices taking place in the Llano Estacado.

To my knowledge, there is not another community-specific space that serves as a virtual repository for information about producers who align with sustainable, environmentally conscious agricultural practices and who have a commitment to supplying consumers within the Llano Estacado region. The Local Llano website serves an important role as a virtual commonplace, to follow Ogallala Commons' guiding vision, to connect local communities—in this case producers and consumers—and to highlight agricultural producers that provide an alternative vision of production to the mega-farm enterprises that dominate the local landscape. Like the food summits, the Local Llano portion of the "Rebuilding Local Food Systems" project is noteworthy for what is does a) within the heavily industrialized Llano Estacado region and b) with a focus on drawing attention to alternative visions of agricultural production while not alienating readers who may be connected to and/or affiliated with traditional agricultural practices. While the approach may be subtle, Ogallala Commons offers space for conversations about local food production that generates dialogue, not alienation. The Local Llano project begins to cultivate readers' critical agricultural literacies through the types of information (i.e., local, sustainable, ground-up approaches) on the website and the ways in which the blog posts encourage alternate visions of agricultural participation with stories of how individuals can produce and consume foods in ways that are sustainable and supportive of local areas and peoples. In this regard, the Local Llano website and accompanying blog move towards food justice initiatives through their attention to equity and inclusion by highlighting producers who may otherwise lack resources and/or avenues to share their stories and, for this region, unconventional agricultural practices.

In my study of the food producer summits and the Local Llano website, I find Ogallala Commons' sponsorship of the "Rebuilding Local Food Systems" project to align with critical agricultural literacies with a move, albeit subtle, towards food justice through its focus on creating equitable and inclusive spaces for agricultural practices that are environmentally, socially, and economically sustainable. However, there is a final component of the Local Llano project that, as of spring 2021, falls short of supporting critical agricultural literacy acquisition and food justice initiatives: the Local Llano social media presence. The most visible component of the Local Llano project is their social media engagement on Facebook. The Local Llano Facebook page has over 4,600 followers, and the posts are frequent, averaging two-to-three times a week ("About"). The Facebook page shares new blog posts and connects readers with the main Local Llano website; however, the engagement reminds readers about planting times and recipes, while offering general encouragement for thinking about, growing, and purchasing local produce. While this is informative, the agricultural literacies supported by the social media engagements are distinct from other Ogallala Commons programs. For example, the local food producers' summits and Local Llano blog posts engage in the inner workings of food production systems, contemplate alternative realities for dominant agricultural narratives, and move toward food justice initiatives by focusing on equity and inclusion of producers, agricultural practices, and consumer access. The social media engagement leans more towards asking questions that may promote engagement but are not structured to promote or support critical contemplation, as is evidenced by the repeated 2021 posts from February 26 and March 11 that ask readers what they're excited about for spring ("About"). Questions about spring could lead to further engagement, but because the Facebook posts start and stop with surface-level questions, the level of engagement is minimal and ends with a commenter's thoughts on spring, albeit the posts did not garner comments in this example.

This begs the question as to what Ogallala Commons aims to accomplish through their Local Llano social media posts. Given the large platform and the potential to engage thousands of consumers, the Local Llano project appears to be Ogallala Commons' most visible opportunity for literacy sponsorship. However, while "social media (SM) tools (websites and applications) have enabled boundaryless two-way communication between the content producer and the consumer," the Local Llano posts do not harness the full capacity of this "two-way" communication (Ihejirika 1). Granted, there is a place in social media for general engagement—likes, clicks, views—and social media posts could interest readers through small actions, like asking for thoughts on spring, to cultivate additional engagement with more substantive matters. For example, Ogallala Commons' sponsorship of the "Increasing Access and Growing Markets: Double Up Food Bucks" session at the 2021 food summit could be expanded from producer-focused at the summit to consumer-focused on social media. The Local Llano Facebook site could share resources to direct consumers to programs that support equitable food access, producers who are food justice oriented, and distribution sites, such as local farmers' markets, that accept food bucks and serve as WIC resources. Instead of focusing on visibility of the project and generating quick-result engagements, the Local Llano project could garner the power of social media to serve as a food justice-oriented repository of resources and a connector of people, places, and ideas to support equitable, accessible food production and consumption in the Llano Estacado region.

However, the surface-level questions on the Local Llano Facebook page reveal a disconnect between Ogallala Commons' sponsorship of critical agricultural literacies and movement towards food justice across organizational programs and initiatives. From my attendance at the 2019 Food Summit, I have direct knowledge that Ogallala Commons outsources its social media creation to a content management company, Primitive, and this company conducted a workshop on social media engagement during the summit. This is further evidenced by the "staff" section of the Ogallala Commons website that lists Kade Wilcox, the owner and CEO of Primitive, as the staff contractor for digital strategies responsible for "building out program structure" and "digital communications platforms." The management company Primitive likely creates posts that they think will garner attention and increase engagement, such as asking followers about their plans for spring, but the social media content creators lack the critical literacy sponsorship that we see through more overt and direct initiatives, such as the summits and blog content. Birkenfeld, Ogallala Commons' executive director, lives in the Llano Estacado region and directly plans, facilitates, and oversees the summits. As the executive director and a fellow producer, he has demonstrated a sense for the needs of local producers and the ways in which the local community engages in alterative agricultural production and consumption. Similarly, the blogs are often researched and written by Ogallala Commons interns, a component of the Ogallala Commons' Workforce and Leadership program. Like Birkenfeld, the interns come from local communities and have insider-knowledge on local producers, practices, and markets for consumers who seek more sustainable, equitable resources and methods of agricultural engagement. Birkenfeld and the blog writers share in the mission of the organization to decentralize knowledge and resources, harness collective knowledge, and create spaces to learn from and with one another.

Conversely, a content management company lacks the same connection to the organization, its objectives, and mission, as is evidenced by posts that center on quick response versus long-term, sustainable, justice-focused impact, which is what I observed from my study of posts up to spring 2021. Granted, just drawing attention to a nonprofit initiative can be an initial goal, especially on social media. However, if the primary goal for the content management company is to garner surface-level likes and general audience engagement and if the content does not eventually transcend into substantive posts and engagement, then this portion of the Local Llano project will continue to fall short in the advancement of food equity in the most public of platforms. When issues of food shortages, supply chain disruptions, and increased prices began to dominate the media with the onset of the COVID-19 pandemic, the Local Llano project missed the opportunity to serve as a central information hub with social media as an outlet for disseminating crucial information for equitable food access and support for local producers. Understanding who creates the content and for what purposes is essential to unpacking how Ogallala Commons' social media has been utilized as a means for visibility versus another avenue to support the development of critical literacies and to advance food justice initiatives. The social media portion of the Local Llano project is where I hope to see growth in the future, for it has ripe potential for reaching vast audiences with this crucial information, so long as the content creators, be it an outsourced management company or Ogallala Commons staff and volunteers, have clear objectives of engagement that transcend surface-level interaction.

Ogallala Commons has demonstrated their sponsorship of critical agricultural literacies and movement toward food justice initiatives in their inclusivity of producers, support of sustainable agricultural practices, and food access for consumers through the "Rebuilding Local Food Systems" program, particularly the summits and Local Llano website/blog. The Local Llano social media presence is one specific area where Ogallala Commons could refocus the Local Llano project with food justice at the forefront of content, and this should look like rethinking their sponsorship of the social media component of the Local Llano project and the impact, or lack thereof, that a management company has, even with the best intentions, on audiences' critical agricultural literacy acquisition. This refocus begins by reckoning with the significance of literacy sponsorship, not just in funding initiatives but in the creation, management, and execution of content and programming that aligns with critical agricultural literacies where audiences read agricultural landscapes with awareness for equitable and sustainable food production and access. Until the Local Llano project can produce such content, its social media component will be unlikely to produce substantive change towards equitable and just food access, production, and consumption in the Llano Estacado.

PLANTING THE SEEDS FOR FOOD JUSTICE

Ogallala Commons' sponsorship of healthy, thriving local food systems for a "more vibrant future" (Ogallala Commons 2020 Annual Report) harkens to Eileen Schell's reminder that "the stewardship of rural lands and a healthy food supply is an issue for us all" ("Rhetorics," 100). While good stewardship and uninterrupted food supply are often taken for granted, especially post-farm crisis of the 1980s, food challenges associated with the COVID-19 pandemic serve as a reminder that there is much work to be done to cultivate agricultural literacies in the United States, as has been long noted by rural literacy scholars (Donehower, Hogg, and Schell 2007; Donehower, Hogg, and Schell 2012; Edmondson 2003).[3] The COVID-19 pandemic provided a catalyst for organically and overtly acknowledging food justice topics that draw attention to the inequalities and injustices faced by producers and consumers alike. The shift towards food justice is certainly timely and, as with any justice-oriented issue, abundantly necessary.

The study of Ogallala Commons demonstrates the viability for nonprofit organizations to sponsor critical agricultural literacy acquisition in local communities and to propel food justice initiatives that, in alignment with Gottlieb and Joshi's (2010) three areas of action, aim to restructure food systems, focus on equity, and engage in social justice activism. While Ogallala Commons serves as an example organization for study, it is far from the only organization or entity doing this work across the United States. It is in this context that the Ogallala Commons case study reveals several essential takeaways for the future of the food justice movement.

First, as noted throughout this chapter, critical agricultural literacies are foundational for the transition from awareness for and critique of inequitable food systems to the re-envisioning of those systems with equity and inclusion at the forefront. Ogallala Commons' "Rebuilding Local Food Systems" program focuses on equitable production and consumption by providing crucial workshops, networking, and educational opportunities for producers and consumers to learn about ways to grow, shop, and support within and for the benefit of their home communities. When organizations, like Ogallala Commons, create programming and initiatives to promote critical agricultural literacy acquisition, they sponsor folks' abilities to question, contemplate, and negotiate content instead of accepting information as fact and affirming the status quo or existing systems that may—and often do—contribute to food injustices. And, as is evidenced in the social media component of the Local Llano project, if a sponsoring agent falls short of producing content or programming that supports critical literacy development, then the organization's sponsorship of food justice initiatives may fall short without this necessary step. In this regard, critical agricultural literacies are the groundwork for the food justice movement, and an organization's success promoting food justice initiatives is largely connected to whether their sponsorship aligns with critical literacy acquisition.

Second, Ogallala Commons' approach reaches diverse audiences through inclusionary, not exclusionary, tactics that support producers and consumers' critical agricultural literacies in a manner that does not alienate audiences through overt or heavy-handed tactics. With the "Rebuilding Local Food Systems" programs, Ogallala Commons is restructuring food systems in a region dominated by large-scale agricultural production. This feat is no small task, for the organization has managed to support small scale producers and the purchasing of local products without alienating interested entities who have connections to neoliberal, large-scale agricultural practices. This point warrants emphasis in the context of the industrial agricultural landscape of the Llano Estacado region but, also, is translatable to other similar environments beyond this specific region. For the food justice movement to gain traction, there needs to be inclusivity across agricultural landscapes and environments, and there is not a one-size-fits-all model for this important work. There must be an awareness of the environments in which folks develop critical agricultural literacies and participate in food justice work and inclusivity for producers and consumers to pursue sustainable and more equitable food justice in diverse locations.

Finally, Ogallala Commons' attention to audience is noteworthy, for it harkens to the interconnectedness of food systems and the ways in which agricultural systems have significant impacts on entire communities. Food access, availability, and affordability are and will continue to be crucially important issues, not to mention the multidimensional impact food production and consumption has environmentally, socially, culturally, financially. There is potential for Ogallala Commons to increase their food justice work across their diverse outreach platforms and programs, especially since they have a demonstrated foundation in cultivating critical agricultural literacies through their programming. For example, this might look like drawing attention to farm worker experiences instead of focusing primarily on owners of production, creating justice-focused materials focused on economic disparities, or acknowledging environmental and ecological concerns in regions that rely heavily on chemical treatments. Regardless of the specific approach, food justice work must consider community impact, and this means expanding discourses, like those that are producer- or consumer-centric and reframing awareness and advocacy. In doing so, sponsors, like Ogallala Commons, have opportunities to move further towards food justice, specifically in an overt turn to naming injustices outright and providing actual steps towards creating more equitable and sustainable food systems.

REFERENCES

"About." n.d. Local Llano Facebook page. Accessed February 1, 2021. https://www.facebook.com/LocalLlano.

"Ag Facts." n.d. Lubbock Chamber of Commerce. Accessed February 1, 2021. http://www.lubbockchamber.com/ag-facts.

Alkon, Alison Hope, and Julian Agyeman, eds. 2011. "Introduction: The Food Movement as Polyculture." *Cultivating Food Justice: Race, Class, and Sustainability*. Cambridge: MIT Press.

Birkenfeld, Darryl. 2003. "A Region Reforming! The Philosophy, Definition, and Brief History of Ogallala Commons." Ogallala Commons. Last modified 2017. https://ogallalacommons.org/wp-content/uploads/2016/01/A-Region-Reforming-paper.pdf.

Brandt, Deborah. 2001. *Literacy in American Lives*. Cambridge: Cambridge University Press.

Brewster, Cori. 2011. "Toward a Critical Agricultural Literacy." In *Reclaiming the Rural: Essays on Literacy, Rhetoric, and Pedagogy*, edited by Kim Donehower, Charlotte Hogg, and Eileen Schell, 34–51. Carbondale: Southern Illinois University Press.

Donehower, Kim, Charlotte Hogg, and Eileen Schell. 2007. *Rural Literacies*. Carbondale: Southern Illinois University Press.

———. 2012. *Reclaiming the Rural: Essays on Literacy, Rhetoric, and Pedagogy*. Carbondale: Southern Illinois University Press.

Edmondson, Jacqueline. 2003. *Prairie Town: Redefining Rural Life in the Age of Globalization*. New York: Rowman and Littlefield.

Gottlieb, Robert, and Anupama Joshi, eds. 2010. "Preface." In *Food Justice*, ix–xvi. Cambridge: MIT Press.

Guthman, Julie. 2004. *Agrarian Dreams: The Paradox of Organic Farming in California*. Berkeley: University of California Press.

"Home." n.d. Local Llano. Accessed February 1, 2021. https://localllano.org.

Ihejirika, Kingsley T., Anne Goulding, and Philip J. Calvert. 2021. "Do They 'Like' the Library? Undergraduate Students' Awareness, Attitudes, and Inclination to

Engage with Library Social Media." *The Journal of Academic Librarianship* 47, no. 6: 1–15.

Masters, Kelley. n.d. "Home." Texas Cottage Food Law. Accessed February 1, 2021. https://texascottagefoodlaw.com.

Ogallala Commons 2020 Annual Report. Ogallala Commons.

"Press Release." 2019, March. Local Food Producers Summit 3.0. Lubbock, Texas.

"Reason No. 8: Because We Live in the Beef Capital of the World." 2013, February 22. *Amarillo Magazine*. https://www.amarillo.com/article/20130222/NEWS/302229755.

Robb, Hattie. 2021, March 30. "Alcove Farms: Regenerative Farming Reaps Egg-cellent Results." *Local Llano* (blog). https://localllano.org/alcove-farms-regenerative-farming-reaps-egg-celent-results.

Robb, Hattie. 2021, May 20. "Ogallala Greens: West Texas' Up and Coming Hydroponic Farm." *Local Llano* (blog). https://localllano.org/ogallala-greens-west-texas-up-and-coming-hydroponic-farm.

Schell, Eileen. 2007. "The Rhetorics of the Farm Crisis: Toward Alternative Agrarian Literacies in a Globalized World." In *Rural Literacies,* edited by Kim Donehower, Charlotte Hogg, and Eileen Schell, 77–119. Carbondale: Southern Illinois University Press.

Schell, Eileen, Charlotte Hogg, and Kim Donehower. 2020. "Introduction." In "Rhetorics and Literacies of Climate Change," special issue, *Enculturation* 32. http://enculturation.net/rhetorics-and-literacies-of-climate-change.

"Staff." n.d. Council for Healthy Food Systems. Accessed February 1, 2021. https://healthyfoodsystems.org/staff.

"Staff." n.d. Ogallala Commons. Accessed June 16, 2022. https://ogallalacommons.org/staff.

Steadman, Jim. 2017, March 13. "Bayer Opens $16.7 Million Southwest Cotton Breeding Station." *Cotton Grower*. https://www.cottongrower.com/cotton-news/bayer-opens-16-7-million-southwest-cotton-breeding-station.

"12 Key Assets of Commonwealth." n.d. Ogallala Commons. Accessed February 1, 2021. https://ogallalacommons.org/about/commonwealth.

"What Is Local Llano?" n.d. Local Llano. Accessed February 1, 2021. http://localllano.org/about.

NOTES

1. For analysis on how organic agriculture "has replicated what it set out to oppose [industrial agriculture]," see Julie Guthman's *Agrarian Dreams: The Paradox of Organic Farming in California* (2004).

2. The "12 Key Assets of Commonwealth" are twelve aspects the organization deems necessary for thriving areas, primarily rural areas, with supported agricultural engagements. The assets align with four corresponding categories: Workforce and Leadership Development (education, spirituality, health), Youth Engagement (sense of place, history, leisure, and recreation), "Rebuilding Local Food Systems"

(foodshed, renewable energy, arts, and culture), and Stewarding Natural Resources (wildlife and the natural world, water cycle, and soil and mineral cycle).

3. Defamiliarization with agriculture is only one of many costs to the current large-scale food system in the United States. For example, there are social, political, economic, and environmental costs, the later most recently noted in Schell, Hogg, and Donehower's introduction to *Rhetorics and Literacies of Climate Change* (2020), a special issue of *enculturation*.

Chapter 7

Once You Sell Us on the Service We Can Render

Agricultural Public Relations, Feminist Food Literacies, and the Rhetorical Power of Women in Ag

Cori Brewster

I attended my first "Women in Ag" workshop in 2015, in the meeting room of my local Extension office, one of about thirty White women connected to several hundred predominantly White others in twenty-seven web-connected sites across five western states. Though I had grown up in agriculture, though I still help out as needed on my brothers' farm, and though I have served most of the last twenty years on the board of a grassroots organization engaged in both local and national food and farm issues, I couldn't help feeling like both an impostor and an intruder, definitely not the kind of "woman in ag" the organizers were aiming for.

My presence was suspect for a lot of reasons, not the least of which were my purpose and my profession. I knew at least a dozen of the other women in the room, many of whom I had worked with on youth gardening projects, issue campaigns, and community-university partnerships related to food—and many of whose connections to agriculture were arguably as tenuous if not more than my own. That morning, however, I was there primarily as an English professor: a landless, unmarried, unmascaraed, salaried skeptic interested in the kinds of rhetorical training currently being provided to "women in agriculture" via public-private partnerships like this one, hosted annually by the Washington State University Extension Service with support from Northwest Farm Credit Services and other industry and institutional sponsors. I had requested permission from lead and local organizers to attend in this capacity and I was upfront with my fellow attendees about what I was studying and why I was there. But while I had been told by the chair of my Institutional Review Board this project didn't even warrant application because I was studying public programming, not its participants, exemption from human subjects protocols hardly erased questions of power or privacy or made this any less strange a thing to talk about in this environment, let alone give up a whole Saturday to do.

The theme of the 2015 workshop was "Making Sense of Marketing: Putting Your Best Boot Forward." The following year, it was "POWER UP Your Communication, POWER UP Your Farm," and in 2018, the last year I attended in person, this time from Salem, Oregon, closer to where my own family had farmed for the past 75 years—and where my mother and her five siblings were then acrimoniously dividing up my grandparents' estate and preparing the farm for sale, half of them unable to buy out the other half at the above market value demanded—the theme was "PUMP UP YOUR FINANCIAL FITNESS!" The "Take Away Messages" I recorded on my exit form from the two sessions that day, "How Does Your Cash Flow?" and "Attention Women: You are a Valuable Part of Agriculture," were "I need more cash" and "I'm not so sure." Three years into studying workshops targeting an imagined farm woman I was no longer convinced anyone identified with entirely, my "Personal Action Plans" were "Go home" and "??"

My focus in this chapter is not just on the identities privileged in workshops like these, or on the disjuncture between the curriculum provided and the lived needs and experiences of the far more diverse set of women actively engaged in, and struggling to engage in, agriculture in the United States, whether they want to or not—though of course these are essential and interconnected threads, especially in thinking about food justice and the multifold inequities women experience across the food system and in agricultural labor in particular. Instead, I want to direct more attention first to the raced and gendered history of agricultural public relations and communications efforts in the United States, of which programs like WSU's Women in Ag conference are an ongoing part; the kinds of rhetorical instruction currently being offered to (predominantly straight White land-owning cis) women in such sites; implications for building common cause and coalition in agriculture and food justice movements; and possible roles writing and rhetoric scholars committed to feminist food literacies and community-engaged pedagogies might play in response.

TEXTS AND CONTEXTS: STUDYING RHETORICAL PROGRAMMING AND PEOPLE

In developing this project, I have thought often of Anne Ruggles Gere's (1994) historic call to better understand and engage the "extracurriculum of composition" (91), on the one hand, and on the other more recent work by feminist food scholars like Abby Dubisar (2018), who envision a feminist food rhetoric that "holds the power to subvert dominant discourses and more fully engage with food's intersectional implications for diverse communities and ecological futures" (126–27).[1] How do these different calls intersect? Where is the "curriculum" or "extracurriculum" of food rhetoric currently happening? Under what pre-existing rhetorical or political conditions? How to study this, on whose terms, and with what possible openings for support, activism, or change? As Ralph Cintron (2003) so well puts it, "Rhetoric is that disciplinary art that imprecisely tracks the making of social imaginaries, including their histories, possible futures, and connections to material conditions" (10). IRB exemption or no, studying "the making of social imaginaries" inevitably requires analysis of both texts and contexts, and both rhetors and audiences, whether a given project works solely from publicly available documents or attempts, as mine does, to further ground textual analysis through rhetorical fieldwork, participant observation, and other informal "field-based research."[2] As Candice Rai and Caroline Gottschalk Druschke (2018) explain, "a renewed interest in field methods [in the discipline of rhetoric and composition] affords opportunities to expand access to objects of study and their complex interrelations . . . and to craft more richly contextualized, deeply grounded accounts of rhetoric in everyday life that are made possible through ongoing proximity to and immersion in the field" (6).[3]

My approach to this contemporary site of rhetorical instruction has been strongly informed as well by feminist researchers in rhetoric, composition, and literacy studies such as Jacqueline Jones Royster and Gesa Kirsch (2012). As Royster and Kirsch remind readers, the most "basic principle" of a "feminist-informed operational framework" is "that there is indeed value to be recognized and appreciated in the lives, words, participation, leadership, and legacies of women" (18). Among the "key values" Royster and Kirsch advocate are "the importance of paying attention to the ethical self in the texts we study, the texts we produce, and the pedagogical frames that we use to instruct and train our students. Such values take seriously the interplay of who we personally are as scholars, teachers, and human beings, what our vantage points are, what we see, how we are conditioned to see, how we engage in sense-making processes, and how we turn those sensibilities into action" (18). This framing has been especially helpful to return to as I have grappled with the differently lived consequences of publicly-sponsored programs like WSU's "Women in Ag"; my outsider-insider, observer-participant status; and what it means to practice an "ethics of care and hope" in a fraught, dynamic, and ultimately dialogical and constitutive rhetorical space (Royster and Kirsch 2012, 145–49).

Royster and Kirsch's framing has been helpful too in thinking about the place of gender in food justice organizing and scholarship (in both of which it remains relatively thinly addressed) and about women's place as rhetorical agents within the food justice movement—not just "at the center of the discussion regarding how, by whom, and to what ends the food system is transformed" but actively leading that discussion on our own terms ourselves (Gottlieb and Joshi 2010, 229).

FROM "SHIFTING THE NARRATIVE" TO RHETORICAL KNOWLEDGE BUILDING

As Alison Hope Alkon and Julian Agyeman (2011) have argued, "Essential to the food justice movement is an analysis that recognizes the food system itself as a racial project and problematizes the influence of race and class on the production, distribution, and consumption of food" (5).[4] The food system is also of course simultaneously a gender project, an economic project, an environmental project, and an ideological project, and one in which differentially raced and gendered divisions of labor, power, land, and wealth are daily made, experienced, rationalized, romanticized, compounded, leveraged, monetized, challenged, shifted, recontextualized, and reinforced. Meaningfully changing this deeply entrenched, densely articulated, highly corporatized, and increasingly global system is no small task.[5]

In developing theories of grassroots change in the face of unprecedented corporate power and consolidation, it has thus been heartening to see progressive food and food justice organizations in the United States return more explicitly over the past two decades to issues of rhetoric. As Robert Gottlieb and Anupama Joshi (2010) call on Antonio Gramsci to explain in their volume *Food Justice*, for instance, creating a more just food system will depend fundamentally on changing the discourse: laying the cultural and ideological groundwork for policy-level change through language that more directly links issues of food to issues of social, racial, and economic justice and helps wider audiences recognize and articulate interests they share (5; 231–33). The Grassroots Policy Project, likewise, has played a lead role in training progressive community organizers and members of grassroots organizations across the United States to think about narrative in particular as "a critical element to building the power to make systemic change" (Mann 2019).

If there is one lesson food justice scholars and activists might take from the Women in Ag workshop I describe in this chapter, and from the longer history of agricultural public relations in general, it is that the movement must support its members in developing new language and new language awareness both. Understanding who is currently being enjoined to speak about agricultural policy and practice, by whom, and in what ways is critical to understanding the broader discourse we seek to shift, as is understanding how, in what contexts, and with whose backing different constituents' agricultural knowledge, narratives, identities, and allegiances have historically been formed. Programs like WSU's Women in Ag conference offer an important locus, I argue, for considering how agricultural discourses form, intersect, and circulate in the United States, how agricultural identities are interpellated by and in response to industry, and how densely articulated the discourses and identities the food justice movement hopes to support, alter, and engage really are. Programs like Women in Ag also cast issues of race and gender in agriculture, agricultural communications, and agricultural movements in important relief, highlighting ways White women farmers and "farm wives" in particular have been enlisted to perform rhetorically for industry—often for free—and what a more just, feminist, agentive approach to discursive activism that continues to build and strengthen our rhetorical capacities might look like instead.

As Bill Ashcroft (2001) calls upon Gilles Deleuze and Felix Guattari to explain, "it is clear that power doesn't operate in a simple vertical way from the institutions [or individuals] in which it appears to be constituted; it operates dynamically, laterally and intermittently." Indeed, "the greatest advancement of cultural hegemony occurs when it operates through an invisible network of filiative connections, psychological internalizations and unconsciously complicit associations" that produce "its effects by a complex, diffracted, discontinuous layering" (50).[6] Fortunately, as many postcolonial scholars would remind us, "No system of control, no discourse, can ever operate with absolute consistency" (52); openings for subjective agency, resistance, and other ways of constituting meaning and identification inevitably remain. No doubt there is a place for English professors in the struggle for fair food, as there is a place for all women in agriculture should we desire it. But in this "rhizomic" context, in which the "operation of power, like the operation of social relations themselves, is both perpetual and discontinuous" (50), we need to work still more intentionally to make it, finding ways to bring our literacies, rhetorical knowledge, and other resources more reflectively and strategically to bear.

Contextualizing "Women in Ag": Leveraging White Women's Rhetorical Power and Labor in U.S. Agriculture

"Throughout the land," Ed Lipscomb writes in the opening to *Grassroots Public Relations for Agriculture* (1950), "group after group is learning that it moves more rapidly ahead when it becomes fully conscious of the all-controlling power of public opinion, and sets out actively to earn and retain public favor" (17). Director of Public Relations for the National Cotton Council and founding member of the Agricultural Relations Council, Lipscomb goes on to detail the voluntary "program of persuasion" White farmers and farm groups will need to undertake if they are to help protect American agriculture from organized labor, "opportunistic political administration[s]" and other racialized, euphemistically-described threats to "basic Americanism" and "the real interests of farmers," such as efforts to set "minimum agricultural wages and working conditions without due regard to farm needs or long-established agricultural practices" (iii; 6; 18; 33).[7] "You don't need special training, and you don't need to be a genius" to defend "brave homes and free lands," he assures "the sons and daughters of wilderness carvers" to whom he addresses the book (iii–iv; 39):

> You are going to be dealing with people—and people are right down your alley. They like you. If they didn't, you would not be an agricultural leader in your area. You would not be preparing to initiate a public relations program for agriculture's welfare. Nine chances out of ten you would not be reading this page.
> Your job of influencing public opinion, however, is not one that can be accomplished overnight. . . .
> Fortunately, the nature of public relations work is such that most people enjoy doing it. Its nature also is such that practice builds proficiency at an exceedingly satisfactory pace. Add to these the fact that in the case of agriculture a great cause is involved, and it becomes logical to expect a minimum of difficulty in obtaining adequate volunteers for sustained activity. Once it is rolling, the job takes on a crusading spirit which neither commercial promoters nor exponents of less fundamental causes can normally achieve. (39–40)

Lipscomb goes on to detail all necessary steps and rationales for carrying out local public relations campaigns in agriculture, effectively enlisting his readers to the same unpaid cause in which he is urging them to enlist others. "This is not intended to imply by any means that you will be able to get by free," he writes in a section titled "The Question of Money" (40). "It means, however, that you are in an excellent position, as a representative of agriculture, to use brains instead of budget and to pay in cooperation rather than in cash. Certainly in your own county and community, the sincerity and diligence of you and your committeemen will more than make up for lack of local money" (40–41).

Rarely spoken to directly, White women appear in several places throughout the book, as "volunteer typists" who can be rewarded with an occasional box of candy, as pass throughs for messaging to others over whom they have influence, and as especially effective cost-free communicative resources to be deployed at male leaders' behest (40; 54–56; 65). In a section on creating public interest stories to feed local media, for example, Lipscomb advises that one source of material "with fascinating potentialities might be a first-hand investigation, or series of them, conducted by members of your own organization or by a women's auxiliary or affiliate if available. A committee of women calling on the freight agents of local railroads and truck lines . . . to determine what percentage of outgoing freight originated on local farms, might not only turn up some interesting information but would rather certainly make quite an impression on the agents" (47). In a section on influencing politicians, he notes, "It will be found, by and large, that women are more effective letter writers than men, and that the members of your auxiliary may do a better job of promoting a successful letter-writing campaign than will their husbands. Certainly their aid should be enlisted" (62–63).

Like major agricultural corporations and public relations firms today, Lipscomb is particularly aware of the higher number of women voters in the United States, the amount of land and household income they control, their influence within social networks, and the importance of harnessing their collective electoral, financial, and rhetorical power (55). "Although women are included in some of the organizations referred to in the preceding paragraphs," he explains, "their direct effect on public opinion is strongest when they are organized in special clubs or groups of their own":

> Being by nature particularly concerned with the welfare of their families, their communities, and their nation, women in general are far more intensely interested in health, security and public welfare than are men. Organize them, give them a cause, and they become an irresistible force before which there are no immovable objects. City and county councils, state legislatures, and the national Congress will all bear witness to the success with which *the hand that rocks the cradle can operate a steam roller if necessary*. (55, emphasis mine)

The power and persistence of women's groups can be viewed as either an asset or a threat, he suggests, depending on who is directing them. Women are "generally more active and aggressive in carrying out group projects than are clubs of men," he informs his White male readers, and when "they start a crusade or set a goal, they are apt to see the job through" (55). Fortunately, Lipscomb concludes, "You will find that your goal of creating better understanding and public support for agriculture appeals strongly to women's organizations. Once you get your story before them through their meetings or otherwise—*once you sell them on the service they can render by helping guard agriculture's welfare and productivity*—you have won an ally whose influence on the public and the polls will stand you in good stead" (55–56, emphasis mine).

Though much has changed across the food system in the seventy-some years since Lipscomb's advice for "protecting agriculture" was first published and circulated through his many speaking events and professional roles, his book remains a useful touchstone, I would argue, for considering the way White women farmers and members of farm families like myself have been imagined, "leveraged," and to some degree interpellated by agricultural public relations strategists and industry groups in the United States. Lipscomb figures White women here as rhetorical vessels and vassals both, operating from a naturalizing and occlusive White supremacist rhetoric that positions White women as uncritical advocates for a set of practices premised on deeply inequitable distributions of land, power, voice, personhood, and wealth.[8]

Now in the public domain and easily accessed free online, the book also provides an especially candid example for teaching about agricultural literacy campaigns and a good reminder to examine closely the kinds of "stories" about self, others, and agriculture that public relations efforts have succeeded in "getting before us" throughout our lives and enlisted our help both directly and indirectly to circulate.[9] To be clear, I'm not suggesting that this kind of communications work in agriculture began with or can be traced solely to Lipscomb, that it has been carried out without contest or competition, that is has always been framed in the same racist and racializing ways, or that individual women and women's organizations have had no agency, awareness, or power to craft messages and identities along the way of our own.[10] What I do want to highlight here, though, are the broad, even if uneven discursive legacies of agricultural public relations efforts past and parallels to ways in which a small, disproportionately more privileged segment of "women in ag" are being asked to think about rhetoric, identity, and duty to protect "the real interests of farmers" via multiple coordinated and competing initiatives today.

Enlisting "Women in Ag": Contemporary Sites of Rhetorical Instruction and Identity

The WSU Extension Service's Women, Farms, and Food program offers a range of programs and services based on the assumption that women "face unique challenges growing viable businesses in farming and ranching," including the annual one-day workshop series I focus on here (Washington State University Extension Service, "Women, Farms, and Food Mission

Statement" n.d.). In 2015, as noted above, this included explicitly gendered training on branding, strategic communication planning, and using social media to build "authentic" relationships with customers by crafting a likeable online identity for participants' own farm families. As 2015 keynote speaker and small farmer Emily Asmus explained while showing a picture of herself and her two young daughters at their market booth, one of her primary marketing strategies is "to play up the idea that we're a family farm. . . . We try to be cute, we try to be likable, and we try to convey to folks that we really like what we do . . . and that we really like the life we're creating for our kids . . . and we do that through lots of pictures and e-newsletters and just demonstrating to folks that this is a way of life that we think people would like." The March 2016 conference, "POWER UP Your Communications," featured presentations similarly grounded in individual women farmers' experience on how women in general can discover our unique communication style in order to "better ourselves," "better the industry," and increase profits. The three prior years had focused even more explicitly on how to "agvocate" online: how to advocate for conventional agricultural policy and practice by telling compelling public stories about one's own family and farm.

Like Lipscomb and other sponsors of "grassroots" agricultural public relations campaigns, the Women in Ag program routinely essentializes women in order to invoke their ostensibly special capacities and responsibilities to promote industry positions.[11] "Why a gender-specific program?" the WSU Extension website (n.d.) asks. Because women "learn differently than men: They like connecting with other women farmers and enjoy sharing resources. Their situations differ from those of men since they generally have responsibilities with children. . . . The number of women in agriculture grows every year—women are natural nurturers and are interested in providing the foods that people want and need" ("Women, Farms, & Food Mission Statement"). Or, as 2018 featured speaker, author, and independent agricultural consultant Sarah Beth Aubrey put it, "Women think differently," as evidenced by "plenty of books" on this topic and the results of the Gallup Strengths Finder assessment tool she has used with her own clients. Women "are the type of people who have a natural tendency to form good relationships," she explained, and are therefore especially "well positioned" to combat public misunderstandings and speak up for ag.

It's important to situate this tack, this program, and the publicly-sponsored cultural work it performs in at least three contexts: the increasing power and participation of women in ownership and leadership roles in agriculture in the United States, the relative success and rhetorical strength of the progressive food movement, and the massive, multi-headed Agvocacy campaign launched in approximately 2009 in response.[12] As has been widely reported in the agricultural press, and repeated at the beginning of the Women in Ag workshop each year, "Women are now the principal operators of 14 percent of the nation's 2.2 million farms" (Mortensen 2013), nearly "triple the share" since 1978, when data was first collected (Hoppe and Korb 2013). When "secondary" operators are included in the count, there are approximately a million women who currently play active, decision-making roles on farms of varying sizes in the United States, whether alongside a partner or on their own (Hoppe and Korb 2013). As Margaret Viebrock, lead organizer of the WSU Women in Ag program tells it, "No other male dominated industry is experiencing such a rapid turnover, as women rise to leadership roles."

This significant shift in the industry, paired with the enormous spending and voting power women have in the United States and increasing public support for sustainable agriculture, organics, local sourcing, farmworker rights, animal welfare, and fair food as it continues to be articulated via popular and social movements and media is of serious concern to the conventional agricultural industry and marketing and public relations firms serving it, as evidenced in part by how intentionally they have worked over the past decade to train individual farmers and ranchers to reclaim the "story of agriculture" on social media. Though campaign organizers have done a far better job than Lipscomb of masking their overall strategy, thousands of agvocacy trainings, blogs, hashtags, and other social media projects have sprung up over the past decade, led in most visible part by Bayer Crop Science, marketer and agricultural public relations consultant Michele Payn-Knoper, Fastline Media Group (parent company of PinkTractor.com), the AgChat Foundation (on whose board Payn-Knoper serves), and countless public and private entities like FFA and Extension since enlisted in various ways to the cause.[13]

As the AgChat Foundation (n.d.) tells the story, they are a "farmer-led," not-for-profit organization founded in 2010 "to empower farmers, ranchers, agribusiness professionals and agriculture enthusiasts to connect society to production of food, fuel, fiber, feed and everyday items. Through [their annual] conferences and online resources, empowerment equips those with an interest in advocating for agriculture with the skills needed to effectively engage and tell their story in social media, face-to-face conversations and on the legislative level" ("Who We Are"). Nearly all of the women selected as featured farmers for the WSU Women in Ag workshop have been trained to agvocate through this network, and while Extension staff report that annual workshop themes are based on requests from women farmers in the region, much of the content and discursive framing in recent years also appears to have been informed at least in part by this campaign.

Each year, the Women in Ag conference has four standard components. First comes an introduction by Margaret Viebrock, in which she describes how women's roles in agriculture are changing, reminds attendees that the public "just doesn't understand agriculture," and explains that "it is very important" in this context "that women be able to express themselves." As is routinely argued by the AgChat Foundation and other "agvocates," farmers are often portrayed negatively in the media; the 98 percent of Americans who don't live on farms are susceptible to all kinds of misinformation; and most consumers, especially moms, trust individual farmers far more than corporations, marketers, or scientists. In the face of all this, Viebrock reiterates, women farmers need to be prepared to tell the story of agriculture themselves.

The second part of the conference each year is a three to four-hour session on the day's theme led by a paid speaker or speakers—typically, a gimmicky web-cast lecture on a proprietary communication or self-assessment tool of some kind, broken up by small group activities to be completed at the separate viewing sites. At the 2015 workshop, for example, the paid facilitator was a self-styled "communication guru" from Seattle named Erica Mills who runs a one-woman marketing firm, Claxon Marketing. Like many of the conference's featured speakers, Mills made a point of stressing that she had "no degree in marketing," and that her trademarked "Claxon Method"—essentially, a series of handouts on analyzing the rhetorical situation—had been developed and "pressure tested" through her innovative work with past clients.

In 2016, the facilitators were both loan officers for Northwest Farm Credit Services whose focus was on working participants through the DISC behavioral assessment, which they often recommend their clients purchase. Like Mills, speaker Michael Stolp emphasized that the communication insights he was sharing were "not things [he and his co-presenter had] learned in a textbook" but "things [they] learned in the real world." Among these insights were "communication is challenging," "communication is important; you have to work at it," "no one communication style is better than another"; "different 'ethnicities'/cultures are no different—all exhibit the same basic communication styles"; and the most important thing to remember is "mutual purpose and mutual respect." (At the site where I was attending the conference, it is worth noting, the thirty-some women there found Stolp so overbearing that we voted to mute the volume for the last hour he was speaking and talk among ourselves.)

The third and most popular part of the conference each year is a 30-minute to hour-long talk by a featured farm woman on how she's applied the ideas discussed that day on her own farm. In 2015, as noted above, "keynote farmer" Emily Asmus advised participants on how to target moms via social media, email, and farm newsletters; how to take cute photos of your own farm family to build a likable brand; and how to build time for drafting farm communications into the work day. She also made a point of emphasizing that communication about food should not be viewed as manipulation like other kinds of marketing because it is providing for a basic need and giving people something that is good for their families that they already want.

In 2016, spokesfarmer and trained agvocate Shelly Boshart-Davis talked about her successful use of the DISC assessment to improve herself and her family business. When she was asked by Viebrock why it is important for women in agriculture to have good communication skills, she explained that this was about "personal betterment": "In bettering myself, I was able to better everything around me." She then turned to her "passion" for "telling the story of agriculture to those around us," which she framed as "bettering the ag industry as a whole." When Boshart-Davis was asked about the difficulty of agvocating online, she told a participant, "Recognize that your audience members may not have gone through the betterment process," and "some people are further along on their journey than others." When asked how to adjust one's communication style in social media so as not to "come across as a bully," she answered, "Some people may be combative . . . if they are coming from an anti-agriculture side." She advised that the women in the audience watch their tone, make sure they can back their points up with facts, and take an "I just want to share" perspective "on what we do on our own farm."

The last part of the workshop each year is set aside for participants to write out their commitments for implementing the day's lesson on carbon copied forms—the "personal action plans" I mentioned earlier. "When we have a written plan of action," the form reminds us, "we are more motivated to follow through." Needless to say, perhaps, there is no room built into the schedule for critical reflection on the tools or ideas introduced, though it sometimes bubbles up, let alone the larger cultural and economic forces that have positioned women in agriculture in these ways or helped move the kind of rhetorical labor and responsibility advocated in these workshops into women farmers' hands. In keeping with much Extension work, the emphasis is on the practical, not the explicitly political—the functional literacies individual actors need to succeed in business, not the critical literacies or tools we might use to interrogate larger structures, explore others' perspectives, build coalition, or advocate for more systemic change.

In sum, while this publicly-sponsored conference is often pitched as meeting women's needs for communication tools that will help them succeed in business, it also routinely seeks to enlist them into performing an embodied, self-metonymizing sort of public relations for the industry as a whole. This for an industry whose interests and troubles individual farm women are assumed to share, on the one hand, despite the very different size, profit margins, and political resources of different operations, and premised on the other on the greater access and credibility they presumably have to reach audiences that larger agricultural corporations and industry groups can't.

"This Program Means Work": Implications for Feminist Rhetorical Activism and Teaching

Though it would be a stretch to say there is a coherent or consistent theory of rhetoric underlying the communications training delivered by featured presenters or the Women in Ag program as a whole, it is possible to identify some of its general features and consider what lessons it might offer for more justice-oriented teaching and activism ahead. First and perhaps most striking is the emphasis on communication as something that has no particular discipline and requires no formal study—something that anyone can and must learn just by doing. While in some sense this is an inviting and democratic message, and one that might reflect in part the inexperience and/or differential access to different kinds of education some individuals selected to speak on this subject by Women in Ag have had, it also seems rather disingenuous in a context in which at least some highly trained, highly paid communications and public relations specialists are asking women to do their "important" cultural and communicative work for free.[14] More importantly, it directs attention away from the additional knowledge, literacies, and tools women rhetors might glean through further study, as well as from language itself, rendering further invisible relationships between language and power even as women are being asked to use language in the service of power—to "protect the industry" our symbol-made, symbol-making selves.

Next, somewhat paradoxically, are the program's emphases on delivery and technical skill, understood in this rhetorical space as the communication tools required to speak more authentically "from the heart" to a public that "just doesn't understand." Again and again, participating women are cast as guardians and truth-tellers and prepared to "diffuse," redirect, and correct rather than consider the lived experiences, evidence, desires, or positions of people who may bring different needs, perspectives, or visions to the table. In this sense, the approach seems decidedly Aristotelian, engaging women in a "rhetoric of the actual," as John Poulakos (1983) put it, in which a pre-existing logos can be embodied and fronted by an already essentialized ethos, as female-identified rhetors are asked to engage far less in invention or deliberation via these trainings than they are handed scripts about food and farming to personalize, self-metonymize, and present unidirectionally to their followers and friends. While the Women in Ag program itself may be aspirationally constitutive—hailing women to hail others in order to constitute and populate a particular vision of agriculture present and future—its curricula renders relationships between rhetoric, identity, and identification less visible rather than more. Among the many consequences of this approach are naturalizing and masking the ways in which straight cis White women's experiences and priorities are authenticated and privileged in public agricultural discourse while the experiences, voices, and priorities of differently identified, identifying, and coalescing others are kept largely off stage.[15]

The extent to which Women in Ag participants agree with such scripts or see themselves as the kinds of women hailed here is typically only addressed from the podium if individual audience members bring it up—though it becomes immediately clear when a speaker's generalizing has gone too far, whether through raised eyebrows or a formal vote to turn off the sound. Participants at all sites can also pass questions off camera to Viebrock, who interjects them throughout the day. Near the end of Aubrey's session in 2018, for example, Viebrock interrupted to pose several questions from the audience, one of which she summarized as follows: "A lot of the talk today has been very broad as far as women getting involved in agriculture and sometimes women of different persuasions, binary, lesbian, whatever, have difficulty breaking into the agricultural world. Have you had any experience with that or any opinions on that of looking at a more diverse audience?" Though she stumbled a bit with her answer, Aubrey ultimately came around to the importance of creating cultures in which uncomfortable subjects can be discussed, advocating "open dialogue about a lot of issues that are different or difficult or not the same as they used to be." While not a particularly radical piece of advice, Aubrey's gesture toward dialogue does represent some break from the "steam roller" approach to agricultural knowledge, identity, and difference speakers typically advocate in this site of rhetorical instruction and in the agvocacy movement overall. In short, whatever our own diverse and shifting views of different food and farm issues might be, there are critical questions we might ask about this model of rhetorical instruction, especially as it is delivered through a public institution in a democratic nation and in the context of a still deeply unjust system of food.

As Gottlieb and Joshi (2010) write, "Food justice, like environmental justice, is a powerful idea. It resonates with many groups and can be invoked to expand the support base for bringing about community change *and* a different kind of food system." While it does not "necessarily create a clear path to advocating for changes to the food system or point to ways to bring about more just policies, economic change, or the restructuring of global, national, and community food pathways," they continue, "it does open up those pathways for social and political action, and it helps establish a new language of social change . . . " (5). The power of this new language manifests in at least two ways, according to Gottlieb and Joshi: in helping build "crossover appeal" as people working on different issues can identify common interests and in laying "the groundwork for broader structural reform as [public] discourse changes" (2010, 232–33).

While there has been important headway in progressive food organizing circles in the United States over the past twenty years in recognizing the role of language and narrative in social change, as I noted earlier, there is still much distance to go. The Grassroots Policy Project has done excellent work in engaging a national network of progressive agricultural groups in trainings that focused on "shifting the dominant agricultural narrative," and in articulating the role of language to a wider organizing public as the "third face of power" in their theory of change (see for example Mann n.d.; Healey and Hinson n.d.). Likewise, the move toward "storytelling projects" among community- and membership-based organizations of all kinds has helped render more audible and visible a far wider range of voices and experiences than historically privileged in public agricultural discourse on or offline. This growing interest in identifying and amplifying shared language and shared values as means of building more powerful and inclusive movements is no small gain in a culture that has for so long de-emphasized formal instruction in rhetoric and so powerfully defined it as the province of dishonest schemers on some less pure or authentic side.

At the same time, I would argue, it is critical that food justice activists and teachers go beyond the same ahistorical, apolitical, and essentializing approaches to the rhetoric of food and agriculture we see in different ways in the work of Lipscomb, the agvocacy movement, and Women in Ag. As we seek to build common cause through new narratives, new paths of identification, and new reckonings with ongoing histories of colonization, slavery, and land ownership in the United States, we would be well served considering more explicitly together what language does, what it has done, and how it does it on all sides of a debate. Otherwise we too risk simply "selling people on the service they can render," fronting with apparently immutable, embodied positions, crafting new narratives without critical examination of where they also already have at least partially come from, and forestalling conversation and other possible identifications, visions, and openings for change. As Plato himself might remind us, the written word—the metonymized, story-told subject or alternately narrativized issue in this case—becomes too easily fixed on the page; members whose values and stories are displayed at a particular moment on organizational websites may hail well to others while being reft of their ability to listen, take questions, consider new evidence, revise their position, rethink or recraft their own identity, analyze or historicize the "new" language they're using, or otherwise continue learning and visioning collaboratively ahead. Uncritically embracing the role of narrative in food justice organizing without inviting all participants to more fully examine the work rhetoric does, in other words, reduces us to the identities, values, and linguistic resources of the moment rather than further building our collective rhetorical capacity, facility, agency, and power.

Perhaps the most important takeaway from the "Women in Ag" workshop for food justice scholars and activists, then, is that telling new stories is not enough. Visibility, amplification, and identification are clearly important, but as strategies for social change they are also easily circumvented, content flooded, and co-opted, as the agvocacy movement and other public relations efforts have shown. Writing and rhetoric scholars would do well to work closely with food justice organizations in addition to identifying the kinds of rhetorical training currently being provided in their communities, if any, the theories of language, identity, and power that inform them, and what needs if any for additional rhetorical knowledge, practice, or instruction remain. I have only marginally addressed here the kinds of cultural work programs like Women in Ag do, and even more briefly the ways they may reify racialized identities, chains of identification and disidentification, and racist, sexist, anti-immigrant, and other discriminatory, dehumanizing attitudes, practices, and policies experienced daily across the agricultural industry. What other kinds of rhetorical instruction are possible in this context? What other kinds of cultural work or collective capacity-building might they do?

I'm persuaded that there is, in fact, "service women can render" in this regard—and I look forward to the power we can leverage in more reflectively organizing and teaching ourselves.[16]

REFERENCES

AgChat Foundation. n.d. "Who We Are." Accessed March 14, 2021. https://agchat.org/who-we-are.

Alkon, Alison Hope, and Julian Agyeman. 2011. "Introduction: The Food Movement as Polyculture." In *Cultivating Food Justice: Race, Class, and Sustainability*, edited by Alison Hope Alkon and Julian Agyeman, 1–20. Cambridge, MA; London: MIT Press.

Alkon, Alison Hope, and Julie Guthman, eds. 2017. *The New Food Activism: Opposition, Cooperation, and Collective Action*. Oakland: University of California Press.

Ashcroft, Bill. 2001. *Post-Colonial Transformation*. London; New York: Routledge.

Brewster, Cori. 2012. "Toward a Critical Agricultural Literacy." *Reclaiming the Rural: Essays on Literacy, Rhetoric, and Pedagogy*, edited by Kim Donehower, Charlotte Hogg, and Eileen Schell. Carbondale, IL: Southern Illinois University Press.

———. 2016. "'Agvocates' for Industry: Citizen-Farmers, Social Media, and the Gendered Production of Food." *The Ecopolitics of Consumption: The Food Trade*, edited by H. Louise Davis, Karyn Pilgrim, and Madhudaya Sinha. Lanham, MD: Rowman and Littlefield.

Cintron, Ralph. 1997. *Angel's Town: Chero Ways, Gang Life, and the Rhetorics of the Everyday*. Boston: Beacon Press.

———. 2003. "'Gates Locked' and the Violence of Fixation." *Towards a Rhetoric of Everyday Life: New Directions in Research on Writing, Text, and Discourse*, edited by Martin Nystrand and John Duffy. Madison: University of Wisconsin Press.

Dubisar, Abby. 2018. "Toward a Feminist Food Rhetoric." *Rhetoric Review* 37, no. 1: 118–30.

Garcia, Mario, ed. 2008. *A Dolores Huerta Reader*. Albuquerque: University of New Mexico Press.

Gere, Anne Ruggles. 1994. "Kitchen Tables and Rented Rooms: The Extracurriculum of Composition." *College Composition and Communication* 45, no. 1: 75–92. doi:10.2307/358588.

Gottlieb, Robert, and Anupama Joshi. 2010. *Food Justice*. Cambridge, MA; London: MIT Press.

Healey, Richard, and Sandra Hinson. n.d. "The Three Faces of Power." Grassroots Policy Project. Accessed March 14, 2021. https://grassrootspolicy.org/wp-content/uploads/2018/05/GPP_34FacesOfPower.pdf.

Hoppe, Robert, and Penni Korb. 2013, April. "Characteristics of Women Farm Operators and Their Farms." Economic Information Bulletin No. (EIB-111). http://www.ers.usda.gov/publications/eib-economic-information-bulletin/eib111/report-summary.aspx#.VDRnZyldWLE.

Jayaraman, Saru, and Kathryn De Master. 2020. *Bite Back: People Taking on Corporate Food and Winning*. Oakland: University of California Press.

Kostelich, Callie. 2019. "Facebook and a Farm Crisis: FFA and Online Agricultural Advocacy." *Open Library of Humanities* 5, no. 1: 1–31. https://www.researchgate.net/publication/330883770_Facebook_and_a_Farm_Crisis_FFA_and_Online_Agricultural_Advocacy.

Lipscomb, Ed. 1950. *Grassroots Public Relations for Agriculture*. Little Rock, AR: Democrat Printing and Lithographing.

Mann, David. n.d. "Is Narrative Strategy a Communications Strategy?" Grassroots Policy Project. https://grassrootspolicy.org/wp-content/uploads/2019/06/Is-Narrative-Strategy-a-Communications-Strategy.pdf.

Mortensen, Eric. 2013, October 24. "Daughters Taking Charge of More Farms," *Capitalpress.com*. http://www.capitalpress.com/article/20131024/ARTICLE/131029935/1030.

Neth, Mary. 1998. *Preserving the Family Farm: Women, Community, and the Foundations of Agribusiness in the Midwest, 1900–1940*. Baltimore: Johns Hopkins University Press.

Ostrander, Carolyn. 2012. "Latent Abilities: The Early Grange as a Mixed-Gender Site of Rhetorical Education." *Reclaiming the Rural: Essays on Literacy, Rhetoric, and Pedagogy*, edited by Kim Donehower, Charlotte Hogg, and Eileen Schell. Carbondale: Southern Illinois University Press.

Payn-Knoper, Michele. 2010, April 29. "Women of Agriculture Week." Cause Matters Corp. https://causematters.wordpress.com/2010/04/29/women-of-agriculture-week.

Poulakos, John. 1983. "Toward a Sophistic Definition of Rhetoric." *Philosophy & Rhetoric* 16, no. 1: 35–48. http://www.jstor.org.access.library.eou.edu/stable/40237348.

Rai, Candice, and Caroline Gottschalk Druschke. 2018. "On Being There: An Introduction to Studying Rhetoric in the Field." *Field Rhetoric: Ethnography, Ecology, and Engagement in the Places of Persuasion*, edited by Candice Rai and Caroline Gottschalk Druschke. Tuscaloosa: University of Alabama Press.

Royster, Jacqueline Jones, and Gesa Kirsch. 2012. *Feminist Rhetorical Practices: New Horizons for Rhetoric, Composition, and Literacy Studies*. Carbondale: Southern Illinois University Press.

Sachs, Carolyn. 1996. *Gendered Fields: Rural Women, Agriculture, and Environment*. New York: Routledge.

Schell, Eileen E. 2011. "Framing the Megarhetorics of Agricultural Development: Industrialized Agriculture and Sustainable Agriculture." In *The Megarhetorics of Global Development*, edited by Rebecca Dingo and J. Blake Scott. Pittsburgh, PA: University of Pittsburgh Press.

———. 2012. "Think Global, Eat Local: Teaching Alternative Agrarian Literacy in a Globalized Age." In *Teaching Writing in Globalization: Remapping Disciplinary Work*, edited by Darin Payne and Daphne Desser. Lanham, MD: Rowman and Littlefield.

Sheridan, Mary P., and Tobi Jacobi. 2014. "Critical Feminist Practice and Campus-Community Partnerships: A Review Essay." *Feminist Teacher* 24, no. 1–2: 138–50. doi:10.5406/femteacher.24.1–2.0138.

Singer, Ross, Stephanie Houston Grey, and Jeff Motter. 2020. *Rooted Resistance: Agrarian Myth in Modern America*. Fayetteville: University of Arkansas Press.

Washington State University Extension Service. n.d. "Women, Farms, and Food Mission Statement." Accessed March 14, 2021. https://womeninag.wsu.edu/mission-purpose-team.

NOTES

1. I recognize that in citing Gere, I'm also already stretching her definition, from which she explicitly excluded "the writing instruction carried out in . . . extension courses" (80). While Gere deliberately centered her study on "self-sponsored pedagogically oriented writing activities outside the academy," she did not plumb very deeply the distinctions between self and other or leader in sponsoring such gatherings or what it means to have agency in a discursive context in which "motivated individuals . . . see [writing and learning] as having social and economic consequences" (80). My point is that the distinction is perhaps a bit too artificial and unattainable, and inapplicable to low-cost workshops currently sponsored by the Extension Service that are advertised as addressing topics local women have requested themselves.

2. For a much fuller discussion of rhetorical fieldwork and "rhetorics of public culture" than I have space for here, see Ralph Cintron's foundational *Angel's Town: Chero Ways, Gang Life, and the Rhetorics of the Everyday* (2007) and Candice Rai

and Caroline Gottschalk Druschke, eds., *Field Rhetoric: Ethnography, Ecology, and Engagement in the Places of Persuasion* (2018).

3. The interest in both informal and formal field-based methods also responds more directly to calls "for critical, activist, and action-oriented practices that not only study the rhetorics of places and people, but also seek to actively *do* rhetoric with others" (Rai and Gottschalk Drushke, 10, italics in original).

4. As Alkon and Agyeman further explain, "Communities of color and poor communities have time and again been denied access to the means of food production," as they have been enslaved, dispossessed, paid no or poverty-level wages for agricultural work, exposed disproportionately to agricultural chemicals and other health risks, and experienced trafficking, physical and sexual violence, harassment, and other injustices in food production and processing.

5. Change is nonetheless possible, of course, as contributors to Alison Hope Alkon and Julie Guthman's *The New Food Activism*, Saru Jayaraman and Kathryn De Master's *Bite Back*, authors in this volume, and many others have shown.

6. See also Ashcroft's discussion of the difference between interpellation and interpolation, and ways in which power, voice, and identity obtain in colonial contexts, 47–48.

7. Though a history of the National Cotton Council and the cotton industry is beyond the scope of this chapter, it is critical to note the racial subtext here and the overarching discourse of White supremacy in which Lipscomb trades. Among the few direct references to race in the text are his warning that national labor organizations are distributing "pamphlets on the place of the Negro in election activity" and his opening celebration of farmers' role in "clear[ing]" the country's "wildernesses, conquer[ing] its savages, . . . and establish[ing] a nation wherein men could . . . expend their energy in expectation that their rewards would be in keeping with the volume and quality of their effort" (1; 10). The entire book is premised, however, on the need for farmers and farm advocates to wage a "second . . . fight for independence" to preserve the social order established by the nation's "founders" (iii–iv).

8. See for example the chapter titled "Special Groups to Be Won," in which Lipscomb draws on an explicitly racist evolutionary framework to illustrate the "psychological principle" through which "American women, in order to conform, feel compelled to discard or remodel perfectly good and appropriate wardrobes. . . . It has been a guiding rule of mass behavior since some primitive African princess stuck a highly polished bone through her hair . . . and thus influenced women of her tribe to adopt a practice which still results in the sale of tens of millions of dollars worth of jewelry each year" (50–51).

9. See for example Eileen Schell, "Think Global," Ross Singer, Stephanie Houston Grey, and Jeff Motter, *Rooted Resistance*, and Brewster, "Toward."

10. See for a few of many examples Mario Garcia, *A Dolores Huerta Reader*; Mary Neth, *Preserving the Family Farm*; Carolyn Ostrander, "Latent Abilities," and Carolyn Sachs, *Gendered Fields*.

11. See for example Michele Payn-Knoper's April 29, 2010, blog post, "Women of Agriculture Week," and the embedded video interview with American Agri-Women

President Chris Wilson focused on how "ladies [can] put their voices . . . to work in bridging the gap between gate and plate."

12. For a more detailed description of the agvocacy movement, see the AgChat Foundation website, http://agchat.org, and Brewster, "'Agvocates' for Industry."

13. See also Callie Kostelich, "Facebook and a Farm Crisis," and Eileen Schell, "Framing the Megarhetorics."

14. It, of course, raises questions too about the role of rhetoric faculty and curricula at the network of land grant institutions hosting such events, and the political, disciplinary, and institutional divisions that might prevent Extension staff from calling on people who teach writing, communication, and media strategy within their own universities to develop programming for "women in ag" rather than diverting public dollars to private consultants with less and/or otherwise interested expertise. Without more research, it's hard to know if Extension staff are aware that these subjects are taught at their university, the extent to which faculty are individually disinclined or structurally disincentivized to engage in such work, and/or if this is part of a larger strategy to direct agricultural messaging work and brand it as "farmer-led" and "grassroots."

15. It also intersects with a third key element of the informal rhetorical curriculum delivered here, which is the ethical absolution ostensibly granted in crafting messages about food. While I recognize that there are many women who have willingly accepted the charge to speak for an industry with which they identify and that they support, the suggestion that speakers are released from ethical responsibility in attempting to direct others' understanding of the politics and practices of something as fundamental to all our survival as agriculture is distressing at best. As Leah Hedberg, Colette Marie, Chelsey Waters, Cheyenne Maszk, Jeannette Benton, Lora Alix, and other students in my winter 2021 graduate seminar on the rhetoric of agriculture powerfully reminded us, the language of food is a profoundly visceral one, especially in writing about hunger, scarcity, and the effects of farming, cooking, and food processing on women's bodies. The emotional affordances of food may thus become a rich resource for rhetors, but should come with greater ethical responsibility, not less.

16. Many thanks to the participants, speakers, and organizers of the Women in Ag workshop, all of the students in my Rhetoric of Food and Ag seminars the pandemic fall and winter of 2020–2021, the members and staff of Oregon Rural Action, and the women in my own farm family, all of whom have contributed so much to my thinking about this project and kept me questioning what this rhetoric and this approach to rhetorical instruction means for us all.

Chapter 8

When the Land Writes

The Rhetorical and Reciprocal Lives of Land and Plants

Veronica House and Kelly Zepelin

Building a just and resilient local food system in the face of extractive corporate production methods and systemic inequities in who has access to healthy, culturally sustaining foods requires expanding our ideas of how to support partnerships across communities through our teaching, activism, and research. Through Veronica's work with farmers in Boulder County, Colorado, and Kelly's work as a forager and cultural anthropologist in Durango, Colorado, we[1] look into types of ethical practice that depend upon reciprocal collaboration with more-than-humans as we consider how the idea of partnership expands if we ask not only *who* but *what* writes.[2]

Community literacy and food literacy scholarship have long centered the concept of reciprocity. But when we discuss reciprocity in community-engaged writing studies, we typically refer to partnerships between community members, faculty, and students. Many Indigenous activists and scholars remind us, however, that knowledge emerges from the land on which it is created (Ríos 2015; LaDuke 1999). Zoe Todd points out that Indigenous scholars have long written about the animacy of other species and objects before higher education's fascination with the ontological turn (Todd 2016). Bernardo and Monberg's discussion of the "long arc" of reciprocity built into the Indigenous Filipinx concept of *kapwa*, "reciprocal being," explains, "When we think of kapwa or of resituating reciprocity within a framework of social justice or food justice, the arc of time expands deep into history and far into the future" (Bernardo and Monberg 2021, 87). In a time of food insecurity, dispossession, culture loss, and the ever-present impact of settler colonization, dislocation from our more-than-human collaborators appears to be perennial and life-threatening. We must partner with land, plants, and people in antiracist and decolonial endeavors, opening ourselves to their rhetorical and authorial agency and knowledge while simultaneously working to build meaningful forms of restoration, reparations, and repatriation.

Centering Indigenous scholarship on reciprocity, we offer a theory of partnership in community-engaged projects that includes more-than-human elements such as plants and land as partners in our work for food justice that *write* about, for, and with us, to play on Thomas Deans' well-known "three paradigms for community writing" (Deans 2000). As our conception of reciprocal partnership expands, is decolonized, and centers Indigenous knowledges often marginalized or delegitimized in white-dominant institutions like industrial food and seed companies and academia, the methods and practices through which we engage, research, and teach must necessarily expand, as well. Part of this expansion of conceptions of reciprocal partnership is due in part to the many decolonialization and reindigenization efforts underway that are revealing/remembering knowledge long suppressed by racist and settler colonial pasts.

In highlighting some of the work happening with farmers and foragers in Colorado, we share approaches to local food work that incorporate the land and plants as writers that help us understand what is just, appropriate, and possible within our ecology. We offer from-the-ground examples of our expanded definition of writing to include nonalphabetic, nontextual, and beyond-human creative agency. We posit more-than-human agential creation as a radical reconception of writing and authorship–one that is part of a larger Indigenous-led movement to decolonize academia and ways of knowing, such as Ruiz and Arellano's conception of "quilting as method" or Robin Wall Kimmerer's discussion of the limits of Western science (Kimmerer 2013, 39). Land and plants partner in creation and help to shape our actions. As Kimmerer reminds us, "To be native to a place we must learn to speak its language" (Kimmerer 2013, 48).

Humans have long struggled to find the language for what this partnership is and for how to explain what it is that the more-than-human world does in its acts of creation. Scholars have used words such as agency, language, rhetorical life, and grammar to describe the creative work of more-than-humans. When we use words such as "writing" and "authorship" in relation to what more-than-humans do, we hope that readers understand that we, too, are grappling with language inherited by Westernized, colonial epistemologies. We could have chosen, for example, cultivating or growing, to draw on more natural terms, or co-creating or communicating or co-shaping. The English language has no word for the creation we seek to explore. As Kimmerer says, "English doesn't give us many tools for incorporating respect for animacy"

(Kimmerer 2013, 56). So we choose "writing," as flawed or partial as the word may be (and understanding that people from other fields or positionalities may choose a different word to get at this inarticulable concept), in order to urge the field of writing studies to *re-vise*, as in to see anew, writing's potential, its scope, its very essence. We ask for a suspension of disbelief from our readers as we envision writing as an animate, always-in-creation force, a capacious view that can help rhetoric and writing faculty, students, and activists understand partnership work with more-than-humans in beautifully rich and unexpected ways.

In expanding our writing partnership model to include the authorial presence of the more-than-human, we can attune to community building and justice-oriented work literally from the ground up. This expansion acknowledges and centers many Indigenous ways of knowing, reciprocity, and more-than-human personhoods and is part of a larger decolonization project that expands food justice efforts. As García and Baca posit, "epistemic alternatives . . . can move us beyond Western categories of epistemology, thought, and feeling" as part of the de-linking project they encourage (García and Baca 2019, 2). We hope that in challenging the field's "story-so-far" of what writing is, we can embrace García and Baca's call for "pushing the 'discipline' to move beyond itself," from what Ruiz and Baca have called the field's 'colonial unconscious' (García and Baca 2019, 24; Ruiz and Baca, 2017, 226). In *Braiding Sweetgrass*, Kimmerer describes a "grammar of animacy," in which, when "listening in wild spaces, we are audience to conversations in a language not our own" (Kimmerer 2013, 48) She calls us to "imagine the access we would have to different perspectives, the things we might see through other eyes, the wisdom that surrounds us . . . there are intelligences other than our own, teachers all around us" (Kimmerer 2013, 58).

For decades, community-engaged scholarship has urged academics to recognize knowledge and expertise beyond the confines of our campuses, to value and share knowledges within and across communities of people. And rightly so. It is a profound hubris for academics to believe our siloed expertise is anything but one contribution in a vast ecology of people working and writing for change. Community-engaged scholars often discuss the importance of an asset-based approach to partnership, "focusing on what already exists, what is already happening in the context, builds on what already exists, acknowledges what *is* present" (Green 2014, 155, original italics). What if, as Kimmerer's grammar of animacy suggests, we approach land, seeds, or plants in the same way, valuing and sharing "grammars" across species and things to include more-than-humans as rhetorically active, knowledge-producing collaborators. What knowledge do they already have, what are they ready to share, what do they want of us?

When we acknowledge land's or a plant's rhetorical life and authorial agency, we draw on Laurie Gries' definition of rhetorical as "something's ability to induce change in thought, feeling, and action; organize and maintain collective formation; exert power, etc.; as it enters into relation with other things (human or nonhuman)" (Gries 2015, 11). She explains that "things become rhetorically meaningful via the consequentiality they spark in the world" (Gries 2015, 3). Gabriela Ríos' theory of land-based rhetorics informs our understanding, as well: "land-based literacies are literal acts of interpretation and communication that grow out of active participation with land. . . . Indigenous relationality recognizes that humans and the environment are in a relationship that is co-constituted and not just interdependent. Additionally, Indigenous relationality recognizes the environment's capacity to produce relation" (Ríos 2015, 64). She explains that this "relationship between land and bodies . . . produces knowledge" that binds us and the land—inspiring a cycle of reciprocity (Ríos 2015, 65). Given these conceptions of rhetoric's force to spark change, we consider what kinds of knowledges are produced between humans and more-than-humans when working toward a just local food system. How does a plant, for example, become rhetorical in terms of sparking consequentiality, and how then does our relationship with it produce knowledge or action? How does the land's response to our activities on it *write about* the benefits or detriments of our actions? We can consider how things pull us into relationships that change our actions, that elicit consequences.

Many writers have described how we and other species adapt and evolve in relation to one another. As we work to build a more just food system, more-than-humans are always at play, co-authoring with us. Certainly, there is text-based writing that we and our students may produce with and for other humans and that can encourage food justice—policies, informational materials, social media posts and blogs, newspaper articles, books, videos, etc. These texts shape how the public understands what local food is, how to access, grow, preserve, and support it. But we believe that the water, the soil (with all of its microbes and nutrients and earthworms), the plants, the animals, the saved and shared seeds, all co-write what is possible for production of local food. We are not talking about writing as static or alphabetic or even human-generated. We are thinking of writing as nontextual rhetorical creation, a beyond-words, generative energy that informs and shapes the world. We are acknowledging Kimmerer's concept of the grammar of animacy and Gries' understanding of "rhetoric as a distributed emergence, an ongoing circulation, and an ever-changing enactment" (Gries 2015, 31). Learning to read and circulate and "co-constitute" these various forms of writing is part of our work as community-engaged scholars, teachers, and activists. Indeed, we believe that broadening the scope of writing to recognize authorship in more-than-human beings is an act of "decoloniality" (García and Baca, 2019, 31–32) that can in turn help us move toward a more just food system.

CULTIVATING RECIPROCITY

I (Veronica) am sitting at a picnic table in one of my favorite spots in Boulder, Colorado, a small neighborhood farm called Dharma's Garden. Founding farmers Tim Francis and Kerry Francis turned just one-half acre of this five-acre property into a productive market garden and have fed my family for years through a CSA of weekly veggies during harvest season. As I've gotten to know Kerry and Tim better, I've been bringing my university writing students for field trips to experience the land's abundance and to learn about ethical land stewardship. As our partnership deepened, I would help purchase supplies for community education workshops at the farm on food preservation and heritage seed saving through a food literacy grant from University of Colorado's Office of Outreach and Engagement. Often on neighborhood walks with my dog, I'll see Tim and Kerry out in the garden, working the rows with a parade of ducks trailing behind. They love this land, and it seems to love them back, giving of itself to them as they give themselves to it. It's a model for feeding community and connecting to land not built on extraction or imposition. I view them and the land as collaboratively composing what is possible for feeding our community and nurturing connection to the earth. In the beauty of this co-authorship are possibilities for expanding our conceptions of deep reciprocity in our community-based practices. Here on the farm on a cool July day, I talk with Kerry and Tim about building partnership with land. I begin by asking what drew them here.

Tim explains, "There was this calling, this longing that started quietly, and we didn't know what to make of it at first. We just felt drawn in toward *this* land, without knowing what it meant, or what would come next. It's very hard to put into words because it's so beyond words, it's pre words" (Francis and Francis 2020). They've told me and my visiting students before that the land has an agency, what Gries (2015) might call a rhetorical life, that expresses itself through their work with it. Kerry explains, "Once we lived *with* the land and lived *on* the land and worked the soil every season, that then led to a kind of conversation. That's also really hard to put into words, but it was some kind of communication where we felt like we could sense something of what the land wanted or that we were being guided in some way. It is a personal relationship and conversation with the land that took time. And then from that conversation, arose a vision that got clearer and clearer" (Francis and Francis 2020). Tim jumps in, "Yes, and I think what we began to experience was an inner receptiveness to a vision of the land that was not solely our own. There was a very real sense that the vision itself arose out of the land. And I think this is partly what makes it hard to put into words, because there's a danger of anthropomorphizing, as if the land is a humanlike person that has its vision and its wants and desires. But it's much deeper than that. It feels to me so relational" (Francis and Francis 2020).

"Not like the land has the vision, per se," Kerry tries to explain. "Rather, we listen, and we become part of a co-created relationship" (Francis and Francis 2020). Tim adds, "We—the humans tending the land—are in this living conversation with the land that is supporting us; and through that the true vision reveals itself" (Francis and Francis 2020).

This communication that they describe is hard to define, harkening back to Kimmerer's awareness of how hard it is in English to find language for more-than-human animacy—it isn't spoken or textual, of course. There is a rhetorical life, to harken back to Gries' definition of rhetoric, that comes through what the land grows and doesn't grow, in which animals thrive on it and where. I'm reminded of Kimmerer's observation on reciprocity, "Something essential happens in a vegetable garden. It's a place where if you can't say 'I love you' out loud, you can say it in seeds. And the land will reciprocate, in beans." (Kimmerer 2013, 127).

Tim feels that disconnection from the natural world that sustains us all is one of the biggest problems so many Americans face and one that perpetuates legacies of extraction and injustice. We believe that our reconception of writing partnerships aligns with Ruiz and Arellano's vision for "medicinal rhetorics"[3] in that it "heals that which was severed through colonial relations and colonial renditions of the human relationship to the Earth" (Ruiz and Arellano 2019, 152). In other words, calling this land-based or seed-based or plant-based agency "writing," as inadequate as the word may be, is an attempt to heal the rift by acknowledging the partnership between us that is so often forgotten and that is a direct outcome of our separation from the land that leads to so much exploitation and destruction. Tim explains:

> If we as a human society were really to honestly have that kind of conversation or relationship with land, we would find that sometimes a particular piece of land is well served by a garden, or maybe it needs to just stay like it is and not have even a garden on it, maybe not have humans on it at all—just remain in a wild state for other creatures to make their homes, or pass through. More often than not, we make our decisions about land use based on some utilitarian calculations, ignoring any kind of real relationship with the land. I would argue that's the very reason that we're so deeply entrenched into so many profoundly disturbing crises around the world today—from climate destabilization to pollution to habitat destruction, and everything else. When we first had this calling here, we didn't quite know what would develop. And then this idea of having a garden just seemed natural, but where would it be? It wasn't until we were here

for a little while that we were drawn to where the borders of the garden would be. And there was certainly some logical reasoning behind it, but it's beyond just logical reasoning. It came out of conversation with the land. Again, it's hard to express, hard to articulate—it seems prior to words and human language. It's more of an intuitive feeling. The creative process of developing our garden started with the felt sense of the garden, then the vision of the garden began to coalesce around that. And as the human will began to engage, to pursue that vision, it looped right back in again to the felt sense: "does this feel contrary to what's happening already, or does it seamlessly merge with what's already here?" (Francis and Francis 2020)

The land *writes for and with* us in partnership, responding to our questions and actions in ways that can alter or confirm what we do. Tim continues:

People ask us if we want to build out the farm more. That's really interesting because—and this is a good example of why it's so important, *so important*, to have this relationship with the land, and to actually live on the land, because it was only through being here and listening to the land that we came to understand the real sacredness of the wild places and the value of finding that balance between the wild and the cultivated. Probably a more typical way to go about starting a new community farm would be to first start with the idea, and then to go find a piece of land to impose that idea upon. Maybe you pull up a Google satellite view of the property and start planning "here is where we could put this or do that." That's the standard way that our modern society works with land. More often than not, I think you'd find that the whole project would start to go astray, because, without the foundation of being with the land and listening and building relationship, all we have are our human intellectual ideas of how to use the land to satisfy our own goals. What we discovered here is that there is another way of being with land, working with land, that turns that paradigm on its head. And to be clear, this isn't new in any way. This is an ancient way of just being with land. And it's also one of the founding ideas behind permaculture: that with any piece of land that you're trying to work, you leave a part of it wild. And then you can observe what's happening there without any human inputs. And you let that help inform the rest of the project. (Francis and Francis 2020)

Tim and Kerry's ideas for rhetorical listening and building relationship with the land before imposing their own ideas on it also align with scholarship on best practices in partnership building. Like Paul Feigenbaum's (2015) conception of collaboratively imagining the *ought to be* with our human partners (44), Tim and Kerry represent the ways in which they collaboratively imagine with the land and animals and plants what *ought to be* for the land and what is being asked of them by the land. It's not through literal talking back and forth, of course, but, as Tim mentions, there is an exchange happening that is beyond human language.

There's a more-than-human rhetorical argument being made for the various choices Tim and Kerry then enact. Tim gives an example:

> Even right here, this little patch of tall grass. For years, we had been mowing it. And then we just realized that it was a different kind of grass from all the other grasses around. And whenever we'd mow it, it would look all hacked-up, as if it was resisting being mowed. And it seemed like maybe it was trying to grow a lot taller than all the other grasses around it. So finally we thought, okay, let's just let it grow taller. And now, there's actually a lot of life that happens there. There are all kinds of insects that live in that little patch of grass. We see dragonflies there, and we see birds going in and getting seeds. It's no hassle to us to have just one little patch of tall grass in the middle of our mowed area. And it's also nice to have some areas that *are* mowed, so that we can sit here at this table like we are now, and have a conversation. So, we just have these decisions that are made out of observation and relationship. (Francis and Francis 2020)

Anthropologist and farmer Devon Peña might refer to this as an example of "relational solidarity with self-willing land+water as vibrant co-actants and shapers of the world" (Peña 2017, 93). The more time I spend with Kerry and Tim, the clearer it becomes that there is rhetorical agency in this grass, the foxes and owls, and the vibrant produce. They are creating in solidarity along with Tim and Kerry, as co-actants and world-shapers. They are involved in nonalphabetic, agential co-authorship of what is possible on this land, and in this way, the reciprocal relationship, which "extends temporally," "means doing the work of revisiting structures of power in continual conversation" (Bernardo and Monberg 2021, 85). Like the best of partnerships, one with the land and plants is incremental, iterative, and evolving, based on respect, collaboration, and love.

Can rhetorical delivery and authorship occur in the form of a vibrant carrot or a creek that cuts a property or a patch of grass? Here we are, sitting at the picnic table, drinking tea made from the garden's herbs, gazing at the grass growing from soil filled with bustling microbes, and the birds cocking their heads looking for grubs, and the deer drinking from the bird bath nearby. We listen as their rhetorical lives write the answer before us.

WILD RECIPROCITY

Giving a pour of water, sprinkling powdered herbs, offering pinches of tobacco, or delicately placing strands of hair at the base of a plant to show gratitude and respect when harvesting are common practices that I (Kelly) have observed working with foragers. These offerings, small gestures, are examples of the many gifts that happen alongside a conscious attention to the *personhood* of the plant—seeing them as a subject, rather than an object. Gifts are acts of reciprocity shared between the living and dying of the plant world. While it would be remiss to not acknowledge that some foragers are negligent and overharvest delicate plants, it is my overwhelming experience working with foraging communities in Colorado that, just as Tim and Kerry are practicing farming methods in partnership with the land, many are actually in deep relationship that involve complex forms of communication and respect. Foragers often describe this communication as a "felt sense," or "somatic knowing," rather than explicit alphabetic articulation.

The famous social anthropologists Marcel Mauss and Bronisław Malinowski were some of the first to publish theoretical research on the power of gift giving and the roles of reciprocal relationships in strengthening social bonds. Here, I theorize that a forager's gifts strengthen social relations *between* species, not just *within* them in the case of human communities. In foraging, consumption and production become gestures of social responsibility and maintenance of social (as well as ecological) bonds. Perhaps counterintuitively, harvesting is a matter of gifting, not extracting in the eyes of many foragers. Often in a forager's cosmology, gifts from the land, (chokecherries, acorns, dandelions, wild rosehips), and gifts from the human hand, (water, powdered herbs, pinches of tobacco, strands of hair, gratitude), enforce interspecies relationships that are intimate, embodied, and, at times, lasting. These relationships orchestrated by gifting bring forth ethical understandings of how to relate to the land.

As Jenine, an urban forager, told me, "When I eat this dandelion, it becomes part of me, *cellularly*. It is food, it heals me. And then I feel motivated to help protect the plant from pesticides, support their environment. I am emotionally and biochemically bonded to the plant and the place where they grow" (Janine 2019). This comment points to the theme of becoming more connected to a landscape through the development of emotional, physical, and chemical bonds, in a way that fosters connection that not only works to bind humans to places, but one that—in the case of this forager—weaves plant matter into the very cells of human bodies. The rhetorical agency of the plant functions both outside of and within the innermost parts of Jenine, an alchemical intimacy that dandelions induce when eaten. How might seeing a plant, to use political ecologist Jane Bennett's words as "vibrant matter" (Bennett 2010), an alive being who is offering you their gifts and who has the potential to powerfully induce change in feelings and actions, change the way people relate to the botanical, ecological world? This idea recalls Bernardo and Monberg's discussion of the Indigenous Filipinx concept of *kapwa*, in which, "If I harm you, I harm myself. If I love you, I love myself. There is a quality of intimacy and shared risk involved. We are not separate. We are connected" (Bernardo and Monberg 2021, 87). Reciprocity binds us in deep partnership.

As a Mohawk ethnobotanist detailed to me, what if we go beyond "just rip[ping] the plant out of the ground," and instead we see our relationship to the world as a process that "requires gifts and attention to survive?" (Mohawk 2019). Perhaps, this dynamic of relationality, personhood, reciprocity, and attention can root humans back in place and connect with the repercussions of inattentive consumerism. Perhaps these gift-giving exchanges can be a form of communication not only *to* more-than-human interlocutors, but also *from* the more-than-human as rhetorical agents, seeing them not only as collaborators, but as "people" who can teach, relate, and reciprocate. Through this kind of vision of reciprocal relationships with plants, and actions to "harvest in a way that minimizes harm" and "sustain the ones who sustain you," as Robin Wall Kimmerer instructs, a wider cycle of giving and receiving is set into motion (Kimmerer 2013, 221).

For example, the authors of the article "Urban foraging and the Relational Ecologies of Belonging" describe, "Foragers developed individual relationships with specific plants; they described listening to these beings in order to learn how best to receive their gifts. The relational acts of giving, receiving, and interacting between foragers and more-than-human others produced a sense of belonging in place regardless of any given species' origins" (Poe et al. 2014, 12). Gift giving appears to not only strengthen a sense of respect and awareness in a forager's harvest, but it also appears to embed the harvester more deeply into the place where they are harvesting. This is not a new concept in Traditional Ecological or Indigenous knowledges, it is merely one that is actualized in the practices of contemporary North American foraging cultures. It places humans and plants in a bidirectional dialogue between harvester and land where both voices are heard and transcend species-based divides. This kind of education is much more fruitful than an extractive monologue of domination, coloniality, and blind capitalism often characteristic of industrialized agriculture.

Seeing the exchange between humans and plants as part of a web of a reciprocal relationship that involves a socially entangled community of actors seems to serve a function in generating an ethical framework that governs many foragers' practices. "Once you learn about the plants being alive, conscious, you suddenly see the whole world expand," a forager explained to me in awe, "like, *everything* is watching you! You learn to tread, watching your feet, much more carefully when this happens. It just takes time and friendship with the plants for the world to explode in aliveness. It takes respect and kindness. I do this with small offerings to say thanks as I pluck wild apples," she says pointing to a scraggly tree up the hill (Forager 2018). As she scrambles up to the base of the tree, I notice small wild apples hanging in the branches and watch her sprinkle some flower petals at its base before biting into the tart fruit.

Foraging for Longitudinal Reciprocity in a Colonized Nation

Robin Wall Kimmerer comments on how this combination of personhood and reciprocity has the potential to widen the legal domain for foraging for plants, can have the ability to ground the forager within a relational ecology: "Killing a who demands something different than killing an it. . . . The deer, the sturgeon, the berries, and the leeks say, 'If you follow these rules, we will continue to give our lives so that you may live'" (Kimmerer 2013, 195–96). Many foragers are having these conversations. My work with foragers has shown me that the practice of seeing the plant world as having personhood often alters their feeling a need to give back beyond the small gestures of water, hair, plant powders, and gratitude, in ways that have a more longitudinal reach.

"I like to think about it as seeds," said a forager at a permaculture conference I attended in 2018 (Forager 2018). "Whenever I harvest something, I say thank you, but then I make sure if there is a plant already gone to seed, to shake those seeds back into the soil. We need to be part of the regenerative cycle, you know? One that requires reseeding. Humans can help reseed the plants, make the soil better, or be an advocate for that ecosystem, practice permaculture. Spreading the seeds is a gift we can and should do" (Forager 2018). Whether it is physically reseeding plots of land or taking actions to support wild spaces, the actions inspired by gift giving can be a form of stewardship, land/food activism, a rhetorical act that catalyzes relationships to deepen over time.

"It is one thing to walk down a trail where there is good wild sumac growing just one time," forager Natalia told me as we ascended a path toward a stand of red sumac glinting in the distance. "It is another thing to come back to the spot month after month, season after season, year after year. It is a really different kind of relationship. You see it go through all stages of life . . . you start to know the rocks, the bends in the trails, the leaves, feel certain trees. Like, I know that the stream we just passed flooded terribly last spring" (Natalia 2019). Similar to a spouse or a childhood friend, time and love strengthens the commitment in a way that can make one feel responsible for their wellbeing. Referencing the flooding steam, Natalia adds, "When I saw the stream was starting to wash out the rocks on the banks, I got in the mud and stacked the rocks day after day, each time I came back, to help ensure the water would get to where it needed to go. I owe this area that much," she says in recognition of the many harvests she does in a place she had grown to love (Natalia 2019).

In a similar feeling as Natalia, Feather, an herbalist who works to protect osha, a sacred and medicinal plant often overharvested by reckless foragers and herbalists, also speaks about this need for a more far-reaching reciprocity and the value of becoming stewards *of a place*, rather than being mere consumers *from a place*:

> I realized, watching plants in Alaska where there are heavy snowfalls, that the umbels of osha would get knocked over by the wet snow turning them upside down and naturally getting the seeds in the right position to reseed. So now whenever osha is harvested, I take the umbel and place an upside-down umbel back into the hole where the root was. . . . We need plants, and they need us too. We are gifts to one another. (Feather 2019)

Such reciprocal worldviews embodied by many foragers extend beyond a short-lived one-time engagement, and are developed through time, communication, and unflinching commitment. What can be seen as an extractive endeavor, has the potential to radically reshape (or perhaps more aptly, *remember*) the human location within an intelligent web of more-than-human actors.

In the case of foraging, longitudinal reciprocity to plants and land is an important remembering of human-plant relations. It is also a largely lost and forgotten experience dulled by the impact of industrialization, colonialism, and economic structures that do not support this kind of intimacy and care. However, in this conversation it is also vital to acknowledge that reciprocity living in a colonized nation like the US, while useful, needs to go beyond just small trailside offerings. Given the history of colonialism, dispossession, and genocide in the U.S., longitudinal reciprocity must extend to larger forms of reparations. In the case of foraging as a traditional foodway, reparations mean *repatriation* of stolen land to Indigenous communities.[4] Restoring land rights and food sovereignty for Indigenous people is, I argue, an essential piece of what reciprocal relationships and food justice looks like in contemporary foraging contexts.[5] The work to remember and reindigenize traditional foodways forcibly lost in settler colonialism, for example, as well as efforts to decolonize foraging laws written as part of a long history of systemic racist oppression of BIPOC communities, are areas of foraging and food justice that need immediate and committed action.

Cultivating intimacies and awareness of the land, the more-than-human beings, and the traumatic histories baked into US soils has the potential to move, change, teach, and inspire action for a more food just world. Foraging for wild plants and becoming aware of the many sophisticated foodways that have been lost in the United States is one example where this dynamic is readily apparent. Repatriation of stolen land, as argued here, is not just a way to practice longitudinal reciprocity, but one that is a mandatory part of dismantling the legacy of settler colonialism.

LITERACY THROUGH RELATIONSHIP

The ethical, relational work that the farmers and foragers practice connects to a larger educational endeavor for food literacy and justice advocates inside and outside of academia. Tim and Kerry share with their community the literacies that arise from partnership with the land, as they counter some of the violences of the industrial food system, which is a living legacy of white-controlled *power over* people, beings, and the earth. Tim argues, "It's only because of the absence of an authentic relationship with the land, and with the plants and animals we eat, that the conditions allowed for an industrial food system to develop. If we are to dismantle that industrial food system and reimagine what it means to have healthy food, healthy planet, healthy societies, it all starts with first having a relationship with the land" (Francis and Francis, 2020). We have an obligation, as part of a decolonial food justice framework, to draw connections between partnering with land and dismantling oppression in the food system—these must go hand in hand. Through classes, workshops, and community events that connect people with land, seeds, and plants as partners, Kerry, Tim, and the foragers we mention share the land's messages with others. Reviving people's reciprocal relationship with land and food is a radical act connecting to food justice.

When we enter into partnerships with farmers and foragers through our scholarship and teaching, we should bring all actors into the project research design and curricular planning. It means turning the typical triangle of reciprocity between human teacher—human student—human community partner into a constellation that includes more-than-humans in intentional design. Attention to context also means attention to the rhetorical life and the authorial power of things as collaborators, and this attention can be incorporated into our course projects and readings for our students, encouraging a food literacy that attunes to all elements of the process of food production and distribution and to the ecology of relationships amongst all involved. When we think of more-than humans as partners in our work, the work necessarily changes.

In their article on decolonizing community writing through community listening, Jackson and Whitehorse DeLaune (Jackson and Whitehorse DeLaune 2018, 43) ask us to consider the ways in which scholars can actively resist the settler colonial force of Western academic moves to quantify, logically "settle" meaning, etc. In a decolonial Kiowa approach, for example, meaning making happens through "co-construction of narrative and communal articulation of meaning" (Jackson and Whitehorse DeLaune 2018, 43). In a related way, this gets at the prelanguage conversations Tim, Kerry, and many foragers describe having with the land. While they can't logically articulate how the conversation reveals itself, they know it is occurring, and that through their co-constructed rhetorical embodiment of their collaborative desires, the farm and the development of wild social bonds emerge. It is akin to what Leanne Betasamosake Simpson has called "land as pedagogy," learning "*from* the land and *with* the land" and understanding that we are "dependent upon intimate relationships of reciprocity, humility, honesty and respect with all elements of creation, including plants and animals" (Simpson 2014, 7–10, original italics).

Settler colonialism and white supremacy are undeniably woven into the industrial food system, foraging laws, our disconnection (and dispossession) from the land, and our education system. This truth calls on us to hold ourselves accountable to the trauma and grief we inflict on other humans, animals, and land. It calls us to do whatever we can to disrupt the violence of educational and research systems that accept certain knowledges and ignore or denigrate others and from food systems that reinforce racist colonial frameworks that place wealthy, white humans at the top, disregard the rhetorical lives of more-than-humans, and allow for extraction and exploitation models to persist.

If we acknowledge that the land writes, how does that writing show up in our teaching and scholarly work for food justice? Listening to the land and what it has to teach us, give us, and ask of us brings to mind Robin Wall Kimmerer's discussion of the Honorable Harvest (Kimmerer 2013, 183). Ask permission first. Only take what you need. Give a gift in return.

For a teacher, the gift may mean studying and building justice-oriented literacy projects around the lands' official and contested histories and original inhabitants (Ruiz 2016, 181); studying worldviews that believe in sacred connection and kinship between species and things; teaching curricula that center (and financially compensate) voices of BIPOC and other frontline food justice advocates, activists, organizers, and scholars; incorporating outdoor classes that connect students' learning to the land and animals we study; helping students build relationships and understanding of the systemic, ecological nature of issues and their localized particularities through readings, research, and physical connection. Through these relationships, we encourage students' awareness of multiple knowledges that break down legacies of indoctrination and call for a reckoning with contemporary realities of the legacies of imperialism and colonization. We encourage their understanding of rhetoric and writing's potential as embodied and distributed decolonial practices across species.

For a scholar, the gift may mean asking the land, and those who have built deep relationships with the land, what is needed. Our human partners are our teachers, too. The foragers, farmers, and activists we partner with can often translate for us, teaching us the languages we haven't yet learned. It means research that brings in multiple voices, not all scholarly, and not all human. It means coming to a project without a set agenda and requires being open to an evolving research process that shifts and transforms along with the land's teachings, histories, and needs. It means advocacy work for or financial contributions to restoration, reparation, or repatriation projects for BIPOC-led farms and food justice initiatives. It means acknowledging our own limited perspectives and pledging to learn more and do more to help resist and shift power imbalances. The return gifts can show up in multiple ways. As we attune to the animate grammars around us, they alter our decisions, they enhance our work, and they transform what would have been had we not listened. To be sure, compared to the abundance offered to us in partnership, these are small gestures of reciprocal gift giving, but they are a beginning, a seed for something to come.

REFERENCES

Bernardo, Shane, and Terese Guinsatao Monberg. 2021. "Resituating Reciprocity within Longer Legacies of Colonization: A Conversation." *Community Literacy Journal* 14, no. 1. https://doi.org/10.25148/CLJ.14.1.009058.

Baca, Karlos. 2018, October 19. "Blue Corn, Bear Root, and Resilience." *PBS*. https://www.nytimes.com/2017/03/08/technology/snap-makes-a-bet-on-the-cultural-supremacy-of-the-camera.html.

Deans, Thomas. 2000. *Writing Partnerships: Service-Learning in Composition*. Urbana, IL: National Council of Teachers of English.

Feather. 2019, June 27. Personal communication.

Feigenbaum, Paul. 2015. *Collaborative Imagination: Earning Activism through Literacy Education*. Carbondale: Southern Illinois University Press.

Forager. Personal communication. 2018.

Francis, Kerry, and Tim Francis. 2020, July 13. Personal communication.

García, Romeo, and Damián Baca, eds. 2019. *Rhetorics Elsewhere and Otherwise: Contested Modernities, Decolonial Visions*. CCCC Studies in Writing & Rhetoric. Urbana, IL: National Council of Teachers of English.

Green, Keisha. 2014. "Doing Double Dutch Methodology: Playing with the Practice of Participant Observer." *Humanizing Research: Decolonizing Qualitative Inquiry with Youth and Communities*, edited by Django Paris and Maisha T. Winn, 147–60. Thousand Oaks, CA: Sage Publishing.

Gries, Laurie E. 2015. *Still Life with Rhetoric: A New Materialist Approach for Visual Rhetorics*. Logan: Utah State University Press.

Haraway, Donna. 2010. "When Species Meet: Staying with the Trouble." *Environment and Planning D: Society and Space* 28, no. 1: 53–55. https://doi.org/10.1068/d2706wsh.

Jackson, Rachel C., and Dorothy Whitehorse DeLaune. 2018. "Decolonizing Community Writing With Community Listening: Story, Transrhetorical Resistance, and Indigenous Cultural Literacy Activism." *Community Literacy Journal* 13, no. 1: 37–54. https://doi.org/10.1353/clj.2018.0020.

Kimmerer, Robin Wall. 2013. *Braiding Sweetgrass: Indigenous Wisdom, Scientific Knowledge and the Teachings of Plants*. 1st paperback ed. Minneapolis: Milkweed Editions.

Kirksey, S. Eben, and Stefan Helmreich. 2010, November. "The Emergence of Multispecies Ethnography." *MIT Web Domain*. https://dspace.mit.edu/handle/1721.1/61966.

Kohn, Eduardo. 2013. *How Forests Think: Toward an Anthropology Beyond the Human*. Berkeley: University of California Press.

LaDuke, Winona. 1999. *All Our Relations: Native Struggles for Land and Life*. Cambridge, MA; Minneapolis: South End Press; Honor the Earth.

Mohawk. 2019, June 25. Personal communication.

Natalia. 2019, August. Personal communication.

Peña, Devon. 2017. "The Hummingbird and the Redcap." In *Wildness: Relations of People and Place*, edited by Gavin Van Horn and John Hausdoerffer, 89–99. Chicago: University of Chicago Press.

Poe, Melissa R., Joyce LeCompte, Rebecca McLain, and Patrick Hurley. 2014. "Urban Foraging and the Relational Ecologies of Belonging." *Social & Cultural Geography* 15, no. 8: 901–19. https://doi.org/10.1080/14649365.2014.908232.

Ríos, Gabriela. 2015. "Cultivating Land-Based Literacies and Rhetorics." *Literacy in Composition Studies* 3, no. 1: 60–70. https://doi.org/10.21623/1.3.1.4.

Ruiz, Iris D. 2021. "Critiquing the Critical: The Politics of Race and Coloniality in Rhetoric, Composition, and Writing Studies Research Traditions." In *Race, Rhetoric, and Research Methods*, edited by Alexandria L. Lockett, Iris D. Ruiz, James Chase Sanchez, and Christopher Carter, 39–79. Fort Collins, CO: University Press of Colorado. https://doi.org/10.37514/PER-B.2021.1206.

———. 2016. *Reclaiming Composition for Chicano/as and Other Ethnic Minorities: A Critical History and Pedagogy*. New York: Palgrave Macmillan.

Ruiz, Iris D., and Damián Baca. 2017. "Decolonial Options and Writing Studies." *Composition Studies* 45, no. 2: 226–29.

Ruiz, Iris D., and Sonia Arellano. 2019. "*La Cultura Nos Cura*: Reclaiming Decolonial Epistemologies through Medicinal History and Quilting as Method." In *Rhetorics Elsewhere and Otherwise*, edited by Damián Baca and Romeo García, 141–68. Urbana, IL: National Council of Teachers of English.

Simpson, Leanne Betasamosake. 2014. "Land as Pedagogy: Nishnaabeg Intelligence and Rebellious Transformation." *Decolonization: Indigeneity, Education & Society* 3, no. 3. https://jps.library.utoronto.ca/index.php/des/article/view/22170.

Todd, Zoe. 2016. "An Indigenous Feminist's Take On the Ontological Turn: 'Ontology' Is Just Another Word for Colonialism: An Indigenous Feminist's Take on the Ontological Turn." *Journal of Historical Sociology* 29, no. 1: 4–22. https://doi.org/10.1111/johs.12124.

Van Horn, Gavin, and John Hausdoerffer, eds. 2017. *Wildness: Relations of People and Place*. Chicago: The University of Chicago Press.

Wildcat, Daniel. 2014, June 10. "Why Native Americans Don't Want Reparations." *Washington Post*. https://www.washingtonpost.com/posteverything/wp/2014/06/10/why-native-americans-dont-want-reparations.

NOTES

1. We are non-Indigenous scholars of the American Southwest writing on traditional Ute, Cheyenne, Southern Arapaho, Pueblos, and Diné lands.

2. While there are several terms scholars use such as "beyond human," "nonhuman," and "other-than-human," we've chosen the term often used in social science and Indigenous writing, "more-than-human." See, for example, Kirksey and Helmreich (2010) and Kohn (2013).

3. Iris D. Ruiz has expanded significantly on the concept of "medicinal rhetorics" in her chapter "Critiquing The Critical: The Politics of Race and Coloniality in Rhetoric, Composition, and Writing Studies Research Traditions" in *Race, Rhetoric, and Research Methods*, edited by Alexandria L. Lockett, Iris D. Ruiz, James Chase Sanchez, and Christopher Carter.

4. For more on why repatriation of tribal lands is preferred by some over monetary reparations, see Wildcat (2014).

5. For an example of a decolonization movement happening in the area where we write, the American Southwest, see Baca (2018).

Chapter 9

Food Justice, Citizenship Right, and Right to Food in Nepal

Pritisha Shrestha

Ever since Nepal's Constitution was promulgated in 2015, after nearly eight years of prolonged deliberation at the first (2008–2013) and second (2014–2017) Constituent Assemblies, the document has triggered factions among the people and political parties due to its description of the citizenship rights provision. Specifically, the crux of the conflict lies in the limited definition of citizenship and the constraints it has posed on the conferral of citizenship on women as well as the naturalized citizens of all genders to their offspring (Mulmi 2017, 135). Already gendered, the constitution through the citizenship act reinserted patriarchal[1] rubrics to grant or deny the citizenship of Nepal. Concerned parties, organizations, and activists, and feminist movement groups have been voicing their dissatisfaction and undertaking protests to lobby and pressure the Nepal government to amend the Citizenship Act, which has made Nepal one of only twenty-seven countries in the world that do not allow women to confer their citizenship or pass their nationality to their children. However, issues pertaining to hunger and food issues have yet to draw a central focus in feminist and equal citizenship right activism in Nepal. The issue of citizenship rights matters to food justice and rights pertaining to food by intersecting other struggles for social justice, racial equality, political rights and representations, land ownership, and geopolitical locations (Herman, Goodman, and Sage 2018, 1075; Brent, Schiavoni, and Alonso-Fradejas 2015; Adhikari 2011, 95), and interlinks with broader discourses surrounding democracy, citizenship, civil society, and social movements (Herman, Goodman, and Sage 2018, 1083). Without the support and enjoyment of other rights and socio-political factors, the journey to achieving food justice halts at a crossroads.

Exploring food justice and Right to Food (RtF) from the gender and feminist lenses in food studies (Dutta, Jyoti, and Thaker 2019; Bellows et al. 2015; Bellows et al. 2016) and feminist studies (Dubisar 2018; Navin 2015; Shiva 2009) is not new. Gender discrimination, whether through domestic, cultural, or policy violence, is a critical element (Awin 2014, 5) that impacts access to adequate nutrition and food. Furthermore, in many cases, being deprived of citizenship means also being denied mechanisms to access food and the RtF. There is a plethora of scholarship that interlinks gender violence and social justice with RtF, including "situating the concept of food justice in border areas of activism and scholarship" (Glennie 2017, 2). However, there is still a huge gap in academic discourses surrounding RtF and food justice with the angle of the citizenship right. Coming from the tradition of environmental justice, the term "food justice" originated in the United States (Glennie 2017, 2) and is "grounded in the notion of citizenship empowerment" (Holt-Giménze 2011, 323) while the discussion on noncitizenship, especially from the global south, is missing in the discourse.

Feminist activism scholars and advocates for the RtF at national and international policy levels have been interlinking gender discrimination with access to food. However, they too seldom (at least in the case of Nepal) mention the connection between citizenship rights to attaining the RtF.[2] Following feminist research methodology that calls for filling gaps and silences (Petersen 2018, 421), I interlink RtF and citizenship rights by bringing in a case study from Nepal to showcase the cause and effect of delayed policy implementation. I argue that with the denial of equal citizenship rights and constraints put on the conferral of citizenship through women, the constitution is in a grave violation of Human Rights, specifically Right to Food (Ghale et al. 2018; Pain et al. 2014; Upreti et al. 2018). While doing so, I prescribe understanding the RtF framework in relation to the "Right to Citizenship" and non-Western context and address what it entails for addressing food justice. And one way to rhetorically analyze RtF in connection to citizenship rights is to rhetorically listen to the narratives and understand the lived experiences of people whose lives are negatively afffected by this lack of legislation. Rhetorical listening provides a means to understand the lived experiences of "peoples' intersecting identifications with gender and race" and to communicate in cross-cultural settings (Ratcliff 2005, 17). For instance, various interviewees I have spoken with in this research mentioned the anger they felt as the policy in question has identified them as second-class citizens by virtue of being women in Nepal. Thus, the conceptual framing of transnational feminism helps in grasping not only such contours of gender-based identities but also interlinking them in relation to policies. My purpose here is to parallel policy (specifically citizenship rights) with personal stories to offer ways to understand intersectionality while conducting food justice, especially in our field.

RESEARCH DESIGN AND METHODOLOGY

Based on the 2015 Constitution of Nepal, I rhetorically analyze the citizenship rights and policy from the lenses of transnational feminism and "Right to Food" as enshrined in 1966 International Covenant on Economic, Social, and Cultural Rights and the Constitution of Nepal 2015. These discourses, as I argue, should not be viewed in a vacuum. As a researcher of transnational feminist rhetorical studies, I aim to demonstrate the impact of citizenship rights on attaining the right to food in Nepal. In order to achieve this, I juxtapose personal narratives with policy to offer the space to listen to the stories of the people while comprehending the erosions created both at the policymaking as well as policy implementation levels. The narratives are based on the IRB-approved interviews conducted in two rounds, stretching over the period of two years: 2019–2021. The majority of the participants identify themselves as feminists who have been working towards achieving equal citizenship rights through their activism in Nepal. The real names of the participants have been mentioned with their consent in the chapter. The interviewees selected for the project hail from various professional backgrounds. Sabitri Gautam, Hima Bista, and Neha Gurung are feminists and woman's rights activists whereas Dr. Binda Pandey and Dr. Yamuna Ghale are political leaders and food sovereignty experts respectively. The first round of in-person interviews with Gautam, Bista, Gurung, and Dr. Pandey took place in Nepal in 2019. Most of the questions pertained to their feminist advocacy work and citizenship policies.

The second round of interviews with Bista and Gurung were follow-ups conducted online via Zoom and Facebook messenger in 2021. This round also included a Zoom interview with Dr. Ghale for the first time. All the interviewees spoke in Nepali and the recordings were turned into transcripts and later translated with the help of my two research assistants.[3] The narrative inquiry worked best for my research as I began this project to inquire how feminist activists in Nepal viewed their citizenship rights while limiting their identities (based on the 2019 interview); and ultimately how they interconnect them with RtF and food justice (based on the 2021 follow-up and new interviews). Through rhetorical listening, their narratives provide implicit connection with achieving food justice and indicates the need for food justice literacy and RtF literacy in feminist advocacies. The chapter captures the pockets of resilience the interviewees (all women) have displayed and unpacks not only the emotional labor but also the aspect of food injustices these policies in question have triggered. Because of the visibility of social media conversation about their work, I was able to identify them for my research.[4] There are countless others whose activism and struggles against and works toward citizenship rights, which have not been mentioned here, that are also equally important, and they need to be listened to as well.

CITIZENSHIP RIGHT AND CHALLENGES IN NEPAL

Nepal is one of the only twenty-seven countries in the world that denies women equal citizenship rights by disallowing them to pass on their citizenship to their children. What this means is that the state asks for the identification of fathers and not of mothers while the children are in the process of obtaining their citizenship. Those who fail to establish or prove that a Nepali man is their father, are denied citizenship despite having a Nepali mother or being born and bred in Nepal. In other words, according to the CEDAW Shadow Report Preparation Committee (2018), there is a "non-recognition of the independent identity of women in transferring the citizenship to the spouse and children" ("The Shadow" 2018, 20). This, in fact, infringes upon and violates the human right to food as the Constitution of Nepal does not recognize its citizens based on gender equality. Nepali women are viewed in relation to their male partners or lack thereof. "The Shadow Report" further points out that Articles 11 (2), 11 (5), and 11 (7) categorize Nepali Mothers as Nepali Mothers with Nepali Men, Nepali Mothers with unidentified men, and Nepali Mothers with foreign men. As a result, there is a gap at the bureaucratic level in recognizing single women's agency[5] for conferring citizenship to their children and spouse, whereas men are granted independent agency to confer their citizenship to their children and spouse. According to a 2013 study conducted by the Forum for Women, Law, and Development (FWLD)—a Nepali organization for the promotion and protection of human rights—it is estimated that there are some four million people in Nepal who do not have citizenship (Shrestha 2013, 7).

"Right to Food" (RtF) in Nepal

The right to adequate food and nutrition (RtFN) is one of the basic human rights enshrined in international human rights.[6] As a member state of the United Nations (UN), the kingdom of Nepal signed and ratified the International Covenant in 1991. In the same year, Nepal signed and ratified the Convention on the Elimination of all Forms of Discrimination Against Women (CEDAW), which states that the member nations grant citizenship regardless of gender. And in 2015, Nepal, now a federal democratic republic nation drafted and promulgated its latest constitution in which it is stated respectively in Articles 36 (1), 36 (3), and 42 that "every citizen shall have the right relating to food"[7], and "every citizen shall have the right to food sovereignty as provided by law" and the "right to social justice" (Constituent Assembly Secretariat 2015, 20), which includes a provision for food, thus offering a human rights-based approach to food security in Nepal. It was also decided then that the Nepal Government would require three more years to translate the rights into policy and laws. Therefore the RtF and Food Sovereignty Bill was proposed and on September 18, 2018, the Food Sovereignty Act was passed by the parliament as a step forward to the progressive realization of Nepal's aim to achieve "zero hunger"[8] by 2030. It could have been a big step towards achieving food justice in a country like Nepal where 2.8 million people are food-insecure ("WFP Nepal" 2021, 2). Enshrining the RtF in Nepal's constitution has been recognized as "a moment of paradigm importance"[9] ("FAO Regional" 2015) as a progressive step towards addressing food justice. This also signifies that based on the constitutional framework, the RtF is justiciable, which means that in cases of violation of RtF, they could be presented before the court of law.

Despite this, these rights–inspired by the UN's human rights framework–remain unfulfilled as the provisions in the constitution are perceived by the policymakers in a vacuum rather than in conjunction with each other and in a perfect sense of the world where everybody is entitled to their rights. Unlike the popular understanding that western-based notions of human rights adopted in the non-West by the local political elites who are often viewed themselves as westernized (Pollis 2006, 68), in Nepal, most of the Constituent Assembly members–and women represented one-third of the assembly–belonged to traditionally marginalized communities. Contrary to most states from the non-west where the western definition of human rights is "rejected or, more accurately, meaningless" (68) these rights have been adopted but have failed to be implemented at policy levels.

Global instances have shown time and again that the so-called progressive legislations for RtF, accessing citizenship, immigrants' rights,[10] refugees and asylum seekers[11] take longer for implementation. Connecting to the situation in Nepal, Richardson posits the universal dilemma and positions that local bureaucrats face in the global-south while "mediating on the ground practice in confused legal settings in Europe and North America " (Gill 2009 and Mountz 2010 qtd. in Richardson 2016, 337). The confusion with constitutional provisions and the new legal framework has been compounded by a lengthy CA process (Nightangle and Rankin 2011, 2012, qtd. in Richardson 2016, 337). When western guided principles and frameworks are adopted in the non-west, it is always warmly welcomed by western organizations. International organizations such as WFP, FIAN, and Amnesty International, have welcomed the Food Sovereignty Act. Amnesty International also puts faith in the constitution, especially Article 36 to guarantee the RtF as it "lies in a robust legislative framework and an effective implementation of that framework" (Amnesty International 2018, 4). Furthermore, the organization has urged the Nepal government to implement its new law on the RtF based on the Act to mitigate food insecurity. Rhetorically, by incorporating internationally accepted tools and principles in the constitution and policymaking, Nepal gets positively reviewed[12] at the UN's Universal Periodic Review,[13] Human Rights index point, and Human Rights Watch. As feminist rhetoricians, we need to pause and ask who creates and implements human rights frameworks and who they serve the most. Feminist scholars have long argued that these frameworks are far from being gender neutral (Sachs et al. 2014, 401). In a developing country like Nepal, developing agencies and their projects bring funding for "reordering" peace and gender equality. As Sachs et al. rightly note, through regulatory bodies, these development projects place men, or rather, "particular forms of masculinity" in charge of guiding networks and policy frameworks at the national level. And it is from these "power relations [in] gendered spaces that the food security framework emerged" (401), which has yet to incorporate the dimensions of gender perspective while addressing access to food. The role of citizenship right in these conversations is next to in-existent.

Unless the people at the grassroots level get to fully comprehend and enjoy these rights and policies, these acts remain performative and are for the optics for the Western humanitarian and donor agencies. The other problem with describing the constitution as "progressive" by national and international institutions and reviewers is that it discourages revolution and tries to persuade the audience to accept what is being offered. The Maoist-led revolution transformed Nepal from a kingdom to a democratic federal nation and introduced a new constitution. Incorporating rights and provisions based in the Human Rights framework is a rhetorical move to show a symbolic gesture to the people of Nepal and international humanitarian organizations that the new governing system is going to be better than the previous one and to also justify their own revolution and position in postconflict Nepal. The 2015 constitution "restructured the country as a federal democratic republic, starting a new era and providing an opportunity for progress towards the 2030 Agenda for Sustainable Development. Every citizen's right to food is enshrined in the Right to Food Act" (WFP 2018). However, Nepal's "Right to Food and Food Sovereignty Act 2018" does not ensure the right to everyone residing within its boundary. Subsection 1, under article 3 of chapter of the Act, shortly states, "Every citizen shall have the right to food and right to food security" (National Law Commission 2018, 2). This means that only the full-fledged citizens of the country have this right, and the government is responsible for facilitating the right for only those who have the citizenship card, vis-à-vis the citizens.

The constitution gave "progressive" provisions on paper but hesitated to implement them in practice through bureaucratic entanglement. To address this, a few policymakers and activists have argued for gender-mainstreaming training for the officers. Binda Pandey, a politician, and a member of the first Constituent Assembly suggested that policy and gender-mainstreaming and gender-sensitivity experts should train the local officers (Pandey 2019). However, Pandey pointed out the inconsistencies of the people seeking citizenship through mothers. Pandey articulated that once there was a group of people who were trying to go to the supreme court with the guidance of other activists and political leaders like Pandey. "Now I don't know why they did not do that. If these eight to nine cases were handled by the Ministry, it would have been easier to circulate the same thing in the lower level too" (Pandey 2019). Pandey wanted to emphasize the importance of reaching out to and constantly following up with their trusted leaders to form an alliance to solve their problems.

Yamuna Ghale, a food sovereignty expert–who explores the RtF and food justice at the policy and implementation levels–has aptly observed the gap in knowledge about the issues pertaining to food justice in policymaking and at the local governance and grassroots levels. She asserts that food from the perspective of rights and social justice is not looked upon as an issue in Nepal (Ghale 2021) despite being incorporated as constitutional provisions. Speaking of the Food Sovereignty Act, she states that there is a lack of realization of the importance and responsibility of food justice by central authorities in the formulation and implementation of the act. During her field visits and training in local areas, she observed a similar gap in knowledge and political commitment about the provision and assimilation of the act and liability amongst the local government representatives. Ghale points out that due to these reasons, there is a greater tendency to misinterpret the right of food justice, thus explaining the delay in policy implementation. The delay had a greater impact during the time of the pandemic.

In the early days of the pandemic, countless stories of migrant workers returning from India and other labor destinations surfaced on social and news media (Suswopna 2021). The responsibility of the state during the time of crisis is to not only rebuild the country economically, but to also provide access to food. Ghale summarizes the plight of several Nepali migrant workers coming back home only to witness and fall victim to the hunger crisis[14]—also dubbed as a pandemic of hunger[15]. Hunger pushes people outside of their houses. Hunger pushes people to take risks. Hunger pushes people to remain dangerously mobile during the pandemic. The collective rhetoric of the people in hunger crisis as Ghale posited was: "I would rather die of Covid-19, than die of hunger" (Ghale 2021). Not all migrant returnees had the privilege to find a safe haven in their own home country during a global pandemic;

some had to take the risk and travel again to feed themselves and their families. Swiftness in food policy implementation from the Food Sovereignty Act could have assisted in delivering food justice and mitigating food insecurity.

On the other hand, it is paramount to also mark those who were able to cross borders from Nepal to abroad during the pandemic. People with citizenship–those who qualify to acquire passports–have the agency to remain mobile and search for alternative ways to acquire food justice. The citizenship card functions as a legal identity document like the way the social security number functions in the United States. The citizenship card upholds the supreme power as it is the prerequisite for obtaining other official identity documents such as passports, driving licenses, voter id cards, land ownership, and many more. Ownership of land is vital, especially in a country like Nepal which has much of the rural population engaged in agriculture activities. Gaining access and control over land, proper distribution of land, and availability of productive land led to food security, whereas putting restrictions on land ownership means impeding access to basic human needs and RtF (Shrestha et al. 2011, 58).

Rarely has the RtF been connected with the citizenship right, especially when it relates to people's access to economic independence. Since the formulation of the constitution, feminists[16] in Nepal have inserted that it is guided "in the male image" (Richardson 2016, 331) and by Hindu patriarchal ideologies to control women. However, the drafters did not take into consideration the fact that these discriminatory provisions do not always and only affect women.

When a person in Nepal does not have citizenship, they are deterred from "accessing opportunities" (Dhamala 2019, 69). There are certain barriers one cannot cross without having a citizenship card. As a result of lack of citizenship, people are not only stateless but "they are also unable to access a range of critical human rights such as education, health, and work" (My Children's 2015, 1). People without such certificates cannot open bank accounts, buy properties/land, pursue higher education, register to vote, apply for government positions, or get a mobile sim card. All these documents directly impact attaining food justice, as they are tied to economic upward mobility which plays a crucial role in accessing food. Neha Gurung,[17] a law undergrad in Kathmandu narrates how her mother and stepfather struggled most of their lives to obtain citizenship for themselves and for their children.[18]

> My stepfather[19] is an artist and loves English literature. He is a schoolteacher, and everyone knows there that he did not have a citizenship card.[20] He did not have a bank account where the school could send his salary. So, the school would hand him his salary un-officially, which means being disqualified for provident fund,[21] unlike his colleagues. The school kept on pressuring him to get

citizenship for the purpose of record-keeping. All his life, he has been robbed of opportunities to pursue his career as an artist abroad. On the other hand, our family of four had him as the sole breadwinner and we struggled to survive. My mother had to leave her well-paying job in the Tourism industry in 2012 to pursue activism for me, my sister, and my stepfather. Not only that, my mother started equal citizenship rights campaign[22] in the country for people like us who felt like living like prisoners/refugees in one's country. (Gurung 2019)

The Gurung[23] family has a somewhat happy ending. After years of fighting against the system, meeting with the head of leading political parties, and battling the case in the Supreme Court, Neha and her sister have obtained a citizenship card from their mother's name in 2016. Neha's stepfather[24] also got his long-awaited citizenship at the age of 45 in 2017. But those years where Neha's stepfather had to live a stateless life cautions us to realize the role played by citizenship rights and undocumented people globally in achieving food justice. Similarly, the dedication and sacrifice that Neha's mother had to put in for their rights imply that activism comes at the cost of time, money, and career. Ideally, it is feasible to do activism in households that can afford to constantly pay a visit to their local representatives and navigate bureaucratic hurdles and form alliances for a cause. And social justice calls for speaking for those who cannot do their own activism or have no access to make their voices heard. Feminist activists in Nepal are quite vocal about women's rights and violence against women. However, issues pertaining to hunger and food issues have yet to be a central focus in feminist activism.

Hima Bist, a women's right activist and an executive director of Women LEAD Nepal—an organization that trains young women for leadership roles for the future—has been engaged in women's rights activism which she admits has yet to undertake the aspect of food justice as a priority. She explains that those who are performing activism need to be viewed from their geopolitical locations[25] and for whom the citizenship right impacts more than RtF (Bista, 2021). She shares that thus, feminist activists are still lagging behind when it comes to logically setting up the connection of RtF with citizenship discourse. Moreover, she narrates her ongoing activism work not without a limitation:

> When we talk about activism, there are legal and non-legal activists who advocate because they have examples, materials, resources, and all legal know-how. So they are the ones who give all of these resources to the policymakers. More than policymakers, the biggest roles are played by activists who advocate for all these things. They can't just be stuck on one thing, so they need to gather all the important materials. Thus, the people who are in the government have created a bunch of round-tables discussions. . . . Activists can advocate with all their effort, but they can only take it up to a certain level and not beyond that.

... They can only go up to a certain point. There should be parliamentarians who should be there to discuss this particular point of the constitution. (Bista 2019)

On the day the constitution was promulgated, thousands of miles away from Nepal, Manjushree Thapa's[26] Colorado reacted by burning a copy of the constitution not out of anger, but in mourning (Thapa 2015). Thapa, a well-educated woman from a privileged family background[27] realized that the so-called progressive constitution was regressive towards women instead. Yet for thousands of Nepalese, "especially for marginalized and oppressed sections of society, including women in Nepal" (Ghale 2018), the constitution has continued to make them second-class citizens. The political awareness of one's identity and the status granted by the state is realized when they cannot function in society with the limited freedom and literacy they possess. Let's look at how these discriminatory policies are translated into lived experience.

Sabitri Gautam[28] recalls the time when she accompanied her son to a district office to apply for his citizenship card[29] (Gautam 2019). The federal officers refused to add her name as the mother of her son. The reason: she did not present her marriage certificate at the time.[30] Despite presenting the son's birth certificate which had Sabitri's husband's and her name as parents, the district officers refused to add her name on the citizenship card. "It felt as if the system did not recognize me to be his mother even though I had my citizenship. When I asked why, they said they needed our marriage certificate" (Guatam 2019). She narrated that the incident was both shocking and stressful to the point that it made her depressed, "I haven't taken my son's citizenship in my hands, and it has been for more than 1.5 years." She reads this incident as a way for the state to define and identify women in relation to others: somebody's wife and the child as from that union. In this case, she was not trying to confer citizenship to her son through her, but just wanted her name on the citizenship papers as his mother. This shows how challenging it must be for those who are applying for citizenship through their Nepali mothers. Sabiti shares:

> The fact that my name on both my citizenship and my son's birth certificate were the same was not recognized by those officials. They know that I am his mother through the birth certificate of my son but they also want to know who I got married to so that they are sure of who the father of the child is. And my husband was not asked for the marriage certificate. (Gautam 2019)

Porrone points out that identifying women as mothers subjugates women's individual identity. She articulates, "Conceiving women as mothers or providers of food contributes in crystallizing the concept of 'womanhood' as a category of subordination," which in turn not only denies other intersectional identities of women, but also impacts women's agency to access their right to food" (Porrone 2020. 9–10). Although the advances achieved in developing legal protections for women specifically in the context of the RtF are undeniable, there are "gaps to the identification of effective narratives and practices able to acknowledge women as social agents and advance women's concerns" (4). Sharma and Daugbjerg argue that at the articulation stage of food sovereignty policies in Nepal, it too had garnered ambiguities (P. Sharma 2020, 312). As the RtF and right to food sovereignty are implicitly related to citizenship rights, P. Sharma raises the question of who gets to enjoy these rights: "There are questions in relation to who the sovereign is in food sovereignty" (312). And because of the ambiguities and lack of a proper path for achieving food sovereignty, time and again the issue has comparatively been raised in Latin America by "social and political actors" but seldom in "Asia and Africa" (312). While the citizenship right acts as the biggest bureaucratic and administrative hurdle for living a free life, women's and citizenship rights activists in Nepal have rarely connected it to RtF. Their mission for social justice remains incomplete because it does not transfuse the intricacies of food justice. Food justice relates not only to "seeking to challenge and restructure the dominant food system" (Gottlieb 2010, ix). It is also related to "providing a core focus on equity and disparities and the struggles by those who are most vulnerable" and "establishing linkages and common goals with other forms of social justice activism and advocacy—whether immigrant rights, worker justice, transportation and access, or land use" (ix).

CONCLUSION

Promulgating the Constitution in September 2015 was not expected to be a somber event. Since April of that year, the country had been reeling from the constant aftershocks and aftermath of the 7.8 magnitude earthquake that took the lives of 8,964 people. Promulgation of the Constitution at that occasion was expected to be a momentous event to unite the citizens of Nepal because for the past eight years, the citizens were growing wary about the prolonged drafting of the constitution. Rhetoricians might note: Who were these citizens? Whose agendas were mostly addressed? What kinds of provisions were prioritized? Which framework was most influential in steering the drafting of the constitution? Rhetoricians might also consider the constitutional provisions as well as their rhetorical meanings that intersected and affected various identities and constitutional provisions. As food justice scholars, we might consider constantly locating and theorizing the rhetoric of policy intersections. Identifying the interlocking systems of policies that persistently entrap people in a loop based on their identities and geopolitical situatedness is equally essential while addressing food justice. Solving issues of food injustices requires acknowledging gaps in our own scholarship and food justice activism about various intersections and regularly drawing the attention of stakeholders, policymakers, and scholars to addressing those gaps.

Although activists for equal citizenship rights have significantly made the public and policymakers aware of the gender-discriminating policies in Nepal's constitutions, a coalition between food justice experts/organizations working for monitoring the implementation of RtF and women's rights activist groups needs to be built to showcase the intersection between citizenship rights and RtF. For Nepal to fully realize the right to adequate food and RtF sovereignty, the government of Nepal should not view these rights in isolation, but rather recognize the stark contrast and parallel with other rights asserted in the constitution of Nepal.

REFERENCES

Adhikari, B. 2011. "Nepalese Supreme Court Decision on the Right to Food." In *Right to Food and Nutrition Watch. Claiming Human Rights: The Accountability Challenge*, edited by S. Oenema, F. Valente, and B. Walter. Heidelberg, 94–95. Germany: FIAN International.

Amnesty International. 2019. *Nepal: Right to Food in Nepal Analysis of the Right to Food and Food Sovereignty Acts 2018*. London: Amnesty International Ltd. https://www.amnesty.org/en/wp-content/uploads/2021/05/ASA3101302019ENGLISH.pdf.

Awin, Narimah. 2014. "Bridging the Divide: Linking Poverty Eradication, Food Sovereignty and Security, and Sexual and Reproductive Health and Rights." *Arrows for Change* 20, no. 1: 2.

Bista, Hima. 2019, June 15. Personal communication.

———. 2021, July 6. Personal communication.

Brent, Zoe W., Christina M. Schiavoni, and Alberto Alonso-Fradejas. 2015. "Contextualizing Food Sovereignty: The Politics of Convergence Among Movements in the USA." *Third World Quarterly* 36, no. 3: 618–35.

Commissioner for Human Rights. n.d. https://www.ohchr.org/Documents/Publications/FactSheet34en.pdf.

Constituent Assembly Secretariat. 2015. *Constitution of Nepal*. Kathmandu: Constituent Assembly Secretariat.

Dhamala, Roshani. 2019. *Gender and Citizenship in the Constitution of Nepal, 2015*. PhD dissertation, Virginia Tech.

FAO Regional Office for Asia and the Pacific. 2015. "Nepal Enshrines the Right to Food in New Constitution." Food and Agriculture Organization of the United Nations. https://www.fao.org/asiapacific/news/detail-events/en/c/334889.

Gautam, Sabitri. 2019, July 4. Personal communication.

Ghale, Yamuna. 2021, October 29. Personal communication.

Ghale, Yamuna, et al. "Gender Dimensions of Food Security, the Right to Food and Food Sovereignty in Nepal." *Journal of International Women's Studies.*

Gill, Nick. 2009. "Presentational State Power: Temporal and Spatial Influences over Asylum Sector Decisionmakers." *Transactions of the Institute of British Geographers* 34, no. 2: 215–33.

Glennie, Charlotte, and Alison Hope Alkon. 2017. "Food Justice: Cultivating the Field." *Environmental Research Letters* 13, no. 7.

Gottlieb, Robert, and Anupama Joshi. 2010. *Food Justice.* Cambridge: MIT Press.

Government of Nepal. 2018. *The Right to Food and Food Sovereignty Act, 2075.*

Gurung, Neha. 2019, June 12. Personal communication.

Herman, Agatha, Michael K. Goodman, and Colin Sage. 2018. "Six Questions for Food Justice." *Local Environment* 23, no. 11: 1075–89.

Holt-Giménez, Eric. 2011. "Food Security, Food Justice, or Food Sovereignty." *Cultivating Food Justice: Race, Class, and Sustainability*: 309–30.

Interim Constitution of Nepal 2007. 2007. Kathmandu: Interim Government of Nepal.

Mountz, Alison. 2010. *Seeking Asylum: Human Smuggling and Bureaucracy at the Border.* Minneapolis: University of Minnesota Press.

My Children's Future Ending Gender Discrimination in Nationality Laws. 2015. London: Equal Rights Trust.

Mulmi, Subin and Sara Shneiderman. 2017. "Citizenship, Gender and Statelessness in Nepal." *Understanding Statelessness* 4: 135.

National Law Commission. 2018. *The Right to Food and Food Sovereignty Act, 2075.* Kathmandu: National Law Commission. https://www.lawcommission.gov.np/en/wp-content/uploads/2019/07/The-Right-to-Food-and-Food-Sovereignty-Act-2075-2018.pdf.

"Nepal Country Strategic Plan (2019–2023)." 2018, November. Rome: World Food Programme Second Regular Session.

Pandey, Binda. 2019, July 15. Personal communication.

Petersen, Emily January, and Rebecca Walton. 2018, October. "Bridging Analysis and Action: How Feminist Scholarship Can Inform the Social Justice Turn." *Journal of Business and Technical Communication* 32, no. 4: 416–46. https://doi.org/10.1177/1050651918780192.

Pollis, Adamantia, Peter Schwab, and Christine M. Koggel. 2006. "Human Rights: A Western Construct with Limited Applicability." *Moral Issues in Global Perspective.* Vol. 1: Moral and Political Theory: 1–18.

Porrone, Arianna. 2020, November. "Gender in the Nepal Right to Food and Food Sovereignty Act, 2075." FIAN International Nepal and FIAN International.

Ratcliffe, Krista. 2005. *Rhetorical Listening: Identification, Gender, Whiteness.* Carbondale: Southern Illinois University Press.

Richardson, Diane, Nina Laurie, Meena Poudel, and Janet Townsend. 2016, May. "Women and Citizenship Post-Trafficking: The Case of Nepal." *The Sociological Review* 64, no. 2: 329–48. https://doi.org/10.1111/1467-954X.12364.

Right to Food and Nutrition Watch: Women's Power in Food Struggles. 2019. Global Network for the Rights to Food and Nutrition.

Sachs, Carolyn, and Anouk Patel-Campillo. 2014. "Feminist Food Justice: Crafting a New Vision." *Feminist Studies* 40, no. 2: 396–410.

The Shadow Report Preparation Committee. 2018, November. *Shadow Report on Sixth Periodic Report of Nepal on CEDAW.* https://fwld.org/wp-content/uploads/2018/11/Shadow-Report-on-Sixth-Periodic-Report-of-Nepal-on-CEDAW-2018.pdf.

Sharma, P., and Carsten Daugbjerg. 2020. "The Troubled Path to Food Sovereignty in Nepal: Ambiguities in Agricultural Policy Reform." *Agriculture and Human Values* 37, no. 2: 311–23.

Shrestha, Lisha, and Bishnu Raj Upreti. 2011. "Reflection on Land-Based Relationship Between Agrarian Tension, Armed Conflict and Human Insecurity in Nepal." *Land, Agriculture and Agrarian Transformation*: 57–139.

Shrestha, Sabin, and Subin Mulmi. 2013. "Acquisition of Citizenship Certificate in Nepal—Estimation and Projection." FWLD, Forum for Women, Law and Development. http://fwld.org/wp-content/uploads/2016/06/Acquisition-of-Citizenship-Certificate-in-Nepal-Estimation-and-Projection.pdf.

Thapa, Manjushree. 2015, September. "Women Have No Nationality." *The Record*, 21. https://www.recordnepal.com/women-have-no-nationality.

Tilzey, Mark. 2018. "Nepal." In *Political Ecology, Food Regimes, and Food Sovereignty*. Cham, Switzerland: Palgrave Macmillan.

Tong, Rosemarie, and Tina Fernandes Botts. 2018. *Feminist Thought: A More Comprehensive Introduction*. London: Routledge.

Tuladhar, Indu. 2014. "Statelessness Among Women and Children in Nepal." *Himalayan Journal of Development and Democracy* 9, no. 1.

UN Office of the High Commissioner for Human Rights (OHCHR). 2010, April. *Fact Sheet No. 34, The Right to Adequate Food.* https://www.refworld.org/docid/4ca460b02.html.

"WFP Nepal Country Brief April 2021." n.d. Nepal: World Food Program. https://docs.wfp.org/api/documents/WFP-0000127664/download/?_ga=2.73119831.555347129.1580827133–520964665.1618363039.

Wickeri, Elisabeth, and Anil Kalhan. 2010. "Land Rights Issues in International Human Rights Law." *Malaysian Journal on Human Rights*.

NOTES

1. Patriarchal values in general and Hindu patriarchal codes in general in which women are identified in relation with men such as father, husbands, and sons.

2. This is based on my reading and understanding of national, parallel, and shadow reports presented by different stakeholders for UPR, ESCR, and CEDAW.

3. Jyotika Rimal and Sarasawti Dhakal.

4. I was back in Nepal for three short months in 2019 when I conducted almost all my interviews that concentrated interviewing people who were already visible with their works and struggles. My plan for the following summer was to go back again to

recover work and the plight of people at grassroot levels. Pandemic has put a pause on that.

5. Divorced, widow, single women, rape survivors, female migrant workers (who come back to Nepal with their children born in a foreign land) are mainly affected by the citizenship policy of Nepal, and by the way the constitution of Nepal sees women as in relation to men.

6. It was back in 1948 that the United Nations General Assembly adopted the Universal Declaration of Human Rights (UDHR) which recognized the RtFN as a part of the Right to an Adequate Standard of Living.

7. The RtF was first provisioned in Nepal's Interim Constitution of 2007. Sub section 3 of article 18 entitled "Right relating to employment and social security," it is stated that "Every citizen shall have the RtF sovereignty, as provided in law." It is also the very first time that the country realized the need to address and incorporate the right in its constitution. Making this as the base, the right to food was further elaborated when the 2015 Constitution was promulgated.

8. Established by the UN, zero hunger is one of the 17 goals of Sustainable Development Goals (SDG). The main themes that are carried by the mission include: "end hunger, achieve food security, and improve nutrition and promote sustainable agriculture." Additionally, it's been estimated that 2.8 million suffer from food-insecurity in the country.

9. As a FAO Representative in Nepal, Somsak Pipoppinyo welcomed the promulgation of the constitution in which RtF is also enshrined.

10. For more, see Mathew Coleman's "What counts as the politics and practice of security, and where?"

11. See McConnell "Citizens and refugees: constructing and negotiating Tibetan identities in exile."; Mountz's *Seeking asylum: Human smuggling and bureaucracy at the border*; Black's "Fifty years of refugee studies: From theory to policy."

12. Civil Societies and organizations also get to share parallel reports to counter state reports/review. Due to the scope of the chapter, they have not been included here.

13. Every four to five years, UN's member states are reviewed for their Human Rights records. The latest review of Nepal took place in early 2021.

14. It's been estimated by the World Food Program that 46 percent of the families reliant on remittance lost their source of income during the pandemic.

15. The Pandemic of Hunger: https://www.nepalitimes.com/latest/the-pandemic-of-hunger.

16. See Manjushree Thapa's "Women have no nationality."

17. The Gurung family stories were widely covered in Media. For more: https://www.ucanews.com/news/nepals-battle-over-identity-gender-and-citizenship/72695#.

18. Mulmi poignantly summarizes: Article 38 (1) of Part 1 of the Constitution of Nepal 2015 has ensured: "Every woman shall have equal right to lineage without any gender discrimination." However, the right of women to confer citizenship only when the father is unidentified not only undermines the independent identity of women but also denies their unquestionable biological role in birthing children. The law also requires that children must be born in Nepal and reside in the country as well. This requirement restricts children born to Nepali working or resident in other countries

and children born to rescued trafficked women from acquiring the citizenship of Nepal.

19. Neha's family case is very complicated. Her biological father ruthlessly abandoned the family when Neha was very young. The state did not recognize the real culprit and disregarded her mother's status as a single mother to confer her citizenship to her two kids. After years of fighting the case at Supreme Court, both daughters have gotten citizenship cards. However, the case did not create a precedent for other cases. Their mother is a vocal activist of the citizenship right.

20. Although he was born in Nepal, the state refused to give him his citizenship through his mother's name as his father had passed away a long time ago.

21. welfare benefit offered by the employment office for its employees.

22. For more: https://womensenews.org/2015/10/nepals-constitution-maintains-fatherhood-bias.

23. Due to the limitation of the chapter, I cannot begin to describe the level of hassles the family underwent at the bureaucratic level. For more: https://myrepublica.nagariknetwork.com/news/sc-orders-citizenship-through-mother-for-gurung-sisters.

24. As a wife, Neha's mother could pass her citizenship to her husband. He was finally granted his citizenship through his own mother's name after intense lobbying, networking, and lobbying at the level of state, local and civil society.

25. Struggles of someone living in urban Kathmandu versus someone living in rural areas will be distinct even if they are fighting for the same cause. Hima suggests that people in Kathmandu comparatively do have more access for conducting activism and do not have to struggle for food as much as someone living in rural areas.

26. A well-known Nepali author who had lived more than half her life outside Nepal and presently resides in Canada

27. Thapa's father worked as a Nepali diplomat, minister, and a governor of Nepal Rastra Bank, while her mother is a doctor.

28. A Nepali feminist writer and activist.

29. To apply for citizenship, usually one has to show a birth certificate, and citizenship card of one's parents.

30. The district office was in another city far from their house and they could not go back home to retrieve the marriage certificate.

PART III

Chapter 10

Students Question the Academic Agrifood Industrial Complex and Promote Food Justice

Abby M. Dubisar

On October 26, 2015, I learned about an instance of students' critical agrifood literacy practices when I read a listserv post about university research on bananas. The post, sent to the listserv of a food and agriculture nonprofit, asked readers to sign a petition expressing concern about the research. This "banana feeding study" was approved by the university's institutional review board (IRB), and the principal investigator recruited human participants to eat genetically modified bananas in return for $900 compensation. The post described a number of ways students had tried to prompt their university to be more transparent about this research and its impacts, including a petition they would soon deliver to their university and those funding the study. These students were engaging in critical agrifood literacies and advocating for food justice.

The students' efforts detailed in the post catalyzed my research for this chapter because they reflected their motivation to engage in critical dialogue on the food research conducted at their institution. My interviews with these students illuminate the strategies they employed while practicing critical agrifood literacies. I join environmental rhetoric scholars such as Gabriela Raquel Ríos (2015), who analyzes place-based activism by farm workers, and literacy studies scholars who have expressed concerns about students' understandings of the global food system (Brewster 2011; House 2014; Schell 2012; Smith-Sitton 2019; Winslow 2012). These scholars have all detailed interventions that teach ways to be ethical, effective stewards of future food systems. Building on such scholarship, I contend that these students demonstrate how to practice critical agrifood literacies and activate food justice work.

In this chapter, I situate my study in food justice and critical agrifood literacy scholarship, describe my methods for collecting data, and offer my findings on consequences and sustainability before concluding with limitations and further questions. Ultimately, my analysis illustrates for food justice scholars how students question the academic agrifood industrial complex by applying frameworks rooted in food sovereignty and sustainability. I show how these students challenge the colonialism and tech supremacy that are often embedded in agricultural research. I claim that the students' engagement with the university's invocation of charity and benevolence, which did not hold up to their questions about research design, transparency, and sustainability, reveals the university's participation in research power structures that can put food sovereignty at risk. Arguing that this case prompts greater attention to student food justice activism, especially to how students question their university's partnerships with private funders that host capitalist expansion, I call on food justice researchers to address the imperialist impulses of the land-grant ethic.

LOCATING STUDENTS' CRITICAL AGRIFOOD LITERACIES AND FOOD JUSTICE ADVOCACY

To define critical agrifood literacies, I follow the tradition started by Eileen Schell (2012), positioning such literacy as "an understanding of the environmental, social, and political consequences of the food system and an endorsement of developing sustainable food systems and sustainable ways of living." Such positioning intends to lead students to learn about "global operations of capital, power, environmental resources, labor, consumption, and literacies" in global agrifood systems (Schell 2012). This emphasis on consequences and sustainability resonates with the perspectives of the students featured here and provides a heuristic for locating such literacy practices, including within land-grant universities (Schell 2012). Locating critical agrifood literacies on campus leads immediately to acknowledging the pressures facing agrifood systems, as scholars write with urgency about the multiple crises facing food systems across the globe. For example, Veronica House contends that "food sovereignty and food justice are some of the most important issues of our time" and universities must adjust to address them (House 2014, 4). To seriously address these issues and center food justice on campus, universities must assess their agricultural curricula. Doing so may immediately reveal conflicting practices created by university research commitments, as this case illustrates. The students here share House's concerns. How they act on their concerns exposes their university's reticence to center food justice in a particular research project: The students' coursework on sustainability and food sovereignty clashed with the university's research pursuits.

Agricultural research pursuits at land-grant universities are known to prioritize goals that do not necessarily include food justice, such as securing patents, grabbing land, and other imperialist endeavors (Vidal and Provost 2011). Such research is often embedded in the motivations of private funding sources, which began to heavily invest in agricultural research in the 1980s, when federal funding for university research started to decrease, prompting professors to become entrepreneurs who could profit from research instead of public employees who pursue knowledge for public gain.[1] Writing in 1999 on the benefits of alternative funding mechanisms for agricultural research, economists Wallace Huffman and Richard Just (1999) conclude that "although state taxpayers continue to account for 50 percent of agricultural research resources, the trend toward private funding is a matter of concern because of the potential to displace research with public benefits and to leverage public funds to the benefit of private concerns" (16). Updating these numbers in 2017, Yoo-Hwan Lee and Gregory Graff claim that universities "provide a good venue for engagement with industry stakeholders, in creating new knowledge that can lead to commercial innovations" (90), a situation that seems inevitable due to the drop in public funding, as recent statistics show. In 2013, for example, public funding sources for food and agricultural research amounted to $3.8 billion (23.3 percent) of a total of $16.3 billion while private funding, from such sources as companies, foundations, and farmer organizations, accounted for $12.5 billion or 76.7 percent (Lee and Graff 2017, 64). Regarding land-grant universities, in 2016 the USDA reported that as of 2013, public research institutions, including USDA intramural research and land-grant universities, state agricultural experiment stations, and cooperating institutions (LGU/SAES/CI), conducted under 30 percent of total agricultural research. Showing the immense impact of private funding for land-grant universities and other public institutions, the USDA reports that "out of $12.4 billion spent by private firms and other non government bodies during the same period, all but $686 million financed industry research, with most of the rest funding research at LGU/SAES/CI. Within the public sphere, LGU/SAES/CI conducted $3.0 billion in research, twice the level of USDA's intramural labs" (Clancy, Fuglie, Heisey 2021). With this funding history shaping the current research context, Huffman and Just's call for concern is increasingly relevant.

THE BANANA FEEDING STUDY CONTEXT AND ITS CONTROVERSIES

The banana feeding study mentioned at the start of this chapter was controversial for several reasons. The term *transgenic* (or genetically engineered) is often used to describe the bananas developed for the feeding study because they contain genetic material from an unrelated organism. These bananas, created to address insufficient Vitamin A and thus enriched with extra beta-carotene, would be fed to women students who consented to participate in the study. Since the body converts beta-carotene into Vitamin A during digestion, the university food science researchers planned to measure the presence of Vitamin A in participants' blood samples, to be collected after they ate the transgenic bananas. The researcher's task in the feeding study, then, was to assess the bioavailability of the nutrient's absorption into the women's bodies. Thus, controversies about genetically modified foods and their safety showed up in concerns about the study.

But the study was also controversial because the university where the study took place is a land-grant university, positioned to promote public science. It frames its mission to conduct research with local, national, and international impact. Further, this land-grant institution is in the United States, far removed from Uganda, where researchers claimed the banana would eventually be eaten.[2] Thus, the colonial implications of U.S. university researchers developing technology-driven, top-down interventions to another country's agrifood contexts also made the banana feeding study controversial. The banana feeding study prompts attention from those concerned about food justice, such as the students here, since the food system itself is a racial project (Alkon and Agyeman 2011, 5) and land-grant universities are rooted in white supremacy (Lee and Ahtone n.d.). Universities have histories of working at the intersection of racism, power, and research through their agrifood pursuits. Winona LaDuke (2007) chronicles how University of Minnesota researchers set their sights on wild rice, the only grain indigenous to North America, and University of Colorado researchers attempted to patent quinoa.[3] In the banana study, the university's power to conduct the feeding trials of the banana and measure its nutrient absorption in the bodies of women students in order to contribute to these bananas being inserted into Uganda's agricultural system reinscribes the racist framework of top-down agrifood interventions that might destroy a food that is essential to Uganda's social identity and its farmers' livelihood.[4]

The study assumed that the transgenic banana would transition seamlessly into Uganda's food system. But to do so, the banana would have to be embraced by both Ugandan farmers, who were accustomed to growing certain banana crops, and local populations, who were used to eating bananas that were familiar to them.[5] The insertion of beta-carotene, for example, could turn the bananas orange, which might be unappealing and even alarming to eaters. As I will illustrate, students' awareness of these accumulating concerns and their desire to learn more catalyzed their critical agrifood literacies and understandings of food justice, compelling them to question their university's involvement in this research. And their university's resistance to their questions and reluctance to engage in dialogue galvanize their growing concern that the banana feeding study operates in problematic ways.

Research Design for Feminist Inquiry: Centering Students' Experiences

I used Kathy Charmaz's (2006) concept of grounded theory to design this study, asking the students open-ended questions about their experiences in addressing the banana feeding study. As a feminist researcher, I design research studies that employ literacy studies methods connected to feminist orientations, paying attention to power structures and how individuals traditionally disempowered by institutions, such as students, use literacy practices to address those in power. As Gesa Kirsch and Peter Mortensen (1996) note, "feminist scholars recognize the multiple and shifting subject positions we inhabit at work and play, and they aim to develop ethical principles that foreground such questions as the following: Who benefits the most from the research? Whose interests are at stake? What are the consequences for participants?" (xxi). Acting on these questions complicates the traditional university hierarchy of student–faculty learning: I position myself to learn from the students in order to extend their knowledge to my field, validate their work, and continue the conversation that their university tried to end.

Three students, Gabrielle, Angie, and Rivka, agreed to do individual interviews with me. I interviewed two of these students in person in 2018 and the other student over the phone in 2019. They had the choice of using their first name or a pseudonym, per IRB protocol. I include an introduction that each person wrote when I first quote from them here. They all had an opportunity to read this work and comment on it. All three students either co-majored or minored in their university's graduate program in sustainable agriculture, an interdepartmental program founded on agricultural science. During the interviews they described events that occurred while they were students, and they had all graduated by the time of our interviews. The sustainable agriculture program in which they were enrolled enables students to study sustainable agriculture in an interdisciplinary setting that accounts for biological, social, and economic aspects of sustainability.

As I coded the students' interviews and identified emerging and recurring themes, I noticed how these graduate students' ideas reflected the practices described and encouraged by literacy and rhetoric scholars in their work on food and agricultural literacies, extending food justice and critical literacy studies to address their university's interventions in agrifood systems—all the more poignant at a land-grant university committed to public impact. While many themes occurred across the three student interviews, the recurring, intertwined themes most relevant to food justice activism are consequences and sustainability.

To fulfill their obligation to conduct science that serves the public good, the students' efforts focus on a growing need to urge powerful institutions to be more transparent about their agrifood research. I argue here that these students' attempts to prompt their university to be transparent about its food research, an aspect of research methods addressed in their coursework, illustrate how such dynamic, literacy efforts toward food justice arise in response to agrifood contexts. Also, their efforts deepen understanding of how students raise awareness of public universities' investment in agrifood development. The students' perspectives provide a counternarrative to universities' position regarding how and why their agrifood endeavors should be articulated to the publics they serve—including their own students—and the communities they claim to aid.[6]

STUDENTS' RHETORICAL STRATEGIES THAT ADDRESS CONSEQUENCES AND SUSTAINABILITY

As I will show, the students' practices of critical agrifood literacies emphasize the banana feeding study's consequences and sustainability as they address the safety of the study, consider the cultural impacts of the bioengineered banana, question the research-funding source, and show the limits of the study's reliance on a single, technological solution sponsored by a land-grant university. They applied knowledge from their coursework, such as about methods for ethical research and the multiple facets of sustainability in agrifood systems. The three students' orientation to the banana feeding study began by asking questions in multiple contexts and conducting basic research about it, both initial steps in practicing critical agrifood literacy.

Graduating with her PhD in Soil Science, Rivka now studies how sustainable farming practices augment soil's ability to fight climate change and teaches introductory courses in soil and environmental science. Safety is the first consequence Rivka addressed in our interview, describing how the students researched the banana feeding study after learning about it from an IRB recruitment email sent by the lead researcher to some women students at her university. When researching the study, Rivka first noticed that no evidence of previous trials existed that addressed the bioengineered banana's safety: "We thought it was strange that [the banana] was considered okay by the university for them to just ask women to participate in this trial without any public evidence of its safety." She also found no evidence that the target population beyond campus had been consulted about the study. Thus, she identified two audiences for whom consequences and safety matter: the research participants who would eat the banana to help test its bioavailability and the population who would eventually eat it. While reporting on the study indicated that Ugandan citizens were the target population for the bioengineered banana, Rivka noted, "we had no indication that [Ugandans] actually wanted a GM [genetically modified] banana." To understand the design and purpose of the banana feeding study, Rivka researched the impacts facing these multiple audiences who would consume the banana. Her observations here connect with questions of food justice and the power distribution embedded in such research and the human right to have access to culturally appropriate foods and foodways.

Rivka and her fellow students also addressed cultural impacts by expanding their initial research to cases beyond this study at their campus. In looking at similar incidents where GM foods were brought into other countries with the support of local governments, they found that the people themselves did not want to grow or eat the GM foods. "The obvious example," Rivka said, "would be golden rice.[7] There were other incidents that we discovered. We thought that if [the banana feeding study] wasn't trying to avoid the public eye, then there shouldn't be any problem having a public conversation about it, to bring these issues into the public light." She thought that if the banana feeding study differed from such other examples, the researchers would want to show how and why in order to distinguish their study from previous, unsuccessful GM food projects.

But Rivka found that addressing cultural impacts was not in the interest of the researchers or administrators, and this disinterest affects safety. She illustrates this point by describing their lack of knowledge or concern about these issues:

> The administrative people didn't know the science of what was going on. They couldn't point us to any evidence of species of banana or any evidence of having spoken with the Ugandan people. Not the government, the people. The administrators [repeated], "This was approved by the IRB, our internal review system deals with this stuff. So if it's gone through therefore it's safe." That's kind of chicken or egg, it's safe because it was approved, but it was approved because somebody thought it was safe. And [that] doesn't mean that it is safe.

Thus, the expertise that Rivka gained from her environmental science undergraduate degree and agronomy graduate degree included knowledge of the safe and culturally appropriate methods that should be used to assess bioengineered foods, and the upper administration seemed unable to answer Rivka and her fellow students' questions about whether these methods were used. (While Rivka was able to meet with the lead researcher once during office hours, that faculty member would not answer any of Rivka's questions regarding her and the other students' concerns about the study.) Feeding GM bananas to college students without knowledge of the food's safety alarmed Rivka because it put developing the GM food ahead of participants' safety and local populations' priorities. Further, the lack of publicly available information about the transgenic banana's safety suggested that the university knew how to conduct feeding trials but did not know—or at least acknowledge—the critical importance of publicly addressing the broader ethical and cultural implications.

Further addressing the cultural impacts of the study, Rivka insisted that the perspective of the targeted public of Ugandan citizens be included in public science endeavors such as the transgenic banana's development. She expressed deep concern that she could not find evidence that Ugandan citizens requested a GM banana—a key concern about the study because the banana was purportedly for Ugandans. She explained the significance of including the targeted public's perspective by defining sustainability, providing a heuristic for ways to assess agrifood research and other food system interventions. Rivka defined the three pillars of sustainability as environmental, social, and economic:

> Environmental [sustainability includes] not overusing resources, for example, past the point where they can't be replenished at the same rate you are using them. Then there's social sustainability. The idea that people are being treated equitably, receiving fair pay. . . . The people involved would be the owners of the farm, the farm workers, and the people. [We ask:] Are they receiving a living wage, do they have medical benefits, and that kind of thing. That's part of sustainability because, if the people cannot continue on in their current line of work due to social constraints, then it's not sustainable in a sense of sustainable being something that can continue indefinitely.

Later she described the third pillar of sustainability, economic sustainability, which in this case involves assessing whether a farm is earning enough money to sustain itself indefinitely.

Cultural values, especially in the Ugandan context, Rivka explained, necessitate an intertwining of these pillars. She addressed the importance of acknowledging why it matters when a particular food has been bred within one nation for a long time: "Those foods, those crops, those seeds that they hand down from one generation to another, are social and cultural capital, and they are ingrained into their cultural system." Thus, it is complex, if not impossible, for an outside entity such as a university to implement a new staple food, especially without considering interlinked factors of economic, environmental, and cultural sustainability. These projects can wrest control from local populations, enacting the university's power over local systems to their detriment. Rivka describes the context in terms of sustainability: "Food sovereignty is part of sustainability, where food sovereignty is defined as self-control of food systems within one's nation or one's culture. This has historically been a problem in Africa . . . where the people lose control of their food systems because the government appropriates their land and/or dictates what has to be grown." Rivka was thus troubled that outsiders, in this case, American university researchers, thought they could replace a nation's familiar banana with a new banana.

Notably, one of Rivka, Angie, and Gabrielle's classmates in the sustainable agriculture graduate program was from Uganda, and he participated in a public dialogue session hosted by students concerned by the banana feeding study. (The students invited the lead researcher and members of the administration to participate in this session, but they declined.) Rivka described what she had learned about that Ugandan student's experience: "He'd actually been . . . doing social work in Uganda with children who had malnutrition, and he felt the banana wouldn't help because the reason for the malnutrition was diarrhea. . . . So you can get more nutrients [through GM foods] that may help a little bit, but the underlying problem was actually parasites and other diseases." In Rivka's understanding of sustainability, then, the solution that the university was developing with its banana feeding study did not align with the needs of the people for whom the GM banana was supposed to aid.

Funding for the study also prompted these students to ask questions about sustainability and consequences, such as the implications of university research being sponsored by private funders. Angie, especially, addressed the funding issue. When Angie, a cisgender, heterosexual white woman currently living in the Midwest and working as a sociologist in academia, received the IRB recruitment email about the study, she immediately was concerned about its funding source. While the students' research did not reveal much about the study itself, the students did find out that the Gates Foundation was a funder of the work. Angie commented that the Gates Foundation's wealth gives it much power to create change. Angie was concerned that it was using its power to "lift up a certain type of agriculture that [sustainable agriculture experts] think is actually really harmful, colonial, imperialistic." She acknowledged that the Gates Foundation has supported productive projects but that so many other agricultural approaches that she had studied in her courses could use such funding for greater impact than what the banana feeding study would yield. Established organizations shared Angie's concern. The Community Alliance for Global Justice in Seattle published a critique of the Gates Foundation's approach to development programs in Africa. Another group, Navdanya, Vandana Shiva's organization in India, does seed sovereignty work, and the students discovered it had a petition expressing concern that the transgenic bananas were an example of biopiracy (n.d.).

Beyond the funding source and its support of technological interventions in agrifood systems, these students also addressed that technological approach directly. Rivka, Angie, and Gabrielle all commented on how such a technology-dependent, intensive intervention, as a single-solution approach, deserved scrutiny since its consequences and sustainability were questionable, depending on the application and desired outcome. Angie explained why a discussion of the consequences of different interventions deserves to happen and why any single solution should be questioned in multiple ways:

> This idea that GMOs [genetically modified organisms] are good or bad I always felt was very simplistic. They're used as a tool for exploitation, colonization, capitalization. They're used as a tool for that, and [our university] packages it as science and development. I'm not saying that they could never be used in a way that was actually grounded in community and used for a development project, maybe they could be, but we're not able to even study them as a possible tool in the toolbox that way because it's so accepted that there's one way to do this and this is how we're doing this. . . . Literally, any kind of technology that everyone says is right all the time or wrong all the time I would question. Let's try to talk about this in more complex terms.

For Angie, a more complex discussion included how bananas are grown. She described how sweet potatoes could potentially better address vitamin A deficiency, which the banana feeding study claims to address. Because sweet potatoes are an annual crop, not a perennial crop such as bananas, their production is less intensive. She detailed how bananas require more land and a longer term of investment. For example, Angie described how sweet potatoes make more sense than bananas in an agricultural system in which land tenure is uncertain; unless a farmer knows they will be on the land in future years, and has title to the land, planting a perennial crop like bananas would be very risky—the farmer might plant bananas only to have the landowner rent the land to someone else in future years, or the farmer might find that once they have made this investment in a perennial crop, their right to farm on the land is contested by others who wish to gain the benefit of their investment. This example is just one of multiple solutions for addressing vitamin A deficiency beyond that of developing technological interventions.

The university's single-solution approach also drew Gabrielle's attention, causing her to reflect on the ways GMOs are positioned as the favored intervention when a range of other agrifood approaches could be used, especially when considering the three pillars of sustainability. I asked Gabrielle, a social scientist who studies climate, gender, and just agrifood systems and directs a national women in agriculture program for a U.S. nonprofit, what she thought about agrifood applications of genetic modification. She answered, "I'm critical of them because they generally tend to prop up this system that is flawed for lots of reasons and it's one more way to use technology to disconnect people from their food and farmers from having access to their seeds, and the technology is highly expensive." Gabrielle noted that since she is not a geneticist, she cannot directly address that particular aspect of GMOs, but she is concerned about how they are used to intervene in agrifood systems and sever relationships between people and their food. She expressed the importance of understanding these applications' consequences:

> It's how we use that tool [of GMOs], and I would say, generally speaking, in ag, it's been used to prop up a system that further disenfranchises people from their food and especially for small holders and people in an international context, that's often created more costly inputs that have drastically reduced their ability to be food sovereign.

Like Rivka and Angie, Gabrielle's application of critical agrifood literacy around GMO technology relied on showing her understanding of the science and social consequences.

Angie addressed in more detail why the single-solution, technology-based intervention taken up by university researchers mattered to its status as a land-grant university, founded on conducting research for the public good. A single question reflected her ongoing concerns: "Why is university time, university faculty, university students being asked to take part in a study for which there's no response to how is this serving the public good?" Connecting the land-grant mission of her school to developing technological solutions to agrifood problems, Angie made this observation, which relates to Rivka's earlier concerns about the importance of consulting the local population for whom the bananas were being developed: "I think that the land-grant mission serv[ing] public good with science and technology is inherently a problem if it doesn't understand that the local knowledge is also a way of understanding the world and recognizing it doesn't maybe look like Western science and what happens in the lab, but that doesn't mean that it's not also a good approach." Angie believed that there are alternative ways that universities like hers could approach agrifood issues beyond the single-solution GMO approach: "They may not make as much money. Maybe they don't even require money." She was concerned that universities working in the interest of industry might not pursue approaches to agrifood problems, such as malnutrition, if such interventions are not profitable.

Gabrielle suggested that universities should prioritize transparency and full disclosure of the complexities of agrifood research, including addressing its controversies and debates:

> I think the land-grant and public institution in my mind would [say], "Yes, we're doing [controversial research]. Let's do it in a transparent way and actually acknowledge the complexity of this topic." Rather than "African women are starving in Uganda and this [GM food] is the solution and you should get behind it and if you don't, then you don't understand science. And you don't respect our institution," which is more the language we heard and more the reaction, and that, to me, isn't representing the land-grant mission, [it should instead say,] "Let's really dig into the ethics of this kind of research at a place like [this institution]. . . . Let's still bring critical thinking skills and questions about the public good to the forefront of the research that we're doing."

Gabrielle's reference to critical thinking skills and questions about the public good reflects a more ethical and open approach to controversial agrifood research that has consequences for communities beyond campus. The students' coursework and extracurricular experiences prepared them to practice this approach, and they expected their university to do so as well.

Together, the students' critical agrifood literacy practices show informed and nuanced inquiry into the broader implications of their university's research. Their attention to safety concerns regarding the GM banana's potential toxicity; consideration of sociocultural contexts of this study, aspects that could both contribute to the banana's success in Uganda and continue the racist, colonial history of unsuccessful agrifood interventions there; concern regarding the funding source of the study; and emphasis on the importance of looking beyond a single solution to complex agrifood issues all show their critical agrifood literacy practices and food justice orientations that shape their broader concerns about the study's consequences and sustainability.

Subverting Student Activism's Ephemerality and Destabilizing Power

Rivka, Angie, and Gabrielle's critical agrifood literacy practices provide illuminating examples of how students address their university's practices, but the fact that these three are the only students who consented to be interviewed limits the variety of perspectives. That said, this case study opens sites of intervention for those interested in food justice questions because it illustrates pathways for students and faculty to address their own institutions' interventions in food sovereignty and food justice, specifically by asking questions about research design and safety. The students' resistance strategies serve as models for other food justice advocates and are teachable examples of how students harness available means of persuasion. Humanities researchers working in food justice can adapt the students' questions to their own universities' agrifood research practices in order to participate in the reenvisioning that House (2014, 4) calls for us to do as we teach about the flawed food system. Likewise, as universities like the one featured here actively contribute to flaws in the food system, faculty can seek opportunities to support students on their own campuses who engage in questioning the academic agrifood industrial complex, looking for coalition opportunities to support student-led campus initiatives.

One lasting lesson of this case study is the ephemerality of student activism. But by centering the critical agrifood literacy practices of students in our food justice scholarship, we archive how students are leading initiatives for food sovereignty and questioning their university's investment in colonial, exploitative practices. Because universities may not be motivated to archive student activism, especially when such advocacy questions the university's research projects, faculty have an obligation to listen to students, take their perspectives seriously, and find ways to ensure that their food justice work does not disappear when they graduate or leave the institution. And by incorporating students' food justice literacy practices into our courses as rich examples of rhetorical strategies, faculty foster the next generation of university students who can learn from their peers and find ways to question existing power structures.

When I first heard about this study, I was struck by the imbalance of the researchers' narratives defending their study and their response to the students who questioned it. In one way, they defended their study using benevolence and charity narratives of white saviorism by promoting its outcome as saving the lives of Ugandan women and children, but in another way, they insisted that they were responsible only for measuring the bioavailability of Vitamin A in women student's bodies, separating out this one aspect of the larger project to evade questions about the project's overall impact. As a feminist rhetorician, I am prompted to critique the tension between the researcher's narratives' reliance on gender and power differentials and the simultaneous attempts to absolve themselves of responsibility for the larger project's consequences. Universities should be subject to questions about their agricultural research and its intervention in other countries' food systems and be ready to respond to how their research projects serve the common good, with ongoing and in-depth contributions by target populations. Especially at land-grant universities, researchers and administrators should welcome, not avoid, questions about the public good and the three pillars of sustainability since food justice is a public good.

Scholars are currently addressing food justice possibilities for land-grant universities. Claiming that "within the colonizing university also exists a decolonizing education," La Paperson (2017) details optimistic possibilities for land-grant universities because each of them is "an assemblage of machines and not a monolithic institution, its machinery is always being subverted toward decolonizing purposes" (11). Educated at the very institution they critique, the students here attempted to subvert the machinery, and for me, reading about their work created glimmers of hope about how students use critical agrifood literacies to promote justice in noticeable, impactful ways. Rethinking land-grant institutions and their relations of conquest, Sharon Stein (2020) writes that white people must "disinvest from our perceived entitlements, certainties and supremacies and face our own roles in the violence of accumulation," a reckoning that few are willing to undertake (224). Thus, land-grant agricultural researchers must be willing to overtly reject white supremacy in their agrifood research in order to fully disinvest from such projects that have been enabled by private funders and others with profit-driven ambitions that do not coexist with food sovereignty and justice. As more information becomes publicly available about private agrifood funding, questioning funders' priorities and practices should include addressing their impact on the research they prompt universities to conduct (McGoey 2021). Since the neoliberalism of scientific research is moving toward privatizing public goods, plenty of evidence has accrued to show how a radical shift is needed. Rural sociologists call for "a democratized science [that] connects the material and ethical dimensions of university research to the extent that it recognizes that society well-being involves more than meeting material needs" (Glenna, Shortall, and Brandl 2015, 455). But here resides the crux of the problem, as Angie describes it: Universities have no motivation to approach agrifood research if such endeavors are not profitable for private funders within an academic agrifood industrial complex that privileges profit over public good.

Destabilizing the power structures of the academic agrifood industrial complex and addressing the need for transparency in agrifood research so that publics can participate in how such research impacts their communities is an ongoing, interdisciplinary project, with plenty of work to do. Students' practices here enact the very food justice concepts promoted by scholars in a range of fields, including critical literacy, since, as Schell (2012) writes, "critical literacy education on the global food industrial complex can become a means toward creating a more just and equitable food system and ... society" (52). This statement reflects the goals valued by Gabrielle, Rivka, and Angie and the aims they called for their university to endorse. Beyond universities,

Angie recalled other contexts in which these conversations are happening and critical agrifood literacies are enacted. When she attended a recent Agriculture, Food, and Human Values Society conference, she was struck by this succinct remark by a keynote speaker, Ricardo Salvador: "We have an agricultural system that takes plenty and manufactures scarcity." Agreeing with his remark, she suggested that the system does so "by design because it is a tool or it's an agent of colonization, of imperialism. It's very much about white supremacy. It's very much about patriarchal control of land." Angie's comments here further align with Schell's (2012) statement, showing how applying critical agrifood literacies is about asking these core questions about the agrifood logics that position power in capitalist, colonial infrastructures.

Ultimately, these students' food justice efforts prompt further questions and research endeavors for literacy scholars to pursue. For example, conducting longitudinal research with individuals such as Gabrielle, Angie, and Rivka as they transition into postgraduate careers would illuminate the shifting identities of students after graduation. Also, future research might examine how critical literacies from various disciplines could be applied together toward food justice work. Literacy scholarship could benefit from initiating cross-disciplinary collaborations such as those shown here in order to explore how communicative knowledge across the curriculum can inform critical agrifood literacies. Such efforts might be inspired by the participants here, who drew upon multidisciplinary knowledge when communicating about science with the public. Rivka, Gabrielle, and Angie show us how students apply their expertise and work to promote food justice at institutions that matter to them. Since students only temporarily inhabit our campuses, their time to impact institutional change is limited. The literacy practices of the students presented here can serve as an invitation for faculty members and researchers to better attend to their institutions' investments in colonial agrifood research and adapt these students' practices to their own campus contexts, seeking opportunities for multidisciplinary interventions that promote food justice.

REFERENCES

Alkon, Alison Hope, and Julian Agyeman. 2011. "Introduction: The Food Movement as Polyculture." In *Cultivating Food Justice: Race, Class, and Sustainability*, edited by Alison Hope Alkon and Julian Agyeman, 1–20. Boston: MIT Press.

Black, Stephanie. 2001. *Life and Debt.* New Yorker Films.

Brewster, Cori. 2011. "Toward a Critical Agricultural Literacy." In *Reclaiming the Rural: Essays on Literacy, Rhetoric and Pedagogy*, edited by Kim Donehower, Charlotte Hogg, and Eileen Schell, 34–51. Carbondale: Southern Illinois University Press.

Chapman, Peter, dir. 2009. *Bananas: How the United Fruit Company Shaped the World*. New York: Canongate.

Charles, Dan. 2013, March 7. "In A Grain of Golden Rice, A World of Controversy Over GMO Foods." *NPR*. https://www.npr.org/sections/thesalt/2013/03/07/173611461/in-a-grain-of-golden-rice-a-world-of-controversy-over-gmo-foods.

Charmaz, Kathy. 2006. *Constructing Grounded Theory: A Practical Guide through Qualitative Analysis*. Thousand Oaks, CA: Sage.

Clancy, Matthew, Keith Fuglie, and Paul Heisey. 2021, May 20. "US Agricultural R&D in an Era of Falling Public Funding." *USDA*. https://www.ers.usda.gov/amber-waves/2016/november/us-agricultural-r-d-in-an-era-of-falling-public-funding.

Enloe, Cynthia. 2000. *Bananas, Beaches, and Bases: Making Feminist Sense of International Politics*. Berkeley: University of California Press.

Food and Water Watch. 2012. "Public Research, Private Gain." https://web.archive.org/web/20120711204603/http:/documents.foodandwaterwatch.org/doc/PublicResearchPrivateGain.pdf.

Frank, Dana. 2016. *Bananeras: Women Transforming the Banana Unions of Latin America*, 2nd Ed. Chicago: Haymarket Books.

Frundt, Henry. *Fair Bananas!: Farmers, Workers, and Consumers Strive to Change an Industry*. Tucson: University of Arizona Press, 2009.

Gates, Bill. 2012. "Building Better Bananas." *Gates Notes*. https://www.gatesnotes.com/development/building-better-bananas.

Gertten, Fredrik, dir. 2009. *Bananas!**. novemberfilm/Oscilloscope Laboratories. DVD.

Glaser, Jason, and Diego Lopez, dirs. 2018. *Banana Land: Blood, Bullets, and Poison, 2014*. YouTube.

Glenna, Leland, Sally Shortall, and Barbara Brandl. 2015. "Neoliberalism, the University, Public Goods, and Agricultural Innovation." *Sociologia Ruralis* 55: 438–59. https://doi.org/10.1111/soru.12074.

House, Veronica. 2014. "Re-Framing the Argument: Critical Service-Learning and Community-Centered Food Literacy." *Community Literacy Journal* 8, no. 2: 1–16. https://DOI.org/10.1353/clj.2014.0008.

Huffman, Wallace, and Richard Just. 1999. "Agricultural Research: Benefits and Beneficiaries of Alternative Funding Mechanisms." *Review of Agricultural Economics* 21: 2–18.

Kirsch, Gesa, and Peter Mortensen. 1996. "Introduction: Reflections on Methodology in Literacy Studies." In *Ethics and Representation in Qualitative Studies of Literacy*, edited by Peter Mortensen and Gesa Kirsch, xix–xxxiv. Urbana, IL: National Council of Teachers of English.

Koeppel, Dan. 2008. *Banana: The Fate of the Fruit That Changed the World*. New York: Plume.

La Paperson. 2017. *A Third University Is Possible*. Minneapolis: University of Minnesota Press.

LaDuke, Winona. 2007. "Ricekeepers: A Struggle to Protect Biodiversity and a Native American Way of Life." *Orio*. https://orionmagazine.org/article/ricekeepers.

Lee, Robert, and Tristan Ahtone. n.d. "Land-Grab Universities." *High Country News*. Accessed April 1, 2020. https://www.hcn.org/issues/52.4/indigenous-affairs-education-land-grab-universities.

Lee, Yoo-Hwan, and Gregory Graff. 2017. "The Production and Dissemination of Agricultural Knowledge at U.S. Research Universities: The Role and Mission of Land-Grant Universities." *Journal or Rural Development/Nongchon-Gyeongje* 40: 63–103.

McGoey, Linsey. 2021, May 25. "Why Billionaires Like Bill Gates Can't Fix the Problems They Helped Create." *New York Times*. https://www.nytimes.com/2021/05/25/opinion/bill-melinda-gates-foundation.html.

Monaghan, Peter. 2004. "Genetically Altered Papayas Pit Scientists Against Activists in Hawaii and Thailand." *The Chronicle of Higher Education*. https://www.chronicle.com/article/genetically-altered-papayas-pit-scientists-against-activists-in-hawaii-and-thailand.

Navdanya. n.d. "GMO Banana Petition." Accessed December 8, 2019. https://www.navdanya.org/site/campaigns/366-gmo-banana-petition.

Philanthropy News Digest. 2014. "Gates Foundation Awards $13.8 Million to Boost Banana Production." https://philanthropynewsdigest.org/news/gates-foundation-awards-13.8-million-to-boost-banana-production.

Philpott, Tom. 2012. "How Your College Is Selling Out to Big Ag. *Mother Jones*. https://www.motherjones.com/food/2012/05/how-agribusiness-dominates-public-ag-research.

Rìos, Gabriela Raquel. 2015. "Cultivating Land-Based Literacies and Rhetorics." *Literacy in Composition Studies* 3, no. 1: 60–70. https://licsjournal.org/index.php/LiCS/article/view/827.

Schell, Eileen E. 2012. "Think Global, Eat Local: Teaching Alternative Agrarian Literacy in a Globalized Age." In *Teaching Writing in Globalization: Remapping Disciplinary Work*, edited by Darin Payne and Daphne Desser, 39–56. Lanham, MD: Lexington Books.

Schooler, Robert. 2016. "The GMO Debate: One Student's Experience of Pro-GMO Propaganda at Cornell University." https://www.independentsciencenews.org/health/the-gmo-debate-one-students-experience-of-pro-gmo-propaganda-at-cornell-university.

Smith-Sitton, Lara. 2019. "Pathways to Partnerships: Building Sustainable Relationships Through University-Supported Internships." *Community Literacy Journal* 14, no. 1: 73–82. doi:10.1353/clj.2019.0029.

Stein, Sharon. 2020. "A Colonial History of the Higher Education Present: Rethinking Land-Grant Institutions through Processes of Accumulation and Relations of Conquest. *Critical Studies in Education* 61: 212–28. doi: 10.1080/17508487.2017.1409646.

Striffler, Steve, and Mark Moberg, eds. 2003. *Banana Wars: Power, Production, and History in the Americas*. Durham, NC: Duke University Press.

USDA Economic Research Service. 2019. "Agricultural Research Funding in the Public and Private Sectors." Last updated August 24, 2021. https://www.ers.usda

.gov/data-products/agricultural-and-food-research-and-development-expenditures-in-the-united-states.

Vidal, John, and Claire Provost. 2011, June 8. "US Universities in Africa 'Land Grab.'" *The Guardian.* https://www.theguardian.com/world/2011/jun/08/us-universities-africa-land-grab.

Winslow, Dianna. 2012. "Food for Thought: Sustainability, Community-Engaged Teaching and Research, and Critical Food Literacy." PhD dissertation, Syracuse University.

NOTES

1. See, for example, Tom Philpott (2012). The Food and Water Watch (2012) research on which Philpott relies is available through the Internet Archive. The USDA Economic Research Service's (2019) report on Agricultural Research Funding in the Public and Private Sectors also provides more information.

2. According to Bill Gates, a funder of this research, Ugandans are the intended recipients of this banana due to the popularity of bananas in their diets. But he describes their bananas as flawed. In his blog post announcing the project, he writes, "Unfortunately, the banana varieties grown in Uganda are low in essential micronutrients, particularly Vitamin A and Iron" (Gates 2012). He describes how researchers will develop a banana that will increase these levels and eventually distribute more nutritious banana varieties to Ugandan farmers. Gates's foundation granted $13.8 million to the International Institute of Tropical Agriculture in Nigeria in order to develop and distribute "higher-yielding disease-resistant hybrid banana varieties in Tanzania and Uganda" (Philanthropy News Digest 2014), a project justified by the notion that banana production only achieves 9 percent of its potential in these countries and that a higher yield variety of banana is needed, one that is more resistant to pests and diseases. Not only a food staple, bananas are described as an "essential economic product" in the funding announcement. Thus, increasing yield would also purportedly increase sales for the farmers who would grow these bananas. The appropriateness of such a banana for Uganda's agrifood context is questioned by the students in this study, as the data analysis shows.

3. LaDuke chronicles the history of the wild rice interventions starting in the late 1800s when a researcher's "perception of the Ojibwe wild rice harvest as a bastion of primitiveness would become the prevailing opinion at the University of Minnesota throughout the twentieth century . . . a sort of battle cry for industrializing agriculture" (2007). Pointing out the conceptual impossibility of patenting a wild food, LaDuke (2007) details the many ways in which the university has attempted to co-opt wild rice. Regarding quinoa, LaDuke (2007) describes how farmers in the Andean region of Bolivia and Ecuador were shocked by this patent, as they had been "cultivating and stewarding the grain for thousands of years." The patent secured the university's power, as it gave the university exclusive control over a traditional Bolivian quinoa variety as well as the hybrids developed from the breeding of forty-three

other traditional varieties. The researchers dropped the patent years later, thanks to efforts by the Bolivian National Quinoa Producers Association and other international groups.

4. Similar contexts of race, power, and agrifood intervention are featured in the documentary film *Life and Debt* (Black 2001), including examples such as how the Jamaican dairy industry is destroyed by the United States (enabled by the World Bank and International Monetary Fund) importing powdered milk.

5. While beyond the confines of my study, as a politicized food embedded in complex agrifood contexts, the banana symbolizes for many an icon of food politics that is enmeshed in multiple oppressive systems, including systemic gender oppression (Chapman 2009; Enloe 2000; Frank 2016; Frundt 2009; Gertten 2009; Koeppel 2008; Striffler and Moberg 2003).

6. I know of a few other cases where university agrifood research has drawn similar attention. According to Monaghan (2004), a transgenic papaya developed by scientists at Cornell University and the University of Hawaii at Hilo prompted concerned citizens and farmers to protest, claiming that the GMO papaya had contaminated organic papaya in Hawaii, potentially ruining the organic papaya industry. Also, Cornell's efforts to patent the virus-resistant papaya plants caused controversy in Thailand, where they were developed and grown even though GMO plants are forbidden by law. Cornell student Robert Schooler (2016) describes Cornell's pro-GMO stance, claiming that "Cornell, as an institution, appears to be complicit in a shocking amount of ecologically destructive, academically unethical, and scientifically deceitful behavior. Perhaps the most potent example is Cornell's deep ties to industrial GMO agriculture, and the affiliated corporations such as Monsanto." Disappointed by the pro-GMO dominance of perspectives in a class he took on the "GMO Debate," Schooler (2016) details an independent course he designed to provide a wider range of perspectives than those endorsed by Cornell.

7. See Charles (2013).

Chapter 11

From Food Security to Food Justice to Civic Engagement

Building an Interdisciplinary Critical Pedagogy

Deborah Adelman and Shamili Ajgaonkar

WHY STUDY FOOD?

Food connects all people in an intricate web to each other and to the larger world, starting with the intimacy of family and community, yet also extending broadly to encompass social, political, economic, cultural, and environmental forces. From the perspective of critical pedagogy, this offers a unique opportunity to engage students. All students eat, and by and large, participate in the industrial food system that prevails in the United States. Thus, the academic study of where and how we obtain our food requires students to acknowledge their individual roles within a system that is characterized by exploitation of human labor, cruelty to animals, environmental degradation, land loss, and displacement and contributes to disease and to climate change. This understanding that an individual student's life is constructed by and within broad social structures is an important goal of critical pedagogy. Inviting students to both imagine and take action to construct a more democratic and equitable future is another important goal of critical pedagogy. As educational theorist Henry Giroux writes:

> Critical pedagogy, unlike dominant modes of teaching, insists that one of the fundamental tasks of educators is to make sure that the future points the way to a more socially just world, a world in which the discourses of critique and possibility in conjunction with the values of reason, freedom, and equality function

to alter, as part of a broader democratic project, the grounds upon which life is lived. (Giroux 2010, 717)

We have been working to develop an interdisciplinary critical food pedagogy that integrates the perspectives of the sciences and the humanities on our own campus, a public two-year college in the western suburbs of Chicago, for more than twenty years. This pedagogy incorporates active learning, including civic engagement and on-campus food production, inviting students to work with others on specific actions and projects to envision and implement an alternative to the current food system. We would like to offer our experience as a case in point to illustrate how the study of food offers great potential to engage students meaningfully in the academic goals of an undergraduate education as well as involve them in working for change in their own food choices, on their own campus and in their communities. By helping students realize the role they play in perpetuating the current neoliberal industrial food system, as well as the potential role they have in transforming it, a comprehensive (both academic and experiential) food pedagogy fits within the broader framework of critical pedagogy. We argue that a critical food pedagogy should become an established part of the undergraduate general education curriculum due to its inherent interdisciplinarity and unique transformative possibilities for twenty-first century students who face a world with urgent multiple crises that must find resolution.

We find resonance with our work in Classen and Sytsma who argue that colleges and universities have a responsibility to offer all students an education both in food literacy and food systems pedagogy, regardless of whether their majors explicitly involve them in learning about food or engaging in food production. Food literacy encompasses functional knowledge and basic skills regarding food. Food systems pedagogy involves critical knowledge, which allows learners to understand their relationship to the broader food system. Attempting to weave the "practical with the political," the "pedestrian with the profound," they define *critical food* literacy as

> a set of skills, knowledge, and understandings that 1) equip individuals to plan, manage, prepare and eat food that is healthy, culturally appropriate, and sustainable, while 2) enabling them to understand the broader sociopolitical and ecological dynamics of the food system, and 3) empowering them to incite socioecological change within the food system. (Classen and Sytsma 2020, 10)

Furthermore, they assert, that institutions of higher education have a crucial role and a responsibility to support the transformation of the industrial food system for three fundamental reasons: (1) as part of the work of preparing active and engaged citizens; (2) because many of their students are not prospering or thriving within that system and are experiencing food insecurity, and (3) pedagogically, food serves as an entry point to ask students to envision and "model many important and progressive practices from prioritizing equity and diversity to pursuing environmental sustainability" (Classen and Sytsma 2020, 15).

It bears mentioning here that even before the COVID-19 pandemic took hold, research had begun to establish the growing amount of food insecurity facing college students in the United States. About 36 percent of university students and 42 percent of community college students reported food insecurity in 2018 (Goldrick-Rab, Richardson, Schneider, Hernandez, and Cady 2018, 3). This problem will only be compounded by the economic and social disruption of the pandemic as it impacts college students, their families, and their communities, particularly on campuses such as ours, where 67 percent of our students attend part-time (C.O.D. Research and Analytics 2021) and must balance multiple responsibilities between school, work, and family. Furthermore, our student demographics indicate a population vulnerable to food insecurity—our college has a higher percentage of Latino and Black students than their overall percentage in DuPage County, and these two groups also have median household incomes that are lower than the County average (IMPACT DuPage n.d.).

Thus, the lessons students take, from studying our current food system, about environmental justice, racial, social and economic injustice, and poor public health outcomes, are not abstractions for them, but part of their lived experience. These lessons will only become more urgent in the upcoming years, and the possibilities for positive change, whether reformist (food security, anti-hunger) or radical (food justice, food sovereignty), will require their attention and their energy.

A FOOD PEDAGOGY FOR IMAGINING AND PRACTICING JUSTICE

We teach general education courses at a college where we often have our students for only one semester, during which we introduce and discuss many topics, integrating the different ways of constructing knowledge in the humanities and natural sciences. We engage in experiential and field learning, and overall, our students work hard to fulfill challenging assignments. We must carefully determine the essential lessons we want students to retain about themselves, the environment, and their future possibilities. Our students are taking their place in the world in a time of multiple crises, most urgently massive ecological decline and accelerating climate change. We want them to leave class knowing that they have an important role to play and actions to take towards constructing their own futures in a world they would like to inhabit.

A major point we emphasize with students is that the type of knowledge a society prioritizes plays a determining role in shaping its life, but knowledge is ever-changing. Even considering the short span of human existence on this planet, we can see that different types of knowledge have been valued at particular times in the arc of the human story. The types of knowledge that were needed for the two major societal transformations, the Agricultural Revolution, some ten thousand years ago, and the Industrial Revolution, less than three hundred years ago, were each distinct and different from each other as well as from that of our hunter-gatherer ancestors. Yet, they both represent a particular type of human domination over resources—land, water, minerals, fuel, animals, and so on.

At present, it is no longer possible for human societies to sustain themselves through this domination of resources. Here is where we educators must intervene and must remake our educational system. What is needed today is an education that provides students the tools, an integrated view that centers on justice on multiple levels, and, importantly, the enthusiasm to make peace with the planet. This is what Paul Hawken advocates when he says, "Inspiration is not garnered from litanies of what is flawed; it resides in humanity's willingness to restore, redress, reform, recover, reimagine, and reconsider" (Hawken n.d.). We would like to believe that the lessons learned in our classroom and in others will encourage students to become part of a movement that Hawken sees as already underway, a movement that "is not burdened with a syndrome of trying to save the world; it is trying to remake the world" (Hawken n.d.).

Food is the perfect lens through which to do this. Despite the limits of a semester, students can leave with an understanding that through food they can engage in this practice of rebuilding the world. To this end, we distill what we study into six general food justice principles that our students can take with them as a guide for a lifetime of making food consumption choices:

1. Understand and respect ecology.
2. Understand their foodshed and the consequences of their food choices: understand modern production practices that provide the food they eat and the impacts of these practices on carbon, nitrogen, and water cycles, biodiversity, waste generation, and the food workers along the food chain.
3. Embrace the complexity in making food consumption decisions
4. Develop personal guiding principles for food consumption and apply them in making food choices.
5. Learn how to grow food and participate in food production

6. Build relationships in the community and engage in justice practices

DEVELOPING OUR PEDAGOGY

At our college, as probably elsewhere, the General Education Student Learning Outcomes (College of DuPage n.d.a) emphasize the development of critical thinking, which occupies first place on the list of seven outcomes. Other outcomes include the ability to reason scientifically and quantitatively, communicate effectively, possess cultural and historical comprehension, and recognize how social-economic institutions shape society and influence individual behavior. But there is no statement about the purpose of this knowledge, no expressed intent that developing these habits of mind also imparts to students the awareness, skills or the imperative to use what they learn for the common good. As David Orr reminds us, the current state of the world (climate disruption, biodiversity loss, food insecurity, economic, social, and racial inequity, and a global pandemic to name a few) "is not the work of ignorant people" (Orr 1994, 7). He further notes "education is no guarantee of decency, prudence, or wisdom. More of the same kind of education will only compound our problems. This is not an argument for ignorance, but rather a statement that the worth of education must now be measured against the standards of decency and human survival" (Orr 1994, 8). Orr advocates for a pedagogy that explicitly acknowledges the limits of knowledge building and seeks to instill a sense of responsibility to use this knowledge well.

Our approach to teaching attempts to enact what Orr asserts: we—professors and our students—are actively responsible for the knowledge that we construct and the world we co-create. We began our co-teaching journey in 2001, combining an English class (Deborah) with Environmental Biology (Shamili). We came together out of a mutual desire to go beyond the limitations of our individual disciplines, recognizing that each offers a different lens through which to make sense of the world, and both are necessary to find our place within it. We also value and enjoy each other's disciplines and have learned from each other alongside our students. We both look to narrative as an important way of understanding the world. Over the years, we have organized our seminars around different course combinations, in particular rotating offerings within the English Department—selecting from composition, literature, and film studies classes. However, common to all our seminars for over more than twenty years, we emphasize education for action focusing on the following four dimensions.

Critical Literacy

Brazilian educator Paulo Freire challenged the notion of literacy as a mere set of reading and writing skills. For Freire, literacy is the ability to "read the world" by "reading the word," that is, literacy is a crucial way to engage symbolic representation to locate oneself within socio-economic, cultural—and we would emphasize, environmental—structures and systems. Developing a deeper understanding of the world can be a step toward becoming an agent of change. Shor and Pari note:

> Critical literacy thus challenges the status quo in an effort to discover alternative paths for social and self-development. This kind of literacy—words rethinking worlds, self-dissenting in society—connects the political and the personal, the public and the private, the global and the local, the economic and the pedagogical, for reinventing our lives and for promoting justice in place of inequity. (Shor and Pari 1999, 1)

Education for Resilience

David Orr asserts "All education is environmental education" since "(b)y what is included or excluded we teach students that they are part of or apart from the natural world" (Orr 1994, 12). But while understanding ecological principles and the pursuit of sustainability remains relevant, it is no longer sufficient. In a postpandemic world, where change is the only constant, resilience thinking is essential. Resilience refers to the ability of ecological systems to cope with the stresses and disturbances of change. Resilience thinking, rooted in the belief that humans and nature are inextricably connected, and thus form "one socio-ecological system," recognizes that unexpected events and crises caused by environmental change are increasingly common and that humans must increase our knowledge and preparedness about how to confront them while also learning to live sustainably within the Earth's capacity (Stockholm Resilience Centre n.d.).

Education for Responsibility

Knowledge carries with it the responsibility to see that it is well used in the world. As David Orr suggests, students must accept the reality that human knowledge, while vast and impressive, has overtaken our ability to see that it is used safely. Much of our knowledge, in fact, cannot be used for "consistently good purpose" (Orr 1994, 13). For Orr, to know something means to understand how it impacts people and communities now and in the future: knowledge is not an abstraction.

Civic Engagement

Students must not only understand that they have the potential to become change agents, but they should also be engaged in the practice of developing the skills to shape the future that they would like to have. Working to make a difference can be inspiring and hope-inducing. Paul Hawken, encouraging students to join with all who are working to reconstruct the planet points out that studying and understanding scientific data about the condition of our planet can certainly lead people to feel pessimistic about the future. However, getting engaged with and working with activists who are determined to restore the planet and improve the lives of the poor leads students to feel optimistic about a better future (Hawken 2013, 269).

INTEGRATING CROSS-DISCIPLINARY PERSPECTIVES

Central to how we teach is the recognition that education must model the world as it exists, a complex, multidimensional system that is beyond the scope of a singular discipline, and that students need to learn how to integrate the various elements of their general education. Students co-register in both an English and Environmental Biology course, engaging the perspectives of the humanities and natural science to develop a holistic reality that models interconnected phenomena. While students may initially wonder how our disciplines, with two distinct methods of knowledge making, complement each other, we share with them our conviction that both English and Biology engage in the same pursuit: understanding life in all its diversity and interconnectedness. The topic of food and agricultural practices has provided a rich focal point to integrate these seemingly disparate perspectives. Over the course of the semester, the material we engage in our classroom and the way we organize our assignments makes the connection apparent.

When we began teaching our seminar in 2001, we started with an exploration of personal food practices, combining texts with a real-world lab inquiry. Students, analyzing the data they collect about their own food choices, realize that they know very little about where their food comes from and how it has been produced, and even their attempts at research will not necessarily reveal much of what is hidden. In our early years of teaching, we organized the class around topics of food production relevant to Environmental Biology: seed, soil, water, energy, pest control, human labor, and animals. Each unit illuminated the ways in which industrial agriculture uses these valuable resources, on both a national and global level. Thus, students began to understand that their personal food choices have an impact far beyond their own lives.

For example, our unit on pest control introduced students to the impacts of the widespread use of pervasive synthetic chemicals on our crops. The scientific perspective of the Environmental Biology textbook was complemented by the texts we read for Introduction to Literature, which was the English Department class that term—the literary scientific voices of Rachel Carson and Sandra Steingraber, as well as the lyrical voice of Helena Maria Viramontes in her coming-of-age novel about a Chicana farmworker, *Under the Feet of Jesus*. The novel vividly portrays the pesticide poisoning of one of the main characters, something that actually happens routinely and frequently to the farm workers who pick our crops, as students had already learned. While the scientific readings caused our students concern and alarm about the dangers of pesticides, Viramontes' narrative led them to feel empathy, sadness, and anger about injustice. The blending of the scientific and the literary made connections apparent and vivid to students, as evidenced in their responses. In a reflection paper, one student wrote, "Before I took this class I never thought about my food choices affecting so many subjects." Another student wrote, "I was appalled and outraged when I heard about the Nike Company using child labor in Third World countries. Many of us were. But not until reading *Under the Feet of Jesus* did I realize that the very same thing is happening in our beautiful state of California."

In 2003, we were able to secure land on campus to dig up and install our first garden site. We imagined that students, by putting their hands in the soil, would observe what they had studied about the complex living nature of soil in Environmental Biology and the joy of growing food depicted in Wendell Berry's poetry come to life. It would also provide a positive experience in the midst of reading about topics that were often overwhelming and demoralizing. Digging the garden space, cutting through turf grass, going through soil preparation, and reading Pablo Neruda's "Ode to the Earth's Fertility" to take inspiration, planting, and harvesting, all gave students an exciting and uplifting experience (Adelman and Sandiford 2007). Thus, the first years of our work gave a clear indication of the value of a food-centered seminar to engage students in academic work and service learning to give back to the community.

Reflecting on this moment in her service learning paper, a returning student with teenage children showed how she integrated our work in the garden with the textbook, essays, poetry, song, and her own previous personal history:

> The exhausting preparation of the soil was the focus for weeks, giving me an appreciation for the valuable resource it is, "of astonishing beauty, complexity and frailty" (Cunningham, Cunningham, and Saigo 236). I never put the concepts of soil degradation and its impact on agriculture together until I read "Letters from the Dust Bowl," by Caroline Henderson. I was a child when I

lived in that part of the country, but the Woody Guthrie songs and the Wendell Berry poetry brought the memories flooding back to me of the harsh existence of living on barren earth, over-cultivated, overgrazed, and overlooked.

Given that our academic term spanned from March to June in our Midwestern climate, we imagined a small lettuce crop might be the extent of our efforts, squeezed in between the end of winter and the end of the trimester. However, we soon realized that we would be able to do much more than grow a small crop of early season greens. Grant funding allowed us to retain a garden manager throughout the growing season, and our college's connection to a large, multiservice nonprofit community organization provided ready access to a food pantry as an outlet for our harvest. The garden project grew at the same time our classroom curriculum expanded. Students planted, tended, harvested, delivered, and helped with the distribution of hundreds of pounds of fresh produce to community members in need. Our garden manager diversified crops to appeal to a wide variety of clients, including people from Latin America, South Asia, and Eastern Europe, with particular cultural food preferences. One important discovery in that early stage, reading our students' reflections on this work, was that many of them had personal family experiences receiving food assistance from a food pantry. Eventually, this realization would lead to an important pivot in whom we serve, as we recognized that the problem of food security was real and present for many of our own students.

BUILDING A SYSTEM OF FOOD JUSTICE

When we began teaching about food in 2001, there was already increasing awareness of the importance of examining the industrial food system to understand fundamental issues of justice and inequity in U.S. society. The term "food deserts" (now referred to as food apartheid), the recognition that the spatial inequality of housing patterns along race and class lines had direct relationships to food access, had recently gained prominence. Books such as Eric Schlosser's *Fast Food Nation*, which views widespread consumption of fast food as evidence of its role as a common denominator that links Americans from all sectors of society, gained mass popularity. In the ensuing years, interest in the topic has widely expanded, including increased scholarship, food-based curriculum, and activism that includes a diverse, multifaceted movement in pursuit of alternative food systems, which contains a food justice sector highlighting the relationship between food production and social and economic justice, including issues of race, class, gender, and other forms of inequality (Alkon and Guthman 2017, 5).

These developments have bolstered and changed our work with students. We have consistently organized our class to move from the personal to connect to broader social, cultural, and environmental concerns, but have made significant shifts in the content, organization, and structure of our curriculum, which we will subsequently discuss. As our understanding of the power of the content matter became more evident, we reconfigured how we teach. While the integral building blocks of our seminars did not change, we reworked how we utilized these components: classroom study, field trips, lab inquiries, and civic engagement.

Classroom Study

The foundation of our work takes place in the classroom, where students learn content based on reading literary and scientific texts, lectures, discussion, film screenings, and doing research. Integration of the two classes is fundamental, i.e., a unit that studies the consequences of turning tallgrass prairie to farmland includes both Willa Cather's *O'Pioneers* and the scientific study of prairie soil and topsoil degradation and loss. However, we have made two major changes to our classroom that represent our growing understanding of the potential of food studies as liberatory studies—in the words of educational theorist Henry Giroux, food studies as part of an overall vision of education as a "force for strengthening the imagination and expanding democratic public life" (Giroux 2010, 715).

The first change concerns our organizing concept, which, for many years, has been food security. Students presented their initial ideas about food security, which generally focused on access to adequate food at all times, aligning themselves with a 1983 definition of the Food and Agriculture Organization of the United Nations (Clay 2002). As we worked our way through the topics or resources used in relation to agriculture, students' definitions of food security grew more complex, with new understandings that it is deeply related to how we use resources and treat participants across the food system. The litany of bad news would build serious environmental problems, worker exploitation, factory-raised animals, lack of access to land and other resources, the health problems for the Earth's "stuffed and starved," the different populations of malnourished people, those who either face an abundance of cheap, disease-inducing industrially processed food or who lack access to food overall (Patel 2012). The last third of the term was devoted to exploring solutions

It became increasingly apparent to us, from our own reading, research, and student responses to class material, that a focus on food security did not adequately identify what is most clearly lacking in the global industrial food industry—not more food, but rather addressing the multiple injustices upon which it is built. Thus, in 2018, we changed our organizing concept from food security to food justice. By the time we made this shift in our syllabus, there was ample documentation across the globe of farmers, workers, and consumers mobilizing to address the issues of the food system, and we were able to organize the seminar around both problems and solutions, that is, around specific actions for food justice rather than organizing it solely around a list of topics that could easily lead students to hopelessness and resignation. So, for example, in recent years, in a seminar where the English class that Deborah teaches is an introduction to Film Art, we show Julie Dash's *Daughters of the Dust*, a film about a Gullah family leaving the Carolina sea islands on the eve of the Great Migration (and which features a sumptuous banquet that highlights Gullah foodways) while we look at historic patterns of land ownership and loss for African Americans, and at the same time introduce students to the work of Leah Penniman and Soulfire farms, an afro-indigenous community farm in upstate New York whose mission aligns it with movements for seed saving, ending food apartheid, and for food sovereignty and reparations.

The second change grew from the first. By introducing the topic of food justice as an organizing principle, we realized that we needed to structure the class around systems thinking—the food system that we do have, and the food system that we could have. Thus, after an initial unit exploring students' personal environmental worldviews, we now immediately introduce the topic of the industrial food system, broadly identifying its key features and the consequences they bring, which we will continue to explore in specific detail. At the same time, we tell students that we will be thinking aspirationally all semester, so that while we examine the industrial food system, we will simultaneously conceptualize our own alternative food justice system, using ecological principles and key points of environmental and social justice as a foundation, including ample evidence of actual food justice projects in the US and around the world. This allows us to consider the alternative food movement's various dimensions, from the "reformist" food security/anti-hunger organizations that deliver food assistance programs and encourage the expansion of corporate retail into underserved communities, to the "progressive" community food security/food justice practitioners who seek to make healthier food available in underserved communities by providing vegetables, garden spaces and knowledge, to the "radical" food sovereignty movement with its goal of redistribution of wealth and resources (Holt-Gimenez and Wang 2011, 97).

We use concept maps as a learning tool, adding an interactive visual element throughout the term. Students map our current food system, side by side with the alternative one we might envision and build. We introduce this assignment at the beginning of the course, and it remains a subject of discussion throughout the term. Reflecting on the major lessons learned from the mapping assignment, one student wrote:

Changing to a sustainable food system, would have major effects on society, the economy and ecology in a lot more ways than it seems. . . . I realized just how much impact this would have on people's lives, it would impact every person in some way. Pretty much everyone would have to work together or would likely have to make some sort of sacrifice to switch to a sustainable food system.

Another student noted:

We all play a role in determining the state of our system, as modern individual consumers. Though this role may seem minuscule in the grand view of the system, our purchasing power, our cultures, our understanding, our willingness to change, and so much more influence the higher-level decisions which shape the ways we acquire, sell, and purchase food and determine how this system will interact with the natural world. Money is a massive driving force within the modern industrial food system, and its significance in our society's decision-making in regards to food system choices cannot be overstated. A lot of wanted change must come from changing our views on what is and is not "profit."

We challenge students to think deeply about the lessons they have taken from class materials. Students realize that the scope of change needed to create a food system based on principles of food justice is vast, but they are able to imagine that even our basic economy is not immutable:

The solutions required for a sustainable food system . . . include the idea of a circular economy to reduce waste and increase resource availability. On a related note, I included the concept bubble {in the map} about a linear economy as a problem in the current system. I suggested a collective economy as a way to organize around the needs of many. I included environmental economics as a way to consider long-term sustainability. I included the green new deal, including its jobs guarantee and unionization as a way to focus on how work relates to the economy.

Field Trips

Experiential learning is a valuable tool for engaging in the food system through direct experience. Although our students live in a world with 24/7 access to food, they have little to no concept of how the food gets to them or the ecological and cultural history of the richest soil in the world that underlies the grocery stores they shop at or the restaurants they work in. We are fortunate to be able to expose them to both the natural history of the Midwest by visiting a restored prairie on our campus and the human history of this landscape by touring a living history farm that is part of the local forest preserve district. The exploration of the campus prairie provides insights into soil formation, the adaptive traits of native flora and fauna, the role of pollinators, and the potential for the prairie to serve as a model for agriculture. A visit to Kline Creek Farm with its sheep, cows, horses, and crop fields introduces students to what this corner of Illinois looked like in the early 1900s on the cusp of the transition in food production from feeding people to growing commodity crops. Students learn about the evolution of farming and the decisions farmers must make between caring for the land and growing cheap food. After visiting Kline Creek and talking to the farmer who runs their operation as his "day job," in order to afford his own family's farm, a student wrote:

> The way we were talking about modern farmers in class made me start not to like them. They were almost depicted like the antichrist because of the damage they create. After I met the second guide (the farmer) I threw all that thinking out the window. That's when I became convinced that something else was the cause of the problem here, not just modern agriculture. I just kept thinking about the farmer playing with his daughter. Why would he want to leave his daughter all the problems we talked about in class? I'm sure he knows of them, but he needs to feed her and put her through school, too.

Lab Inquiries

The environmental biology class is a lab science class and the necessity to include assignments that require data collection and analysis provides an opportunity for students to conduct a meaningful investigation into their relationship with food. One lab engages students in understanding their "foodshed" and the consequences of their food choices on biodiversity, energy flow, and nutrient cycles. Another lab asks students to explore the grocery store they shop in so that they can understand how the marketplace shapes how they eat and to consider the role of food labels as a way to help consumers make more informed decisions about what they purchase.

Civic Engagement

Recognizing that students need a mechanism to apply what they are learning to make a difference, we incorporated service learning into our class. There were opportunities to volunteer at a local food pantry, and to work at the garden we started on campus, which supplied produce to the pantry. We found the service-learning model limited in scope because direct service is far from the only path to social change. Discovering the Pathways of Public Service and Civic Engagement (Stanford University n.d.) has allowed us to reshape this crucial element of our work and provide multiple avenues for students to work towards the public good. The framework offers six pathways along which individuals can take action to contribute to the common good:

1. Community Engaged Learning and Research: Connecting coursework and academic research to community-identified concerns to enrich knowledge and inform action on social issues.
2. Community Organizing and Activism: Involving, educating, and mobilizing individual or collective action to influence or persuade others.
3. Direct Service: Working to address the immediate needs of individuals or a community, often involving contact with the people or places being served.
4. Philanthropy: Donating or using private funds or charitable contributions from individuals or institutions to contribute to the public good.
5. Policy and Governance: Participating in political processes, policymaking, and public governance.
6. Social Entrepreneurship and Corporate Social Responsibility: Using ethical business or private sector approaches to create or expand market-oriented responses to social or environmental problems. (Stanford University n.d.)

While the Civic Engagement assignment provides opportunities for students to take individual action, at the same time we stress to students that addressing social and environmental problems requires collective action by an educated and engaged citizenry. One student connected the experience of her own family garden to her work in the community garden on campus:

> Farming is in my family line, and I continue it now on a smaller scale. I take pride in my garden when it comes time to harvest, and I think more people should get to know this feeling at least once in their lives. . . . I also see gardening as a social benefit, as well as environmental. . . . I know the satisfaction of turning a seed into something much bigger. I know gardening is tedious at times and some people lack the resources (or physical ability), to make this happen, that's why it's imperative that community gardens continue to thrive. I also believe that our generation and the children beneath us should share the same passion for bettering the environment around us, by growing produce instead of buying processed groceries from big-name industries.

Environmental historian Neil Prendergast argues that the key to remaking the food system lies first in mobilizing public imagination to acknowledge that all parts of the food chain are connected, from farms to supermarkets to those who work in it yet often remain unseen. We have found that including concept mapping in our seminars in recent years has greatly helped us bring students to this awareness, as mapping allows students to visually represent the content of what they are studying and to establish or represent relationships between the ideas in that content. As one student wrote about our collaborative efforts to map out an alternative food system based upon principles of sustainability and justice:

> This map paints food sustainability as a very complex issue. Some of the problems might bear easy solutions but there are many subtle interconnections that complicate the issue. Problems are connected in networks with other problems and some solutions rely on the success of other solutions.

For Prendergast, with public awareness, alliances can be built between citizens rather than between specific groups whose identity is shaped by an economic role such as "supermarket consumer," or "crop manager." Taking direction from critical geographers, he argues "Citizens should place their hope and energy in the public . . . to combat inequality, there has to be a healthy, vibrant public" (Prendergast 2017, 272). To that end, one student noted the role of education, specifically our seminar, in transforming public awareness:

> The effectiveness of education in its ability to shape sweeping changes in behavior is crucial. Most of the solutions require knowledge that we've had for a long time. When this knowledge gets shared through documentaries, essays, features, texts, and lectures, it lets people know that these things are beneficial, tested, and profitable in an ecological sense.

Thus, our work in civic engagement, which focuses on developing student awareness of their role as citizens, is of equal importance to classroom study.

TAKING ACTION: THE FOOD SECURITY INITIATIVE

As evidence about the reality of hunger among college students was emerging in the national conversation, in the 2015–2016 academic year members of Phi Theta Kappa (the National Honors Society for Community Colleges) embarked on a research project to investigate the need and feasibility of a food pantry on campus. Their data was in alignment with the national data that more than a third of our students either were food insecure or knew someone who was. This led to the establishment of the Fuel Pantry on our campus in Fall 2018, and growing recognition on our campus that the basic need for food was not met for a good number of our students.

Building on this initial research, we integrated our learning community class with a Speech class to investigate the nature of food pantries and whether they adequately serve student needs. In the culminating public presentation of their project, the students concluded that pantries generally lack fresh produce, which our students deemed necessary as part of a healthy diet. Unfortunately, at that time the campus garden had disappeared for a few years, a victim of campus politics and a new facilities master plan that put buildings on top of the garden plot. However, knowing the previous history of years of bountiful campus harvests, a small group of students were inspired to apply to a local community organization for raised garden beds, simultaneously securing permission for the space on campus to install them. The garden, under a different college administration, returned, now linked to the campus pantry, and the Food Security Initiative emerged (FSI)—a campus-wide project made up of a team of students, faculty, and staff working to provide food directly to students and other members of the college community. This was a significant pivot for the garden, a recognition that our first iteration of the garden had overlooked the possibility that significant numbers of our own students (and staff, including adjunct faculty) were food insecure.

The FSI mission statement is multifaceted: "Build food security in our community. We cultivate and provide nutritious food, educate through academic study, and direct participation, and engage the local population to access and meet its nutritional needs" (College of DuPage n.d.b). Eventually, we view our work as building a food system on campus, where we assess our own needs and provide them to the extent possible locally. However, we face considerable obstacles, including the fact that our campus, like so many, awards corporate contracts to provide basic food services and thus far has been uninclined to consider changing that.

The pantry operates out of a small room near our bookstore. It is open to any student, faculty, or staff member with no requirement to demonstrate financial need. Clients can receive 15 points of food per week for nonperishables. We offer fresh produce, grown on campus, for no points. Since March 2020, when the campus became restricted due to COVID-19, we have moved to a curbside distribution model with clients placing their orders online. This shift in distribution practices has changed the demographics of our clientele, which now includes families, and members of our custodial staff. Clearly the need for food assistance is significant among the various members of the college community, although we do not yet have research or data that would help us understand its full scope.

Over the past four years we have made a deliberate effort to reach out and include other disciplines and departments within the college. Some examples of the outcomes of this effort to involve people from across the campus include:

- We served as the client to a design-build class in architecture, which built a garden pavilion as a gathering space. Post-COVID-19 in Summer 2022 they will be building a garden shed.
- A graphic design class designed the logo for the Food Security Initiative.
- Culinary faculty and students have been helping us extend the summer and fall harvest by converting surplus tomatoes, peppers into marinara sauce, beans into chili, and donated heritage apples into pie filling.
- Sodexo (the campus food service) has worked with our team to run a salad and soup bar made with our campus garden produce as an awareness generator and fundraiser for the project. They also donate unsold sandwich bread and bagels (some of which the Culinary program makes into bagel chips and croutons) to the Fuel Pantry.
- Horticulture donates what their students grow and have shared their high tunnel for us to plant an early spring crop.
- We have collected wild rose hips from the restored prairie on campus to dry and package as a tea, bringing wild foods into the mix.
- We may be a demonstration site for solar-powered portable refrigerators designed by HVAC faculty and students to keep produce from spoiling in the warm weather.

The Food Security Initiative, as the hands-on component of our food pedagogy and a site of civic engagement for service learning students and student interns, has served to promote and develop connections between the campus silos—between disciplines, between academic and technical/vocational programs, between Academic and Student Affairs (the only project on campus that is housed in both of those divisions) and between academic programs and basic student services, in this case, the food that is available on campus for students as the sustenance they need for success. In past years of our project, we had to overcome the opposition of a surprisingly hostile administration, and we did prevail, due to public support from much of the college and wider community. General awareness of the issues of food security among college students and the growing movement of campus gardens across the country have helped to create a new environment in which our project is now able to thrive. We have been both surprised and gratified by the growing interest extended to us from across campus. For us, this is yet another example of how food joins us all, and has the potential, in sometimes unexpected ways, to make connections, build bridges and unite diverse constituencies, as has been the case on our campus. We want students to know that the work of remaking the world is not optional. It must be done. And we want them to embrace being part of that work.

REFERENCES

Adelman, Deborah, and Shamili Sandiford. 2007. "Reflections from the Garden: Developing a Critical Literacy of Food Practices." *English Scholarship*, Paper 36. http://dc.cod.edu/englishpub/36.

Alkon, Alison Hope, and Julie Guthman. 2017. "Introduction." In *The New Food Activism: Opposition, Cooperation, and Collective Action*, edited by Alison Hope Alkon and Julie Guthman, 5–27. Oakland: University of California.

Classen, Michael, and Emily Sytsma. 2020, July. "Student Food Literacy, Critical Food Systems Pedagogy, and the Responsibility of Postsecondary Institutions." *Canadian Food Studies* 7, no. 1: 8–19.

Clay, Edward. 2002. "Food Security: Concepts and Measurements." *Trade Reforms and Food Security: Conceptualizing the Linkages*, edited by Food and Agriculture Organization of the United Nations, chapter 2. Rome: FAO. http://www.fao.org/3/y4671e/y4671e06.htm#bm06.

College of DuPage. n.d.a. "General Education Student Learning Outcomes." Accessed March 1, 2021. https://cod.edu/academics/programs/general-education-outcomes.aspx.

———. n.d.b. "Food Security Initiative Mission Statement." Accessed March 1, 2021. https://www.cod.edu/student_life/cod_cares/pantry/index.aspx.

Giroux, Henry A. 2010. "Rethinking Education as the Promise of Freedom: Paulo Freire and the Promise of Critical Pedagogy." *Policy Futures in Education* 8, no. 6: 715–21.

Goldrick-Rab, Sarah, Jed Richardson, Joel Schneider, Anthony Hernandez, and Claire Cady. 2018. *Still Hungry and Homeless in College*. Wisconsin Hope Center. https://hope4college.com.

Hawken, Paul. 2013. "You Are Brilliant, and the Earth Is Hiring." *The NAMTA Journal* 38, no. 1 (Winter): 269–71.

———. n.d. "To Remake the World." *Orion Magazine*. Accessed March 16, 2021. https://orionmagazine.org/article/hawken-article-may-june-text-in-place.

Holt-Gimenez, Eric, and Yi Wang. 2011. "Reform or Transformation? The Pivotal Role of Food Justice in the U.S. Food Movement." *Race/Ethnicity: Multidisciplinary Global Contexts* 5, no. 1 (Autumn): 83–102.

IMPACT DuPage. n.d. "2021 Demographics." Accessed October 29, 2021. https://www.impactdupage.org/index.php?module=DemographicData&controller=index&action=index.

Orr, David W. 1994. "What Is Education For?" *Earth in Mind: On Education, Environment, and the Human Prospect*, 7–15. Washington, DC: Island Press.

Patel, Raj. 2012. *Stuffed and Starved: The Hidden Battle for the World Food System*. Brooklyn, NY: Melville House.

Prendergast, Neil. 2017. "Food and the Environment." *The Routledge History of American Foodways*, edited by Michael D. Wise and Jennifer Jensen Wallach, 261–75. New York: Routledge.

Shor, Ira, and Caroline Pari. 1999. *Critical Literacy in Action*. Portsmouth: Boynton/Cook Publishers.

Stockholm Resilience Centre. n.d. "What Is Resilience?" Accessed March 5, 2021. https://www.stockholmresilience.org/research/research-news/2015-02-19-what-is-resilience.html.

Stanford University. "Pathways of Public Service and Civic Engagement." Accessed March 3, 2021. https://haas.stanford.edu/about/our-approach/pathways-public-service-and-civic-engagement.

APPENDIX

Sample Assignment Sequence #1 for "Seed, Soil, and the Soul: Food Justice for a Sustainable Future"

This assignment is one we have developed over the last two years in our interdisciplinary seminar "Seed, Soil, and the Soul" using concept maps—mapping is a great way to have students visualize the relationships that exist in the current food system. This assignment also asks them to imagine and envision an alternative food system that has healthier and more ethical connections.

Mapping a Sustainable Food System

As a semester-long class project, we will envision and map out a sustainable food system that offers solutions for feeding ourselves in a way that respects ecology, values diversity, builds resilient communities and is based on social justice. We will build our map on the basis of class materials that include film, labs, research, field experiences, and readings. Over the course of the semester you will submit the following assignments (some to be completed independently while others will be assigned as group work):

- ASSIGNMENT A—Mapping *Food Inc.*
- ASSIGNMENT B—Mapping your personal foodshed (from Lab 3)
- ASSIGNMENT C—Concept maps of two selected documentaries
- ASSIGNMENT D—Mapping a sustainable food system and class debrief

Assignment A—Mapping Food Inc.

This assignment asks you to develop a concept map of the industrial food system of the contemporary United States as depicted in the documentary *Food Inc.* This map will serve as the foundation for our subsequent mapping assignments. Throughout the semester, we will examine our industrial food system, identifying the problems it poses and the consequences it leaves us, all with an eye toward identifying points of intervention. These interventions will ultimately help us map an aspirational sustainable food system for our future.

A concept map is a visual representation of information or a set of ideas. It can take various forms such as charts, graphic organizers, tables, flow charts, Venn diagrams, timelines, and so on. These visual representations help you organize, connect and synthesize information.

To complete this assignment:

1. View the documentary *Food Inc*.
2. Take detailed notes as you watch the film.
3. Use your notes to develop a concept map of the film. This concept map will show the industrial food system in the United States today as depicted in the film. To make this map, your organizing idea, or central theme is "the industrial food system." This central theme is your concept "bubble," the overarching organizing point of your map. From this bubble, branch out in various directions to map out the ideas of the film, which presents our food system and the interconnections between the elements of this system. Your map should show these connections. The film covers a broad number of issues—animal farming, labor conditions in food production plants, health consequences of the industrial diet and so on. The film is organized into nine chapters, but this is not necessarily the organization of your map. There is no one correct way to make this map, so approach this assignment with an open mind knowing you not constrained to one way of viewing the system and organizing the information presented in the film. Keep in mind, however, that we are mapping out this system based on the ideas presented in the film. There will be time to revise, augment, challenge, and so on. these ideas as we continue through the mapping project and examine many other sources with many more ideas.
4. After completing your concept map:
   - Identify the three most important ideas you take from the film
   - Identify two big questions this film raises for you.

Assignment B—Mapping Your Personal Foodshed

This assignment is a continuation of our mapping activities working towards the mapping of an aspirational sustainable food system for the future. For this part of the mapping project, you will be turning your focus from the overall societal industrial food system towards your own participation in it, by examining your personal foodshed. This will be based on the data from Lab 3 (Exercise 12 in the Environmental Biology Lab Manual) that explores what you eat, how it is grown, packaged, processed, transported, and so on.

You will examine your own (and your family's) practices as eaters and consumers. The photos above come from a book that explores families around the world, highlighting what unites and what distinguishes people living in distinct places, cultures and economic circumstances. Each photo represents the family's food consumption over the course of a week. Look carefully at these photos and you will notice differences not only in what is consumed, but how it is processed and packaged. Think about what your own family's photo might look like as you approach this part of the mapping assignment. Feel free to include any visual representation (images, clips) with your map!

To complete this assignment of developing a mind map of the ideas that emerge from your lab activity:

1. Complete Lab 3 (Exercise 12 in the Environmental Biology Lab Manual)—Exploring Your Foodshed.
2. Prepare detailed notes from the lab data and analysis and use your notes to develop a concept map of your foodshed.
3. Decide on the central organizing theme. As in previous maps, your identification of the central theme of your lab will be your concept bubble. From this bubble branch out in various directions to map out your foodshed and show the various connections.
4. After completing your concept map:
   - Identify the three most takeaways from this map of your foodshed.
   - Identify two big questions this personal foodshed map raises for you.

Assignment C—Concept Maps of Selected Documentaries

You will work in four groups to complete this work, and each group will be responsible for mapping two from this list of eight documentaries.

This assignment is a continuation of our mapping of *Food Inc.* and our eventual mapping of an aspirational sustainable food system for the future. Each one of the following eight documentaries discusses problems posed by our current industrial food system. They also contain ideas and examples of how these problems can be addressed, as do many environmentally focused documentaries. Keep in mind that *points of intervention* discussed in these films will be up for consideration in our subsequent project to develop a sustainable food system.

For each film, your group will develop a concept map (mind map) of the ideas presented.

To complete this assignment:

1. View the documentary.
2. Take detailed notes as you watch the film.

3. Each film has a subject it explores, and within this subject, there is a central idea (theme). Discuss and agree on the film's central idea. This will be more clearly identifiable for some films, so this will take some collaboration.
4. Use your notes to develop a concept map of the film. Your identification of the idea (theme) of the film will be your concept bubble. From this bubble, branch out in various directions to map out the ideas of the film and show their connections.
5. After completing your concept map:
    - Identify the three most important ideas you take from the film
    - Identify two big questions this film raises for you.
    - Discuss how this film can be helpful towards reshaping our current food system into a sustainable food system.

Films

Each group will be responsible for one of the following four for the first part of the assignment:

- Growing Cities http://www.growingcitiesmovie.com/the-film/
- Seed: The Untold Story https://www.seedthemovie.com/
- The Pollinators https://www.thepollinators.net/how-to-watch
- Dirt! The Movie http://www.dirtthemovie.org/

Each group will be responsible for one of the following four for the second part of the assignment:

- Harvest of Shame https://www.npr.org/2014/05/31/317364146/in-confronting-poverty-harvest-of-shame-reaped-praise-and-criticism
- Dolores https://www.doloresthemovie.com/
- A Place at the Table http://www.magpictures.com/aplaceatthetable/
- *Wasted*! https://www.hollywoodreporter.com/review/wasted-story-food-waste-1047319

Assignment D—Mapping a Sustainable Food System

The syllabus identifies our major class project: to envision and map out a sustainable food system that offers solutions for feeding ourselves in a way that respects ecology, values diversity, builds resilient communities, and is based on social justice.

This assignment is the culminating step of this sequenced mapping project.

We will start from the knowledge we have been acquiring of our current industrial food system, starting with our viewing of *Food Inc*. This study of this food system identifies its unsustainable and damaging environmental, social, and cultural consequences. At the same time, we have identified current projects and proposed alternatives to the way we currently grow and produce food.

Our task is to take this knowledge and imagine ways to intervene, reshape or transform that food system. As all our mapping assignments have asked, we want to see that major concepts and ideas and major problems are identified, as well as proposed or actual solutions (i.e., the projects identified in *Growing Cities*), and we want to see connections and relationships between the points of the map.

While we do not have a fixed idea of what this map should look like, we want to broadly integrate class materials, including all the documentary films from this mapping assignment, relevant lab assignments, relevant feature films, field trips, material from the Bio textbook, and relevant supplementary materials.

Everybody will need to contribute and show clearly what their contribution is to the creation of the map. However, we want each student individually to identify in writing key takeaways and major questions, as we have in all previous mapping assignments, and submit that to us individually.

We need to make two decisions as a class before we can finalize this assignment:

1. What is the central concept bubble?
2. How do you want to structure your work on this assignment (i.e., small group or one large group, breakout into work groups for different parts of the map, etc.)?

Sample Assignment Sequence #2 for "Seed, Soil, and the Soul" Course

This experiential learning assignment illustrates how we incorporate hands-on experience into our interdisciplinary seminar. Students work in one or both of our campus sites that promote food security, the Garden and/or the Food Pantry. Integrating their service-learning experience with what they are learning in the classroom students produce short videos—also a reflection of our desire to incorporate multimodal assignments. We have our Media Lab Manager work with students to support the video production.

Experiential Learning Project

This joint assignment integrates academic instruction with real-world experiences. The purpose of experiential learning is two-fold: (1) learn about the application of ecological principles and cultural representation through engaging in 15–20 hours of service-learning activities at the Fuel Pantry and the Fuel Garden on campus; and (2) to connect your research and service experience to deliberate societal priorities regarding food production and consumption. Over the course of the semester you will submit the following four assignments:

- ASSIGNMENT A—Video essay on your food choices
- ASSIGNMENT B—Food biography
- ASSIGNMENT C—Video essay on food security at COD
- ASSIGNMENT D—Class debrief on the seminar and your service learning experience

Assignment A—Video Essay: You Are What You Eat

The main purpose of this assignment is to create a three- to five-minute video essay in which you analyze your own eating practices.

Specifically, we would like you to record, reflect on, contextualize (within the issues we are studying in class) and analyze your own eating habits and practices. Though it may be a cliché, the expression "you are what you eat" will be the guiding focus of this video essay. That is, what does a careful consideration of what, where, how and how much you eat reveal about who you are? Your lifestyle? Your values? Your economic status? Your social status? Your understanding of the environmental impact of food production and consumption? The extent to which intentionality guides your most basic life practice? Do your eating practices reflect the larger social and cultural patterns we are studying in class?

The material for this video essay will come from several sources:

- You will be collecting data on your eating practices for Lab 2 (Exercise 12 in the lab manual). Through your analysis of this data, we expect that you will gain insights on your individual food choices as well as on the broader social, cultural, economic and environmental forces that impact on and shape those individual choices.
- Wendell Berry's essay "The Pleasures of Eating," which you will be reading for Lab 2 (Exercise 12) as well, offers a framework for you to consider your own practices. His contrasting categories, "industrial eater" and "responsible eater" suggest that most of us could be considered one or the other. Do you fit into one of these categories? Is there another category you know of that better suits who you are? Berry writes, "A significant part of the pleasure of eating is in one's accurate consciousness of the lives and the world from which food comes.

The pleasure of eating, then, may be the best available standard of our health." To what extent does your diet represent your "consciousness of the lives and the world from which food comes?" What does your diet reveal about who you are?
- Other class materials including readings, films, class discussions, field trips, your service learning experiences, and so on.

We suggest that you begin capturing footage throughout the term that could be included in your essay. While we would like you to create your own footage and images for some of the material, found footage and images is also acceptable as a source.

Additionally, please write a brief reflection that addresses the following:

a. Explain why you chose to tell the story as you did.
b. How did the ecological concepts and principles that we have discussed influence how you made the video? Make some specific connections in your response—i.e., which biological concepts/principles would say most influenced you in making this video? Explain.
c. In film making, while you decide what to include, what to exclude, and the point of view to present, you are also limited by the length of the film and the time in which you have to tell your story. Reflect on both the possibilities and the limits of film making with regard to your food habits. Discuss how your video connects to the films we have seen and/or reading from the film texts. Again, make specific connections and in your response be sure to explain how any ideas you encountered influenced your video essay.

Assignment B—Food Biography

Potato chips, apples, coffee, steak, and bread—our daily lives are dependent on many such agricultural food products. Food, in fact, is the basis of life. Thus, by studying the food we consume we can come to better understand our lives—who we are as individuals as well as a society. Since food connects us with others through cultural and social interactions, ecology, economics, and politics, we also learn about gender, family, and community relationships when we study food production and consumption. For the most part however, we tend to use food products without complete knowledge about the impact the product has on the environment and on the people whose lives are central to its production.

In this assignment you are being asked to think beyond the final food product you consumed, to explore these factors that we often are unaware of from the history of the food item, to how it is cultivated, harvested, and processed, to the impacts of producing and consuming this food product on the environment and human society. You could also consider whether the benefits that the food product provides justify the environmental and other costs and to explore ways in which to improve the food product's record—i.e., reduce its negative impact.

1. Select one food item. You could pick an item in its raw form (e.g., a potato, milk, an apple, beef, sugar, etc.) or in the form of a product (e.g., potato chips, milkshake, apple pie, burger, candy, etc.).
2. Write a story or a short piece of prose or a poem for the food item you select—like a biography. You could choose to write from the perspective of the food item, the perspective of you as the consumer, or a combination. As suggested in the introduction above your writing should make reference to at least *five* of the following:
   - history of the food product (i.e., wild relatives, evidence of first domestication, where and why domesticated, how the cultivation of the crop spread, etc.)
   - methods of cultivation, processing, and distribution (both past and present)
   - uses of the food product (both past and present)
   - examples of how the food item is tied to particular human cultures (in both production and consumption)
   - economic importance (both past and present)
   - social and political issues (both positive and negative) connected to the cultivation, processing, and use of the food item
   - environmental impacts (both positive and negative) connected to the cultivation, processing, use and disposal of the food item
   - health consequences (both positive and negative) of producing and consuming the food product
   - suggestions for how we might mitigate (reduce the negative effects of) the environmental, health, social, and other impacts of the cultivation, harvesting, processing, use and disposal of the food item
3. In addition to the prose or poem respond to the following questions:
   a. Explain why you selected the food product that you did.
   b. How did the ecological concepts and principles that we have discussed thus far influence what you wrote? You must make three specific connections to the biology text. In your response be sure to explain the biological concept/principle and explain how it influenced your writing.
   c. Writing the story of food is akin to film making and can have similar limits in what we can imagine and speak to and the point of view presented. Reflect on the limits of what can be imagined with regard

to your food item. Discuss how your writing connects to the films we have seen and/or reading from the film texts. You must make three specific connections to the film texts. In your response be sure to explain how the idea influenced your writing.

Assignment C—Video Essay: Food Security at COD

Food security is central to what we are studying this semester. Over the course of the term we will be exploring the concept of "food security" and learning what it means to be food secure, or food insecure, from a variety of perspectives. Our work throughout this semester will also ask you to reflect on how worldview shapes the ways in which we as individuals and as a society approach understanding food security and solving issues concerning food production and consumption in the world today—for humans as well as other species.

So, how can we define the term food security? The current widely accepted definition states: *Food security exists when all people, at all times, have physical, social and economic access to sufficient, safe and nutritious food that meets their dietary needs and food preferences for an active and healthy life.*

We can ask this complicated and perhaps confounding question at national and global levels. However, it is a question that deeply concerns people on a local and personal level, as food insecurity negatively impacts people's daily lives. Recent studies have indicated that food security is a growing concern among college and university students throughout the United States, and in particular among community college students. The scale of the problem can be evidenced by the increasing attention being given to addressing it. For example, last year, New York governor Andrew Cuomo mandated that all public colleges and universities in the state have campus food pantries.

This semester you have been involved in experiential learning at three sites that exist on our campus: the Fuel Garden, Fuel Pantry, and the COD Prairie. The Garden and the Pantry were established by COD students on the basis of research they conducted that found that food security is an issue for a significant number of COD students. You will have looked at the results of that research, and you will have participated in student-initiated responses to address the problem. And that brings us to the central concern of this assignment: Why does food security matter at College of DuPage, and what can we do to achieve it? You will answer this question in the form of a short video essay of two to five minutes.

Step 1: Research

To explore connections between science and film studies through the lens of food and agriculture, we believe necessitates a deep curiosity about life.

Thus, we are including the opportunity to step outside the classroom, to involve you in experiences that connects your life to those of others through food, with an emphasis on the issue of food in/security as it exists on our own campus and in our local community.

Thus, for the research that you are expected incorporate in your video essay, in addition to including all that you have learned in this seminar from the texts we have read, the films we have viewed, our field trips, the labs, and class discussion, will also include a *required service learning component*, and any other *optional library or experiential research* (such as independent community explorations of farmers markets, grocery stores, etc.).

We expect the primary benefit of participation in service learning to be that it promotes the integration of academic instruction with real-world experiences. Furthermore, we hope that this experience helps to engender critical and reflective thinking as well as promote civic responsibility. The service learning requirement is that you complete a minimum of 15–20 service learning hours no later than November 30th at a combination of three service learning sites that exist on campus:

- the Fuel Pantry
- the Fuel Garden
- the COD Prairie

Work in the COD Prairie will be connected to prairie restoration including seed collection, seed processing, brush cutting, and so on. While this might not at first sight appear to directly connect to food and agriculture, it does connect to issues of food security through the role of prairies in soil formation and reducing soil erosion, habitat for pollinators, the prairie as a model for agriculture, and so on.

Since this work will be incorporated into your video essay you should keep track of your experiences throughout the term. We suggest you find a system that works for you—your class notes from lectures, film screenings and discussions will all form an important part of the material you need for this project. So will some form of notes of your service learning activities, so record your activities at the food pantry, garden and prairie. Similarly record your observations about the food pantry (the food available, the clients, etc.), garden (food grown, etc.), and prairie (tasks involved, restoration challenges, etc.); and document connections you see to the seminar (biology material, specific films, etc.). Please consult with us if you would like guidance on how to keep track of all these diverse activities that will be crucial for successful completion of this video essay.

Also make sure you obtain video footage as well as photos of your experience. (We will discuss the issue of getting releases signed if necessary in class).

Step 2: Video Production

Work together as a group throughout the term to create a three- to five-minute video essay that:

1. Represents your group's collective answer to the question—Why does food security matter at College of DuPage, and what can we do to achieve it? In answering this question be sure to
   - Provide a definition of food security (you can select something from your research and our discussions in class, develop one based on your experiences, or some combination thereof).
   - Discuss why addressing issues concerning food production and consumption in the world today is important for humans as well as other species. That is, why does food security matter? We are particularly looking for you to explore the biological/environmental consequences that can both cause and result from a lack of food security. Consider using specific examples/case studies to highlight your response.
   - Identify ways in which we can achieve food security and discuss the biological/environmental and consequences that result. Consider using specific examples/case studies to highlight your response.
   - Pay attention to the process of developing your answer. Incorporate some reflection on this process into your video.
2. How you organize and develop your video to respond to the question will be determined by your group. We would like you to be creative! You will need to find and/or create the images and footage that will comprise your video. In short, there are many ways to approach this assignment. Here are some suggestions
   - You might get started by recording each group member's answer to the question as you begin this project, and reflect later on how this answer may have changed over the course of the semester.
   - You might want to document the process by which your group came to this answer. This means that you should start your collection of material soon, and do so throughout all our class activities. We would suggest that you place a particular emphasis on the experiential activities (i.e., service learning), documenting them as you engage in them as much as possible, so that you can capture the moment and the process involved. (You should expect to gather more footage than you will incorporate into the video.)

- You might want to account for what activities, films, and course readings were instrumental in developing your answer and include relevant film clips, selected readings, and field trip and service learning footage.
3. Once you have collected your material, including all footage, images, and any materials you plan to include, you will need to think about the structure of your essay. What narrative structure will best answer the question? How will you turn shots into scenes? How will you turn scenes into sequences? Will you use chronology (how you developed the answer over the course of the semester, from beginning to end) or use a nonlinear sequence—flashbacks, flashforwards, episodic structure? How much of your essay will consist of images? How much will contain text? To do this, we would like you to develop:
    a. A script—your basic narrative—who will say what—your video should not be an unplanned monologue)
    b. A storyboard—a graphic organizer consisting of drawings and images in the sequence you intend them to appear in your video essay. This is a way to "previsualize" the video before you make it.
    c. A shot list—all shots you plan to include in your video. Some of these you will have already taken (hopefully) throughout the semester. Some of these you will still need to shoot. This is a detailed checklist that will organize your video essay and give your group a sense of direction. Identify the types of shots to be included (close-up, medium, long shot, high or low angle, moving camera, etc.).

These steps are not extra work—they are part of the process and will greatly assist you in putting together your final essay. We will collect the script, storyboard and shot list with the video—one copy per group.

Remember that there is more than one "correct" response to the question. What we are looking for is an answer that demonstrates you have read, reflected upon and in general seriously contemplated the material we have read, viewed and discussed in class, and can find some meaning and relevance in it.

Although we are studying film in this seminar, we do not expect you to be filmmakers to complete this assignment. While many of you are probably quite adept at digital communication, and may not need full guidance throughout this project, the COD Digital Media Lab, located in the library, has all the necessary equipment and advice to guide you. The Lab has film equipment, support staff, offers workshops, provides editing programs and most anything you will need to create your video.

Assignment D—Class Debrief

This portion of the assignment is a class discussion on your individual and collective experiences in this seminar and specifically on the role of interdisciplinary and experiential learning in engaging in food issues.

The discussion will focus on the question of food security by exploring both food production as well as food consumption, and is intended as an opportunity to deepen your thinking about the connection between various assignments and the course material. As preparation for the class discussion develop a one- to two-page response that addresses the following questions—

- Land and water are limited resources and the way we use them today has consequences for present and future generations. Considering this reality, what are our responsibilities to present and future generations regarding how we produce food today? Be sure to define who is included in present and future generations.
- In what ways has the overall seminar with its diverse perspectives altered your knowledge, thinking, and perhaps lifestyle? Give specific examples to support your answer.
- Did you find the interdisciplinary and experiential learning relevant? If so why? If not why not?

Sample Assignment #3

We sometimes use *Hungry Planet*, a book by Peter Menzel, that offers visual representation of families from around the world sitting with a week's worth of their food. The book offers a fascinating comparative look at the diversity of foodways, from refugee families to U.S. suburban families, making clear the differences and disparities that exist worldwide. We generally have students work in small groups, selecting a group of families, and presenting an anlysis and reflection of what they read to their classmates.

Hungry Planet Assignment

Text: *Hungry Planet* by Peter Menzel and Faith D'Alusio
https://menzelphoto.photoshelter.com/gallery/Hungry-Planet-Family-Food-Portraits/G0000zmgWvU6SiKM/C0000k7JgEHhEq0w

Each group will select a group of families from the text and an essay from the text from a list I distribute. Your group's task will be to analyze and synthesize the family stories and what they tell us about world food practices. You will present this material to class in written and oral form.

The goal of this assignment is to expand and further our discussion of world food practices. Thus, while your response should address the material from *Hungry Planet* first and foremost, it should also reflect the other materials we are discussing in class. That is, how can the material we are reading and discussing in class serve as background for this report?

Directions for teams:

1. Form groups of three.
2. Select your group of families/essay.
3. As individuals, read the assigned materials (photos and accompanying explanatory text, essay)
4. Meet as a group. You will probably need to meet more than once to do this well. As a group you need to: a) discuss what you learn from the material and what it tells you about world food practices b) organize a presentation to the class about what you learned from the material and what it tells you about world food practices and c) write a summary of your conclusions. You will distribute this to all class members. It should be approximately one page. d) in writing, individually, reflect on how this assignment incorporates and/or expands your understanding of the seminar topic and the materials we are studying in class.
5. On the scheduled date, you will present your work to your classmates. You may create a PowerPoint, but more importantly, be prepared to discuss the visuals provided to us by the text (photos). And remember, your presentation is not intended to repeat what you provide in your summary. It should complement your summary.

Here are examples of written essays assignments where students were enrolled in Introduction to Film Art. (We also have some assignments where students wrote essays on the basis of texts from Introduction to Literature but haven't included them here.)

Writing Reflections

Over the course of the semester you will write two documented essays based on questions we provide. The purpose of this assignment is to provide you an opportunity to integrate biology with film in critically analyzing how we feed ourselves. In additional to class material you are also expected to incorporate in your essay responses information from field research that you conduct and service learning that you engage in. We will provide you more detailed instructions for completing this assignment.

Writing Reflection 1 — Exploring Food Worldviews

General Directions

Please respond to the following question in essay form. As a genre, essays represent an author's attempt to put forth a personal perspective on an issue (thus the common use of first-person in essay-writing). Thus, there is no "correct" response to the question below. Rather, we are looking for an essay that demonstrates you have in general seriously contemplated the material we have viewed, read and discussed in class, and can find some meaning and relevance in it. Since this question encompasses both biology and film, we are looking for a) evidence that you have understood key scientific concepts, b) evidence that you can provide a compelling (well-supported) "reading" of a film and c) evidence that you can make connections between the two.

The Prompt

From the texts we have read, the films we have viewed, and our/your field trips to the COD Prairie, Kline Creek Farm and a Farmers' Market, it is already clear that the advent of agriculture has had significant consequences for humans as well as other species. We have looked at how the shift from hunter/gatherer and settled societies to agricultural societies has impacted on how we live, and on our relationships to the ecosphere. That is, an agricultural lifestyle both shapes human worldviews and understanding of the ecosphere, and defines our relationship to it. We have also seen that agricultural societies change over time, up to the present, leading to our primarily industrialized system. Given this, address the following question:

> *How have changes in food practices shaped human worldviews and our relationship to the ecosphere and to each other? Where do you fit into this historical continuum?*

To answer this prompt, use the guidelines described below to organize your essay:

a. Briefly summarize how the human acquisition of food has changed over the history of our species (i.e. how we went from hunter/gatherer societies to early agrarians to the agriculture of today) and how these changes in food acquisition shaped/reflect human worldviews.
b. Today, regardless of how we get our food, we are all connected to agriculture. Furthermore, our food procurement preferences reflect a particular "agricultural worldview." Define/describe your "agricultural worldview." While we would like you to provide a personal description

of an "agricultural worldview," it should be based on your understanding of the variety of ideas and perspectives offered by the films, readings, and field trips. Make reference to the most influential sources that shaped your definition/description in your essay.

c. What we believe and how we act can often be in tension and that may be true of your "agricultural worldview" as compared to your actual food procurement practices. Discuss both the confluence and contractions between your "agricultural worldview" and your food practices. In addition discuss the biological/environmental and cultural consequences of your food procurement practices making reference to specific examples from the sources (film, texts, field trips) you select to delineate particular ecological and cultural consequences—for our relationship to nature, to work, to health, to community, and so on.

Sources

In your answer you will need to make specific reference, through a combination of summary, paraphrase, and/or direct quotation, to several of the films we have viewed and the texts we have read for class. We would like a minimum of: *the biology textbook and one other reading, three films—narrative or documentary, the field trip to Kline Creek Farm, and your exploration of a farmer's market.*

Text sources to include (select at least two—one must be the Biology text):

- Anne Houtman, Susan Carr, and Jeneen Interlandi—*Environmental Science for a Changing World* (required)
- Jared Diamond—"The Worst Mistake in Human History"
- Wendell Berry—"The Pleasures of Eating"
- Anita Endrezze—"Corn Mother"
- Any of the Hungry Planet readings and the families we have looked at

Films to include (select at least three):

- Snow Walker
- The Environmental Revolution
- Collapse (TED talk)
- Nanook of the North
- America's Lost Landscape: The Tallgrass Prairie
- The Plough that Broke the Plains
- Dirt! The Movie
- *On the Brink*—Haiti
- Understanding Suburban Sprawl (case study on California)
- *Save the Earth, Feed the World*—Australia and North Dakota

- Extinction!
- *Remnants of Eden*—Thailand
- The Future of Food
- King Corn
- Food Inc.
- Days of Heaven
- Any film clips we see related to energy use and consequences of our energy choices

Field trips (Kline Creek Farm and Farmer's Market must be included):

- Kline Creek Farm (required)
- COD Prairie
- Farmers' market (required)
- Service learning experiences

Writing Reflection 2—The Future of Food

General Directions

Please respond to the following question in essay form. As a genre, essays represent an author's attempt to put forth a personal perspective on an issue (thus the common use of first-person in essay-writing). Thus, there is no "correct" response to the question below. Rather, we are looking for an essay that demonstrates you have in general seriously contemplated the material we have viewed, read and discussed in class, and can find some meaning and relevance in it. Since this question encompasses both biology and film, we are looking for a) evidence that you have understood key scientific concepts, b) evidence that you can provide a compelling (well-supported) "reading" of a film and c) evidence that you can make connections between the two.

The Prompt

From the texts we have read, the films we have viewed, our/your field trips to the COD Prairie, Kline Creek Farm and a Farmers' Market, and also your service learning experience it is already clear that feeding 7 billion people presents a complex challenge. Throughout this class we have explored various dimensions of agriculture from food production challenges such as land ownership, pollution, access to water, overgrazing, loss of biodiversity and use of chemicals in food production to food consumption challenges such as overnutrition, malnutrition, hunger, safe food supply, and food miles. Given this, address the following question:

What do you think is the best approach to producing and consuming the food we all need in order to go on living?

To answer this prompt, use the guidelines described below to organize your essay:

a. Discuss what you consider to be the three biggest problems in agriculture (i.e., food production) and food consumption today. For each of the problems you have identified, discuss the biological/environmental and social/cultural consequences that result. In your discussion make reference to specific sources to describe the problems and their consequences.
b. In regard to the three problems you identified above, identify how you think we can better approach the human endeavor of food acquisition (production and consumption). In your discussion make reference to specific sources you select to delineate some possible solutions.
c. What is your personal perspective on the importance of food production and consumption in the human story (beyond the basic biological necessity which is a given)? Is there an author or text that you see as most closely reflecting your perspective?
d. How has your understanding of food and agriculture issues been enhanced by the interdisciplinary nature of this class which combines film and biology?

Sources

In your answer, you will need to make specific reference, through a combination of summary, paraphrase, and/or direct quotation, to several of the films we have viewed and the texts we have read for class. We would like a minimum of: *the biology textbook and one other reading, three films—narrative or documentary, the field trip to Kline Creek Farm, and your exploration of a farmer's market.*

Text sources to include (select at least two—one must be the Biology text):

- Anne Houtman, Susan Carr, and Jeneen Interlandi—*Environmental Science for a Changing World* (required)
- Jared Diamond—"The Worst Mistake in Human History"
- Wendell Berry—"The Pleasures of Eating"
- Anita Endrezze—"Corn Mother"
- Tony Hoagland—"Candellight"
- Alan Durning—"Just a Cup of Coffee?"
- Any of the Hungry Planet readings and the families we have looked at

Films to include (select at least three):

- *America's Lost Landscape: The Tallgrass Prairie*
- *Captured Rain*—Colorado River
- *Chinatown*
- *Collapse* (TED talk)
- *Days of Heaven*
- *Dirt! The Movie*
- *Dive! Living Off America's Waste*
- *Do the Right Thing*
- *End of the Line*
- *The Environmental Revolution*
- *Evolutionary Arms Race*—ants and fungi gardens
- *Extinction!*
- *Food Inc.*
- *The Future of Food*
- *Grapes of Wrath*
- *Harvest of Shame*
- *Hot Enough for You*—plant response to carbin dioxide
- *King Corn*
- *La Cosecha*
- *Nanook of the North*
- *On the Brink*—Haiti
- *Only one Atmosphere*—climate change modeling
- *Our Daily Bread*
- *A Place at the Table*
- *The Plough that Broke the Plains*
- *Queen of the Sun*
- *Remnants of Eden*—Thailand
- *Rivers of Destiny*—Jordan River
- *Salmon Fishing in the Yemen*
- *Save the Earth, Feed the World*—Australia and North Dakota
- *Save the Earth, Feed the World*—California and Indonesia
- *Seas of Grass*—Mongolia
- *Snow Walker*
- *The Story of Stuff*
- *Supersize Me*
- *Tulpan*
- *Understanding Suburban Sprawl*—California
- *Waste Not, Want Not*—Peru
- *World in the Balance*
- Any film clips we view in class

Field trips (Kline Creek Farm and Farmer's Market must be included):

- Kline Creek Farm (required)
- COD Prairie
- Farmers' market (required)
- Service-learning experiences

Chapter 12

Food Justice and Garden Writing in First-Year Seminars at Bates College

Stephanie Wade

In this chapter, I describe how permaculture and antiracist writing pedagogies enabled me to create a curriculum for writing-intensive, first-year seminar classes that addresses food justice through community-engaged writing in school and community gardens. This curriculum interrogates conventional literacy practices and conventional agricultural practices that perpetuate systemic inequities in food systems and school systems, and it uses permaculture to begin to employ alternative approaches to agriculture and education that honor social justice. Motivated by my commitments to decolonial epistemologies, aesthetics, and ethics, I follow Catriona Rueda Esquibel and Luz Calvo, who open their essay "Decolonize Your Diet: A Manifesto" by calling on their ancestors; by urging readers to unite mind, body, and spirit in liberatory work; and by directing us to labor collaboratively "With our heart in our hands, and our hands in the soil" (El Plan Espiritual de Aztlán 1, quoted in Esquibel and Calvo 2013). In the classes I describe below, I aimed to teach writing with my heart in my hands and my hands in the earth, and I learned so much from the relationships that grew from this work. In this spirit, I conclude by inviting you to participate in a public writing project that aims to build relationships and create more inclusive spaces.

Having experienced both privilege and precarity in regard to education and to food, I have lived through and witnessed the limits of conventional food systems and education systems. Studying antiracist pedagogies and food justice, I have learned about alternatives. In this chapter, I describe how I came see these alternatives, how I put them into practice, and how my students responded. All of the students mentioned, quoted, and photographed gave me permission to share their work and images after the classes had ended, and I had submitted final grades; IRB approval was not deemed necessary by the chair of the IRB Committee at Bates College.

CRACKS IN THE CONCRETE

Permaculture—a design system popularized by Bill Mollison and David Holmgren based on their observations of indigenous practices and healthy ecosystems—reminds us that preindustrial principles of sustainable living embrace diversity in living ecosystems. Permaculture teaches us to turn abandoned lots into gardens; offers us the tools to break up the concrete of conventional agricultural practices and literacy pedagogies; and asks us to plant vegetables, flowers, herbs, trees, and ideas based on the material at hand in reciprocal relationships in our work. Antiracist pedagogies—which emerged globally along with movements against colonialism, gained visibility in the United States via the civil rights movements of the 1960s, and are receiving more attention today as a result of increasing attention to institutional racism, violence against Black people, and the Black Lives Matter movement—address the deep historical and contemporary connections between education, colonialism, and racism. Antiracist pedagogies demonstrate the epistemological, aesthetic, and ethical limits of conventional western education practices; and they offer alternatives that enact equity and inclusion by the selection of course material, assignment design, and assessment practices (Fanon 1968; Thiong'o 1986; Hu-DeHart 1993; Condon and Young 2016).

In my teaching, I apply permaculture and antiracist pedagogies by designing classes around the theme of food justice; integrating community engagement throughout the semester; assigning multigenre, public writing rooted in cultural rhetorics; teaching about linguistic justice and code meshing; and modeling inclusive citation practices. I am interested in literally breaking up concrete and asphalt, in cultivating healthy soil, and in growing gardens of vegetables, flowers, and other plants to feed our neighbors and create sustainable habitats for all people, for pollinators, other insects, birds, rabbits, and more. I am also interested in breaking up the ideological concrete and asphalt of modernist thought and conventional literacy pedagogies that constrain healthy thinking, inhibit diversity, and feed the school-to-prison pipeline, practices such as assigning ossified forms of writing like the five-paragraph essay; relying on standardized tests and machine-graded assessments; employing monocultural curricular materials that reify a narrow canon of texts primarily by white, western male authors; and marginalizing most dialects.

The problems embedded in conventional approaches to agriculture and to education parallel each other because both agriculture and education have been shaped by colonialism, capitalism, and neoliberalism in ways that privilege white, western epistemologies, aesthetics, and identities in cultural, ideological, and material ways—thereby displacing, erasing, and cannibalizing other forms of knowledge, beauty, and life. Work in antiracist pedagogies, food justice, and ecological approaches to education clearly illustrate the destructive effects of these parallels and demonstrate the alternatives necessary to build an inclusive, sustainable future in an increasingly small, hot, connected world (Williams and Brown 201; Kimmerer 2013; Nocella 2016). In the following pages, I explore what it means to crack the pavement of neoliberal education and agriculture.

Rooted in three overlapping principles of care for the earth, care for people, and care for the future, permaculture offers conceptual, ethical, and technical tools for applying ecological approaches to our work and navigating the end of the Anthropocene in inclusive ways. Permaculture aims to achieve ecological balance rather than short-term economic profit by advocating slow observation over time and the cultivation of mutually beneficial relationships. It situates humans within ecosystems rather than above them. It cultivates living systems that aim to benefit all, that turn waste in energy, and encourage approaching every problem as an opportunity for creative thinking. For example, the permaculture designer would begin by studying the site itself: the soil, water, wind, human, animal, and plant communities that comprise the place, the patterns, habits and needs. Then, the permaculture designer would use this information to assemble an aesthetically, ethically, and ecologically pleasing environment. In this way, permaculture attends to the material world, it pays serious attention to the elements, it situates human needs and desires in relationship to the needs and desires of environmental factors (Hemenway 2009).

Because the pressures of racism, efficiency, and economies of scale have had similar effects on education and agriculture—diverse histories and the contributions of BIPOC people marginalized and erased; small farms and schools consolidated and closed; human labor stolen, undervalued, and increasingly replaced with technology; and assessments narrowed to easily quantifiable data that fails to account for significant metrics of ecological, cultural, and personal progress—permaculture is one way to begin to address the damages caused by these changes. Wendell Berry explains the similarities of consequences of these changes in both agriculture and education in *The Unsettling of America*:

> As machines have grown larger and more complex, and as our awe of them and our desire for labor-saving have grown, we have tended more and more to

define skill quantitatively. How speedily and cheaply can a person work? We have increasingly wanted a *measurable* skill. And the more quantifiable skills become, the easier they were to replace with machines." (Berry 91)

Similarly, in *Reign of Error: The Hoax of the Privatization Movement and the Danger to America's Public Schools*, Diane Ravitch writes: "the reformers define the purpose of education as preparation for global competitiveness, higher education, or the workforce. They view students as 'human capital' or 'assets.'" The industrialization of agriculture and of education funnels money away from farmers, teachers, and students; it moves farms and schools towards monoculture; and it erodes soil health and the health of our critical and creative thinking abilities.

David Kirkland and Valerie Kinloch's research illustrates the particularly harmful impact of industrial education on Black youth. When situated in school settings dominated by the white, monocultural language and culture of conventional English language arts classes, Black youth are often deemed illiterate by their teachers, but the same Black youth demonstrate a wealth of knowledge about place, literacy, and rhetoric outside conventional classrooms. In Kirkland's study, the knowledge is of the virtual space of social networks like MySpace (2009). In Kinloch's work, it is knowledge of community and the pressures of gentrification in Harlem (2009). In both cases, conventional educational settings do not allow these students to demonstrate the knowledge that they have, and so the students are labeled illiterate, which perpetuates racism and barriers to student success. Both advocate for attention to third spaces outside conventional classrooms, which primed me to consider school gardens as alternative sites for antiracist literacy instruction.

In an early piece, Kirkland uses the language of gardening to provide context for his critique of monocultural curricular materials when he writes "it is important to question how texts and textual traditions that we in English education embrace lead ELA teachers to abide by the failed assumption that roses (our students) only bud in fields (our classrooms) well-manicured by standards and traditions" (2008, 74). In a co-authored later piece, Kirkland directs us to look at the lived experiences of our students, which often requires reckoning with "realities of trauma, hunger, and poverty" (Kirkland 2017, 468). Engaging in the permaculture practice of slow observation over time moves Kirkland beyond calls to dismantle the school-to-prison pipeline, as they illustrate that everyday life for the black youth they have studied is like a prison, so we must go further and dismantle the conditions that create the trauma, hunger, poverty in these communities.

Leah Penniman presents means to dismantle trauma, hunger, and poverty via food justice initiatives. In her book *Farming While Black*, she recovers agricultural knowledge that enslaved people brought from Africa, reclaims the contributions of Black scientists to organic agriculture, reconnects liberation to the land, and offers instructions for building food sovereignty and for building movement for racial equity. She writes "In addition to mass incarceration, one of the most insidious and pervasive forms of state violence against our people is the flooding of our communities with foods that kill us" (224). Penniman, an activist-practitioner, works in a tradition of food justice that links access to healthy food with liberation, a movement that dates back to initiatives run by the Black Panthers in the 1960s and continues today as embodied by Catriona Rueda Esquibel and Luz Calvo in "Decolonize Your Diet: Manifesto," a code-meshed, translingual text and compelling example of rhetorical action. They invite all readers to reach back to their ancestors for cultural knowledge about food in order to find alternatives to the Standard American Diet. Esquibel and Calvo connect the return to precapitalist ways of eating to social justice because, as they state, "We cannot fight for our people and our culture if we are sick and sluggish" (2013, 1). They conclude with instructions for cooking a pot of beans, and a reminder:

> In our call to decolonize food, we aim to create mental, spiritual, and physical healthiness in our communities so that we can collectively grow strong and healthy. We need strong and healthy warriors who can effectively engage in the social and revolutionary struggle against the global economic elites, who maintain control by keeping us sick, weak, and dependent." (4)

In their attention to farming and cooking as material, political, cultural, and personal acts, these BIPOC food justice activists enact the root permaculture principles of engaging the head, the hands, and the heart.

GARDENS AS THIRD SPACES

Veronica House pioneered significant attention to food justice in writing studies with her 2014 *Community Literacy Journal* essay "Reframing the Argument," where she situates food justice projects directly in the tradition of community writing, connects these projects with the well-established pedagogical benefits of community engagement, and forcefully argues that food justice projects in particular require attention today because the very topic of food justice "ties to topics of ecological collapse, peak oil, racism, poverty, corporate capitalism, overpopulation, disease, and hunger" (4). In response to House's argument for community-engaged writing about food justice; Kirkland and Kinloch's call for teaching literacy in third spaces; and Penniman, Esquibel and Calvo's articulation of culturally relevant farming and gardening as antiracist practices, I began to imagine opportunities for community writing projects in school and community gardens.

School and community gardens have the potential to represent and enact alternatives to industrial agriculture and education—replacing the concrete and asphalt of conventional agricultural spaces with healthy soil and biodiversity and replacing the concrete and asphalt of conventional education with practices that cultivate creative and critical thinking and build community, practices that enact antiracism in content and form. According to Devon Peña, an anthropologist and food justice scholar who studies indigenous agriculture in rural and urban settings, community gardens provide third spaces for immigrant communities to maintain their traditional farming practices and preserve their home cultures. Gardens are spaces where all of us can learn more about preindustrial foodways and epistemologies that predate the contemporary practices and the systemic racism that shapes conventional, contemporary approaches to food and to education. In his 2006 paper "Farmers Feeding Families: Agroecology in South Central Los Angeles," Peña situates community gardens in the context of world-wide, cooperative, indigenous agricultural practices. He notes:

> Urban community gardens embody a pattern of resistance and the re-codifying of space wherein local neighborhoods assert control of places for communal uses that lie outside the purview or control of the market. These gardens are thus heterotopias in the making. There are interesting ties between urban agriculture and what I understand is a struggle for food sovereignty, a concept that combines the rich notion of local food security with the idea that food sources are consistent with cultural identities and involve community networks that promote self-reliance and mutual aid. (3)

Peña proposes that urban community gardens allow immigrants and environmental refugees a third space where they can practice food sovereignty by growing their own healthy food, often from seeds that they saved from their home countries, thereby contributing to biodiversity, and maintaining connections to their home cultures. Peña's work aligns with Donehower, Hogg, and Schell's by illustrating the persistence of rural practices and culture in urban spaces, troubling the dichotomy between rural and urban, and pointing to gardens as sites of mutual identification (9). In addition, the gardens that Peña describes and those that my students and I worked in in Lewiston also trouble the dichotomies between political borders. With strong community practices rooted in Central America and western Africa, these gardens are transnational spaces where alternative economies, cultures, and literacies grow.

In education literature, school gardens and community gardens have been identified as important sites for multicultural education and education for social justice because they are spaces where immigrants exercise skills from their home cultures in a new place, which allows them to maintain ties to their home culture and also build capacity to navigate their new homes (Cutter Mackenzie 2009). Additionally, school gardens are one of a number of experiential pedagogies that engage students in authentic learning, proving an alternative to teaching to the test and other rigid curricular initiatives (Williams and Dixon 2010).

Because the percent of K–12 schools with gardens have more than doubled from 2006–2014, they increasingly offer opportunities for educators, but more gardens appear in affluent school districts and current practices have yet to fully integrate writing into garden-based education (Turner, Sandoval, and Chaloupka 2016). For example, a review of school garden websites in Maine revealed only two references to writing in garden-based education curricular materials. Searching the literature reveals a similar gap. For example, Melanie Stewart's bibliography of garden-based education research mentions writing four times and science fifty-five times (2014).

PRACTICE

Starting in the spring of 2015, I began to address the gap of writing in school gardens by teaching theme-based creative writing classes that included community writing in school gardens. In the fall of 2018 and 2019, I connected this with the topic of food justice in two writing-intensive first-year seminars that included community engagement in local school and community gardens at Bates College, in Lewiston, Maine. Bates, a small liberal arts college of approximately 1800 undergraduates founded in 1855, promotes an origin narrative that roots the school in the work of abolitionists, the mission commits the school to social justice, and the administration has recently assembled a team to improve the ways they enact equity and inclusion in the curriculum. For these reasons, the school attracts students who care about social justice, which the residential life staff build on by integrating principles of equity and inclusion into the orientation material and programming. While predominantly white, Bates has been working on recruitment and retention of students from BIPOC backgrounds and on community engagement.

On the first day of the semester in August of 2018, my students and I walked from campus—a small, residential, liberal arts college in New England centered on a grassy, tree-lined quad ringed with ivy-covered brick buildings—through the Tree Street neighborhood of Lewiston to a community garden. This one-mile walk took us through the occupied land of the indigenous Wabanaki people, transformed in the middle of the 19th century to create housing for mill workers, many of whom traveled from Quebec to Maine for work, where they found diminished opportunities, faced discrimination, and endured decades of economic hardship, which deepened as neoliberalism disrupted domestic manufacturing. More recently, immigrants from Somalia, Eritrea, Kenya and other parts of western Africa, many fleeing violence and poverty in their home countries—instability that continues to ensue from colonial occupation and policies—also face discrimination in Lewiston, as they transform the city again. My students and I passed an elementary school where 98 percent of the students qualify for free and reduced lunch vouchers. Down the street, in one direction, corner convenience markets feature Somalian food and clothing. In the other direction, a short string of upscale spots cater to the college crowd, to artists, and to a growing number of professionals, some of whom have been priced out of Portland. Our walk begins to illustrate the layers of history, politics, culture, and economics in our small city and the coexistence of multiple worlds all around us.

In taking this walk together, I aimed for the students to move outside the classroom together and to begin to build relationships with each other and with our neighbors. I wanted them to see the work of our class as intimately intertwined with the life of the community on the Bates campus and beyond, connected in time and place to what has come before and what will come next. Taking this walk together, we begin to unpack artificial binaries about place, following Donehower, Hogg, and Schell, whose book *Reclaiming the Rural* deconstructs artificial dichotomies between rural and urban; represents the social, economic, and political interconnections that bind our different communities together; and illustrates the positive work accomplished through collective action. We begin to build physical, social, and intellectual connections to the community and with each other, thereby enacting a community-engaged, place-based pedagogy in the tradition of Eli Goldblatt, Nedra Reynolds, and Derek Owens.

Lewiston, Maine, a place that initially looks urban and is typically categorized as an urban space, includes many rural features. A number of people who settled here from Somalia and other parts of western Africa have brought with them the deep knowledge of rural living and agriculture as well as rich literacies about alternative economies, family arrangements, and other values. Among the industrial buildings and the dense housing, community gardens, side yards, nature preserves, and the riverfront offer a range of diverse ecological communities and rural niches. Lewiston also borders Auburn, one of the largest agricultural areas in Maine, and is surrounded to the northwest and the south by more farmland and rural communities. Taking a long historical perspective reveals the original rural Wabanaki communities, who persist today. Beginning to apprehend these communities expands our understanding of community work, our understanding of our work, and our understanding of ourselves, which is necessary for us to engage in social justice work (Mares and Peña 2011).

The following year, in 2019, on the first day of the term, my students and I visited two gardens on the Bates College campus: one a new garden managed by Bates students and staff and the other an established educational garden managed by our community partner. While the impact of these walks was smaller, I borrowed and adapted an activity I had learned from the Highlander Institute when they ran a workshop at the Conference on Community Writing in Boulder, Colorado in October of 2017 that served a similar purpose. For this activity, participants are given sheets of paper with photos on one side and facts on the other, each sheet offering a unique identity that participants adopt, quickly learning about their character by reading the facts, and then engaging in conversations with others in character. I selected historical and contemporary people from a range of communities: Wabanaki, Quebecois, contemporary and historical Bates students and faculty, Somali, and even ecological communities, including our plant and animal neighbors. This activity connected the Bates students in my class with our community partner: a group of twelve high school students enrolled in a paid leadership program run by the same organization whose community garden we had visited the prior autumn. The high school students had already finished a summer leadership program, so they were experienced gardeners, which equalized their relationship with the college students, who were older and more advanced in their academic studies.

The next class, we sketched maps of the places we care about, and we used sticky notes to jot down memories. In small groups of about three, students shared and described their maps to each other, primed to look for similarities and differences. Then, I asked them to write about what they learned about each other and to share their insights on additional sticky notes. We stuck the notes to the whiteboard at the front of the classroom and observed our similarities and our differences. We began to build a collective sense of shared identity across difference, encompassing difference, and mutual identification in this way following the work of Eileen Schell, Nedra Reynolds, Kristie Fleckenstein, Eli Goldblatt, Patricia Dunn, Malea Powell, Valerie Kinloch, Jody Shikpa, and others who connect the work of college writing with communities beyond the classroom, who direct writing faculty to draw on the various types of knowledge students bring to college, and who urge us to acknowledge embodiment and to make room for multimodal means of communication. This work also follows Paul Lynch's 2012 call for compositionists to view our work in the context of the end of the Anthropocene—a transition that poses dramatic material, ideological, social, and cultural challenges and also creates opportunities for rethinking the conventions imbricated by racism and classism that undergird institutions such as agriculture and education.

Both the 2018 and 2019 classes met twice a week for an hour and twenty minutes and included a three-hour afternoon lab for community engagement once a week. Our primary partners were the Bates campus garden, and a group of local teenagers called the Fall Gardeners who were enrolled in an environmental leadership program that was run out of the Nutrition Center by Eliza Huber-Weiss, a recent Bowdoin graduate. In addition, we worked in local community gardens both semesters, and during the 2019 semester, the Bates students also spent one hour a week volunteering in an elementary school next to the college campus. These opportunities allowed the students and I to learn about our neighbors and each other in a variety of ways. Because the Fall Gardeners had worked in the gardens over the summer, they had expertise to share with the college students, which balanced out the educational disparity between the two groups and made our work more reciprocal. Each of our meetings with the Fall Gardeners began with an ice breaker or two, and the Bates students and Fall Gardeners alternated facilitating these activities. Then, we gardened together in the Bates Garden and a community garden on campus. To build community, we had the students draft conversation starters on index cards, and most weeks we drew on these to get students talking with each other. I also referenced readings and writing processes whenever possible. Students tracked what they learned from the experiential components of class in journals, which became material for projects that evolved over the course of the semester. To celebrate our work with the Fall Gardeners, we had a pumpkin carving party at the Nutrition Center with a carrot cake made from carrots from the campus garden, local apple cider, local cheese, and crackers.

To frame the experiential parts of class, we read and analyzed a range of texts about literacy, food justice, the school-to-prison pipeline, and garden-based education. In 2019, I deliberately selected texts primarily written by BIPOC authors and texts in a range of genres that enacted inclusive citation practices, illustrated cultural rhetorics, and employed code meshing; and I used labor-based grading contracts. In addition to the manifesto by Esquibel and Calvo that I cited above, we read poems by Langston Hughes and Joy Harjo, an ACLU study of food justice and structural racism, an essay by Leah Penniman of Soul Fire Farm, opening remarks by a local food advocate from a conference on local food systems, an opinion essay published in the *Atlantic* and a response in the form of a meta-analysis of educational research, plus an academic study of a class similar to ours. In this way, students practiced rhetorical analysis of various texts written for a range of audiences and purpose. You will find the entire syllabus on my website: https://stephanie-wade.com.

Students analyzed the rhetorical moves employed by the writers; they compared the content of the texts with their experiences and their observations, including their community-engaged work; and they noted questions that the texts raised. After composing literacy narratives, students began to create research questions related to the course texts and their community engagement for a two-part assignment I called the DIY (design it yourself) project. Just as I aim to disrupt their expectations at the start of the semester by walking, drawing, and playing, here I aim to disrupt their expectations of the traditional research paper. The purpose, I told students, was for them to craft a question that will allow them to explore an aspect of the course theme more deeply and to share what they learned with the rest of the class, broadening all of our understanding of food justice, and preparing all to create projects to cultivate social justice in school and community gardens. While students' questions went in a range of directions, as listed below, four (numbers 1–4 below) of the fifteen projects explicitly address issues of racial, cultural, and/or economic equity; such issues were embedded in all of the projects at least implicitly, and, as students engaged in peer review and listened to each other's presentations, they learned more about the significance of garden writing in relationship to racial justice.

1. How might gardens interrupt the school-to-prison pipeline?
2. How can school gardens address the problem of deficit thinking in public schools?
3. How can the Bates Garden partner with the Nutrition Center to address food security?
4. What is the status of food security in Japan?
5. How might a review of university-nonprofit collaborations generate ideas for Bates to increase our collaboration with the Nutrition Center to expand community gardening?
6. What role does companion planting play in garden-based education?
7. What roles do bees play in garden-based education?
8. How might garden-based education address stress and contribute to wellness?
9. What is the role of art in garden-based education?
10. How does fishing relate to food security in Maine?
11. What role does cooking play in garden-based education?
12. How might school gardens address food security in urban environments in the United States?
13. How might the middle school after school provide more community?
14. How does experiential education in school gardens increase interest in STEM?

During peer review and class presentations, I directed students to pay attention to what they were learning from each other both about the topics as well as about their use of rhetorical appeals, and students wrote about what they learned about this in their plans for revision and their reflections on their speeches. In addition, students choose whether to document their research as a paper, a website, a Prezi, or another form.

The next project—which I called the public project—built on the DIY project by asking students to use what they learned from their research and from each other to identify projects for our Bates campus garden that would allow it to serve as a site for social justice. Through public, collaborative processes facilitated by the students, they formed teams of three based primarily on their interests, and they set to work to review the research they had already completed, to review course texts and resources, to identify gaps, and to fill those gaps with more research. The formal assignment was comprised of three parts: each team created a poster that used evidence-based persuasive writing as well as imagery to advocate for their project, each team described their projects during a poster session, and each individual wrote a reflection about what they learned, how they contributed to the group effort, what went well, and what needs improvement. The poster project ideas are below:

1. A summer camp to foster food justice.
2. A pollinator garden to teach middle school students about ecology.
3. A hoop house as a physical site for more collaboration between Bates and community groups such as the Nutrition Center.
4. A proposal to integrate art into the garden to make the space more welcoming and encourage more events and activities there.
5. A proposal for a stand at the Lewiston Farmers Market where Bates students could connect to the community and offer garden-based educational opportunities.

The students presented their posters in the atrium of our dining commons to a public audience as well as invited guests, who included people from our grants office, our community engagement office, and our academic support center. For this event, I made a large vat of bean dip, a culinary allusion to the conclusion of Esquibel and Cavlo's manifesto. At least fifty people attended this event.

The posters led to two projects that continued beyond the semester. One group of students received a campus grant to create a pollinator garden in the campus garden, which, when we have the pandemic under control, will be the first step towards creating a space for after-school programming for local school children in the garden. Another pair of students developed and completed an independent study to design a summer camp for middle schoolers that would use our campus garden to teach them about food justice, to provide culturally relevant education, and to interrupt the school-to-prison pipeline. While this project was interrupted by COVID-19, the depth and professionalism of their work indicate they will be able to follow through when the pandemic subsides.

SAVING SEEDS: REFLECTION AND NEXT STEPS

In students' coursework and final reflections, I observed other visible effects of this class, mostly notably their understanding of themselves as community members in a variety of ways that included the beginnings of the development of antiracist understanding and the development of agency.

When generating material for the DIY project, one student, who had grown up in a neighborhood subject to what Leah Penniman calls food apartheid, applied Esquibel and Calvo's decolonial framework to her own experience. She began with the general question of what she could do to bring food justice to her home community. While brainstorming, she identified the cultural significance of food and neoliberalism as factors to address, and she determined that drawing on her own experiences as well as research about successful programs "will give me a better idea of what I can do to help play my part" (Student 1 2019). The next semester, this student was one of a pair who continued their research via an independent study. In these ways, she demonstrated her commitment to collaborative relationships and her emerging sense of her own agency.

On reciprocity and language diversity, another student wrote in their final reflection:

> Getting to know a little of some of the fall gardeners takes on life and what they were interested in was very interesting to learn. Many of them actually taught me a lot about the garden. For example, which vegetables I never heard of that were edible and other vegetables that were not. The coolest thing was learning some words and phrases from the different languages that the fall gardeners knew. (Student 2 2019)

Another student used the language of permaculture (slow observation over time to build relationships) to describe the learning that occurred via community engagement:

> Being an active member of the community has always been a goal of mine, and being in this class helped establish that. This was one of my biggest goals before entering college, and I am very thankful for what this class has taught me and the connections I've made. I feel engaging with members of the community; in

this case, the Lewiston/Auburn community firsthand is the best way to build relationships . . . I learned a great deal from the lab sessions, which is all in my lab journal, but to summarize it into one word, I learned to become observant. I was observant of the Fall Gardeners, by learning to respect them, their diverse backgrounds, and to recognize their talents and aspirations. Many of them spoke multiple languages and had entirely different cultures. Despite this, we still got along very well, and I was reminded that friendship is universal. I was observant of the Lewiston Middle School students by learning to take a step back from the moment and become patient. Each kid is different in their way, but by being observant, you could recognize their characters and personality, and ultimately build stronger relationships. (Student 3 2019)

Of the fifteen students in the fall 2019 class, only one was a white male. In the beginning of the class, he struggled to connect with diverse perspectives, even as he acknowledged the importance of doing so. In conversation with me, he noted that listening to his classmates during small group discussions helped move him to see alternative perspectives, particularly those from marginalized backgrounds, a point I nudged him towards in my feedback on his reflections.

In his lab journal, he noted that the combination of reading texts by BIPOC authors and working with the Fall Gardeners and the middle school students, many of whom were Black, contributed to his ability to rethink his perspectives.

A connection between classwork and the lab this week, was seeing the world from others' perspectives. In our readings in class, I experienced many views other than my own, which was enlightening because I could realize the errors in my way of thinking. It is important to see the perspectives of others to understand the problems that arise in society. (Student 4 2019b)

In his final reflection, this student concluded that this class helped him understand himself as a community member who needs to spend more time engaging with diverse perspectives.

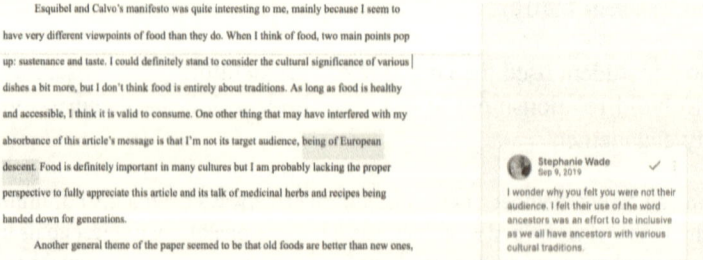

Figure 12.1. Instructor feedback on student reflections paper. Credit: Author.

As for becoming a better community member, I feel that I have managed to be proficient in this area as well, although certainly I can stand to learn a lot more about other cultures and perspectives which are equally important when considering modern issues. In order to come up with solutions which work for as many people as possible, I must continue to embrace points of view which I wouldn't immediately consider otherwise. This class has taught me a lot about verbal and written literacy, as well as social justice; and I have become a better person because of it. (Student 4 2019a)

In these ways, this student demonstrates his evolving understanding of and critique of his own whiteliness, an important step in moving to antiracist perspectives (Condon and Young 2017).

I close with a reflection from a student who overcame initial frustration and ultimately advocated for the power of listening. This reflection demonstrates both the positive impact of these pedagogies and signals next steps:

Every Monday I spent an hour at the Lewiston Middle School helping students with their homework. In my first few reflections I express great frustration because many of the students did not need help so I felt that I was wasting my time. I also felt some hostility from the teachers because they did not acknowledge my presence. Furthermore, at times I overheard students say grossly inappropriate things to one another but I did not intervene because I did not know how to do so in a constructive way. It was not until the last two Mondays that I felt I was being helpful. In both occasions two separate students opened up to me about their lives. Looking back on the time that I spent at the middle school, I was mostly focused on providing homework help when I should have focused on forming connections with the students by just asking them questions and listening. This student continued by quoting from her lab journal: "my conversations with the two students led me to realize that sometimes academic support is not the only support that students need. I now strongly believe that just listening to students and connecting with them is just as important. In fact I think it is something that is overlooked in schools, and that teachers should spend more time listening to their students." (Student 5 2019)

In listening to this student, I see the permaculture principle of slow observation over time in practice. While I aim to better prepare my students for community work, to place them in settings where they are less likely to experience hostility, and to review restorative justice practices so they will have tools when difficult situations emerge, this student points to the significance of time in the process of learning hard lessons. This student also points to one of the hard spots that emerge when we do real work and when we pay attention to the limits of what we can do in one semester, which motivates me to think more expansively. For me, then, next steps also include collaborating with education faculty at my institution as well as the staff who work on community partnerships to improve communication with site partners and to make placement where students do not experience hostility. I am working on a panel with one colleague from our education program in the fall, and I am also planning to offer a winter class on the topic of community writing, which, once it is approved, would allow for year-long collaboration and partnerships.

More ambitiously, but with the collaboration of many partners, I am working on a collection of seasonal writing prompts related to food justice and to gardening as well as the infrastructure to support the publication of writing generated by these prompts. This project, called *the Almanac of Garden Writing*, draws on the historical role of almanacs to empower farmers and gardeners and their particular use to advocate for abolition during the nineteenth century. Like the *American Anti-Slavery Almanacs*, which argued for an end of slavery by appealing to the hands, hearts, and minds of readers with practical information about farming along with stories, images, and essays that illustrated the immorality of slavery, *the Almanac of Garden Writing* will offer opportunities for public, multimodal, multigene writing about food justice (Gustin).

Right now, *the Almanac of Garden Writing* includes prompts created by participants in workshops at the 2019 Conference on College Composition and Communication, the 2019 Conference on Community Writing, and a workshop that was to have been held at the 2020 Conference on College Composition and Communication, which was facilitated independently when that conference was canceled due to COVID-19. Below, I offer a sampling of the prompts developed so far followed by a link to a webpage where you will find more prompts as well as a collaborative document where you can add your ideas.

Chris Thaiss, professor emeritus at the University of California, Davis, and co-author of the blog *A Sacramento Valley Kitchen Garden* contributed a series of general garden writing prompts that could be used to introduce garden writing to writers from a range of backgrounds, whether they have experience with gardening or not.

> Do you have a garden?
> Do you have a garden?
> What do you have in your life that is a literal garden or that is like a garden, as you define it?
> Why do you have it?
> What do you gain from it?
> How has it changed for you?
> What are some surprises that have come out of your garden?
> How is this garden related to the rest of your life?

If you didn't have this garden, what would you be missing?
Have you ever been without this garden?
What happened?
Before you found or built your garden, who were you?

Mark Houston, a doctoral student and instructor at the University of Nebraska, offered a series of prompts related to the practice of starting seeds indoors, an activity that typically begins in the late winter and early spring and might be used near the start of a winter/spring garden writing class, and a set of prompts that could accompany cooking activities anytime.

- Set 1: seed starting
  - Ecosystem education
  - Writing about heritage + histories of place and people
  - Informative writing on eco-relationships
- Set 2: cooking
  - Women's labor, feminization of cooking and devaluing of women's work, honoring ancestors' work and lives through interviews and profiles.

These prompts connect to activities outside the classroom, they address a range of topics, and they include a range of genres, such as research, informative, and persuasive writing as well as creative writing. For these reasons, these prompts—and other garden writing assignments—can be used in alignment with many conventional writing pedagogies, and they can create space for ecological and antiracist pedagogies. This both/and approach enacts the important permaculture principle of starting with the material at hand by accounting for the material conditions in which a number of writing teachers work, conditions circumscribed by workload issues, labor inequity, and assessment dictates, and this approach also enacts the important permaculture principles of cultivating diversity and honoring knowledge garnered by the heart and hands as well as the mind.

The second stage of the Almanac project will include a template so schools and community groups can document and preserve their work and bring garden writing and garden writing projects to diverse communities, thereby enacting the permaculture edict to produce a yield and aligning with what Veronica House calls a rhetoric of abundance in her forthcoming book. It will support ongoing collaborations between colleges, school gardens, and communities; it will provide real audiences and purposes for writers; it will bring the work and the voices of young writers outside the classroom; and it will contribute to food justice by sharing knowledge, raising awareness, and offering practice information about gardening and cooking; so more people can decolonize their diets and their minds. As climate change and movements for racial equity make visible the collapse of industrialism, colonialism, and racism, educators are reckoning with their complicity in these systems of oppression and looking for alternatives. I propose food justice classes that center the work of BIPOC writers and that include community engagement as one way forward. I invite you to join me by sowing seeds in ways that serve your communities, and I hope you will add your thoughts to the collaborative document on my website (https://stephanie-wade.com).

REFERENCES

Alkon, Alison Hope, and Julian Agyeman. 2011. *Cultivating Food Justice: Race, Class, and Sustainability.* Cambridge: MIT Press.

Broad, Garrett. 2021. *More Than Just Food: Food Justice and Community Change.* Berkeley: University of California Press.

Condon, Frankie, and Vershawn Ashanti Young. 2016. *Performing Antiracist Pedagogy in Rhetoric, Writing, and Communication.* Fort Collins, CO: The WAC Clearinghouse.

Cutter-Mackenzie, Amy. 2009. "Multicultural School Gardens: Creating Engaging Garden Spaces in Learning about Language, Culture, and Environment." *Canadian Journal of Environmental Education* 14, no. 1: 122–35.

Donehower, Kim, Charlotte Hogg, and Eileen E. Schell. 2011. *Reclaiming the Rural: Essays on Literacy, Rhetoric, and Pedagogy.* Carbondale: Southern Illinois University Press, ProQuest Ebook Central.

Esquibel, Catriona Rueda, and Luz Calvo. 2013. "Decolonize Your Diet: A Manifesto." *nineteen sixty-nine: an ethnic studies journal* 2, no. 1: 1–4.

Fanon, Frantz. 1968. *The Wretched of the Earth.* New York: Grove Press.

Gray, L., J. Johnson, N. Latham, M. Tang, and A. Thomas. 1968, June. "Critical Reflections on Experiential Learning for Food Justice." *Journal of Agriculture, Food Systems, and Community Development* 2, no. 3: 137–44. DOI:10.5304/jafscd.2012.023.014.

Gustin, Kelsey. 2016. "The American Anti-Slavery Almanac" The Boston Public Library. https://www.bpl.org/blogs/post/the-american-anti-slavery-almanac.

Hemenway, Toby. 2018. *Gaia's Garden: A Guide to Home-Scale Permaculture.* 2nd ed. White River, VT: Chelsea Publishing.

House, Veronica. 2014. "Reframing the Argument: Critical Service Learning and Community-Centered Food Literacy." *Community Literacy Journal* 8, no. 2: 1–16.

Hu-DeHart, Evelyn. 1993. "The History, Development, and Future of Ethnic Studies." *The Phi Delta Kappan* 75, no. 1: 50–54. http://www.jstor.org/stable/20405023.

Kimmerer, Robin Wall. 2013. *Braiding Sweetgrass.* Minneapolis, MN: Milkweed Editions.

Kinloch, Valerie. 2012. "Politicizing, Placing, and Performing Narratives of Gentrification in an Urban Community." In *The New Work of Composing*, edited by Debra Journet, Cheryl E. Ball, and Ryan Trauman. Logan: Computers and Composition Digital Press, Utah State University Press.

Kirkland, David E. 2008. "'The Rose That Grew from Concrete': Postmodern Blackness and New English Education." *The English Journal* 97, no. 5: 69–75. www.jstor.org/stable/30046887.

———. 2017. "A Dance of Bars: Rethinking the Role of Literacy Education in the Age of Mass Incarceration." *Journal of Adolescent & Adult Literacy* 60, no. 4 (2017): 467–70. https://www.jstor.org/stable/26630757#metadata_info_tab_contents.

Mares, Teresa, and Devon Peña. 2011. "Environmental Justice and Food Justice: Towards Local, Slow, and Deep Food Systems." *Cultivating Food Justice: Race, Class, and Sustainability*, edited by Alison Hope and Julian Agyeman. Cambridge: The MIT Press.

Nocella, A. J., P. Parmar, D. C. Sawyer, and M. Cermak. 2012. "Hip Hop, Food Justice, and Environmental Justice." In *Environmental and Food Justice toward Dismantling the School-to-Prison*, edited by A. J. Nocella, K. Ducre, and J. Lupinacci. New York: Palgrave Macmillan.

Lynch, Paul. 2012. "Composition's New Thing: Bruno Latour and the Apocalyptic Turn." *College English* 74, no. 5: 458–76.

Peña, Devon. 2006, March. "Farmers Feeding Families: Agroecology in South Central Los Angeles." Keynote Address. *The National Association for Chicano and Chicana Studies*. Washington.

Penniman, Leah. 2018. *Farming while Black: Soul Fire Farm's Practical Guide to Liberation on the Land*. White River, VT: Chelsea Publishing.

Student 1. 2019. *Whiteboard*. Lewiston, ME: FYS 493.

Student 2. 2019. *Final Reflection*. Lewiston, ME: FYS 493.

Student 3. 2019. *Final Reflection*. Lewiston, ME: FYS 493.

Student 4. 2019a. *Final Reflection*. Lewiston, ME: FYS 493.

———. 2019b. *Lab Journal*. Lewiston, ME: FYS 493.

Student 5. 2019. *Final Reflection*. Lewiston, ME: FYS 493.

Thiong'o, Ngũgĩ wa. 1986. *Decolonising the Mind: The Politics of Language in African Literature*. Portsmouth, NH: Heinemann.

Turner L., M. Eliason, A. Sandoval, and F. J. Chaloupka. 2016, December. "Increasing Prevalence of US Elementary School Gardens, but Disparities Reduce Opportunities for Disadvantaged Students." *Journal of School Health* 86, no. 12: 906–12. DOI: 10.1111/josh.12460.

Williams, Dilafruz, and Jonathan D. Brown. 2012. *Learning Gardens and Sustainability Education: Bringing Life to Schools and Schools to Life*. New York: Routledge.

Williams, Dilafruz, and P. Scott Dixon. 2013. "Impact of Garden-Based Learning in Academic Outcomes in Schools: A Synthesis of Research 1999–2010." *Review of Education Research* 83, no. 2: 211–35. https://doi.org/10.3102/0034654313475824.

Index

Page references for figures are italicized.

activism: feminist, 6, 10, 12, 72, 133, 141–44, 169, 175; and food justice, 11, 58, 73, 80; political, 65–66, 72–74, 110, 167–7, 175–78, 186
Adekunle, Dali, 51–52, 66
AgChat Foundation, 138–39
agency: definition of, 19; rhetorical, 20
agriculture: defamiliarization with, 128n3; and land-grant universities, 186–88, 198; organic, 5, 27–28, 87, 109, 127n1, 247; and public relations, 11, 130, 133–44; and resistance, 9, 60, 133, 197; women in, 129–32, 136–44
agrifood industrial complex, 186, 198; transnational, 12
agvocacy, 137–38, 142–44, 148n12
Agyeman, Julian, 45, 73, 109, 116, 119, 132
Alkon, Alison Hope, 73, 109, 116–19, 132
The Almanac of Garden Writing project, 258–59
Alvarez, Stephen, 28–29, 32
America Eats (FWP), 55–56
American Anti-Slavery Almanacs, 258

animacy, 149–50, 154; grammar of, 151–52
Arellano, Sonia, 150–51, 154
Ashcroft, Bill, 133

Bell, David, 33
Bennett, Jane, 157
Bernardo, Shane, 149, 157–58
Berry, Wendell, 212–13, 228, 245
Bigelow, Martha, 21
biopiracy, 194
Birkenfeld, Darryl, 113–16, 122–23
Bista, Hima, 169, 175–76
Bloomberg, Michael, 55
Braiding Sweetgrass (Kimmerer), 150–51, 154, 159
Brandt, Deborah, 23, 26, 110
Breslauer, Gus, 64
Bruner, Michael, S., 7, 73

Capital (Marx), 58
CaribBeing, 51
Carney, Judith, A., 101
Cather, Willa, 214
CEDAW. *See* Convention on the Elimination of all Forms of Discrimination Against Women

Charmaz, Kathy, 189
Cintron, Ralph, 131, 146n2
Cochran-Smith, Marilyn, 93
Cockburn, Cynthia, 29
code meshing, 13, 244, 252
Community Alliance for Global Justice (Seattle), 194
community gardens, 8, 60–61, 218, 243; as transnational spaces, 248–54
confianza, 28–29
Convention on the Elimination of all Forms of Discrimination Against Women (CEDAW), 170
critical literacy, 190; acquisition of, 117, 125; agricultural, 110–13; definition of, 3, 88, 210; food justice and, 198; sponsorship, 122
Culcasi, Karen, 20
cultural continuity, 20, 22, 26–28, 33

Dash, Julie, 215
Daughters of the Dust (Dash), 215
Deans, Thomas, 150
"Decolonize Your Diet: A Manifesto" (Esquibel and Calvo), 243
Deepak, Sharanya, 79
Denzin, Norman K., 19
Dharma's Garden, 153–56
Dialogics of the Oppressed (Hitchcock), 20
discourses: agricultural, 153; mainstream migration and refugee, 20; resistance in, 20
Donehower, Kim, 7, 23, 128n3, 248, 250
Druschke, Caroline Gottschalk, 131, 146n2
Dubisar, Abby, 6, 12–13, 131

Facer, Keri, 99, 103
FARFA. *See* Farm and Ranch Freedom Alliance
Farm and Ranch Freedom Alliance, 118–19

Farming While Black (Penniman), 61, 246–47
Fast Food Nation (Schlosser), 213–14
Federici, Silvia, 60
Feigenbaum, Paul, 155
feminism: in research design, 189–99; transnational, 4, 168–69
fermented foods: and "the smell of the Other," 74–81; Syrian, 25, 29, 36n8
Flatbush Eats writing workshops, 51–62, 65–67
Flatbush–PLG. *See* Flatbush–Prospect Lefferts Gardens
Flatbush–Prospect Lefferts Gardens (Flatbush–PLG), 9, 52, 54–55, 59–60, 63–65
Flowers & Bullets, 47–48
food apartheid, 213, 215, 255
food deserts. *See* food apartheid
food insecurity, 58–59, 172–74, 207, 209, 231; and COVID-19 pandemic, 1–3, 9, 44–45, 52, 56, 117, 123–24, 220–21
Food Justice (Gottlieb and Joshi), 11
food justice: and citizenship, 167–68, 170–78; community writing, 247; and decolonial rhetorical frameworks, 10, 150, 153, 161–62; foodie tourists, 40, 44; and gender discrimination, 168, 181n18; and health literacy, 89; and Jamaican dairy industry, 203n4; and land-grant universities, 186–88, 198; Nepal, 167–78; Ogallala Commons, 124–26; and quinoa, 202n3; and papaya, 203n6; "the smell of the Other," 71–79; Uganda, 188, 190–94, 196–98, 202n2; and white supremacy, 73, 162, 188, 198–99; and wild rice, 202n3
food literacy: agency in, 19–20; critical, 87–89, 101–2; definition of, 19–20; feminist, 130–31; scholarship, 149; and women-led entrepreneurship, 25–26

Index   265

food sovereignty, 8, 12, 88–90, 247–48; and agrifood industrial complex, 186–87, 193, 196–98; and alternate futures, 47–48; and citizenship rights policy, 169–78; for Indigenous people, 160; and mutual aid, 65; and right to food policy, 170–78; scholarship, 207, 215; and silenced experiences, 81, 91, 100, 168; and "the smell of the Other," 72; and Syrian culture, 19–20, 22, 26, 28; and urban gardens, 248

food systems: global agrifood systems, 186; industrial, 205; pedagogy of, 206

foodways: African Diasporic, 87; cultural, 43; Indigenous, 42–43, 74–75; Mexican, 32, 42–43

foragers, 10, 12, 150, 156–63

Forum for Women, Law, and Development, 170

Foster, John Bellamy, 59

Francis, Kerry and Tim, 153–56, 161

Freebody, Peter, 89

Frye, Joshua, J., 7, 73

FWLP. *See* Forum for Women, Law, and Development

FWP. *See* New Deal Federal Writers' Project

Gallagher, Kathleen, 90–93, 97–99

Gallegos, Danielle, 88

Gates Foundation, 193–94

Gautam, Sabitri, 169, 176

genetically engineered. *See* transgenic

genetically modified organisms, 203n6; banana feeding study, 191–96; Ogallala Commons, 113–14

gentrification, 44, 52, 55, 59, 246

Ghale, Dr. Yamuna, 169, 173–74, 176

Ghouta, Syria, 28, 36n7

gleaning, 4

Glenn, Cheryl, 38

Glissant, Édouard, 91

GMO. *See* genetically modified organisms

Goldblatt, Eli, 250–51

Gottlieb, Robert, 59, 66, 109–10, 124, 132, 142

Gramsci, Antonio, 66, 132

Grand Army Green Market, 53

The Grassroots Policy Project, 131, 143

Grassroots Public Relations for Agriculture (Lipscomb), 134–38

the Great Acceleration, 58

greenwashing, 87

Gries, Laurie, 152–54

Gullah, 57, 215

Gurung, Neha, 169, 175, 181n17, 182n23

Haraway, Donna, J., 97

Hawken, Paul, 199–209

heritage: co-option of, 40–42; cultural, 20, 38, 48; definition of, 37; for economic development, 39–40; food practices, 37; intangible cultural, 37, 39–41, 43, 46, 48; production of, 37–39; and rhetorical strategies, 39; as persuasion, 38–39; silences in, 38, 43, 45, 48

Hitchcock, Peter, 20

Hogg, Charlotte, 7, 23, 128n3, 248, 250

Holmgren, David, 244

Honorable Harvest, 162

Hyland, Ken, 92–93

industrial education, 246

Jackson, Rachel, C., 161–62

Jacobson, Kelsey, 91, 93, 97

Jeffersonian ideology, 27

Jeffrey, Julie Roy, 22

Jones, Naya, 91

Joshi, Anupama, 59, 66, 109–10, 124, 132, 142

Kadosh, Yagil, 58

kapwa, 149, 157

Ketoure, Nadia, 51–53, 61, 66–67
Kimmerer, Robin Wall, 150–52, 154, 158, 162, 245
kinema, 74–76
Kinloch, Valerie, 246–47, 251
Kiowa approach. *See* writing, and Kiowa approach
Kirkland, David, 246–47
Kirsch, Gesa, 131–32, 189
Kropotkin, David, 63–64

labneh, 25, 29, 36n8
Lefebvre, Henri, 63
linguistic justice, 13, 244
Lipscomb, Ed, 134–38, 147nn7–8
literacy: critical, 3, 88, 117, 210; critical food, 87–90, 206; rural, 7, 22–26, 33; sponsors, 26, 110–12, 114–16, 121–26; taco, 32; transnational, 19–20, 30–33, 101–3
literacy practices: critical agrifood, 185, 196–97; gendered, 20–22; nonacademic, 23
literacy teaching: with community gardens, 243, 247–57; in third spaces, 246–48
Luke, Allan, 89
Lynch, Paul, 251–52
Lytle, Susan, L., 93

Mabry, Jonathan, 41
Malinowski, Bronislaw, 157
Maple Street Community Garden, 51, *57*, 61, *62*
Marx, Karl, 58–60
Mauss, Marcel, 157
McEntee, Jesse, 45
McKittrick, Katherine, 91
Mollison, Bill, 244
Monberg, Terese Guinsatao, 149, 157–58
more-than-human, 149–54, 156, 158, 160–62, 165n2
Morrison, Tony, 61

Mozaic nonprofit organization, 30–32; and SafarTas project, 30–32, 36n10
muda, *71*
mutual aid, 9, 40, 47, 248; and Flatbush–PLG, 52–54, 59–66

Nabhan, Gary, 41
nanglo, *71*
Native seeds/SEARCH, 41
Navdanya organization (India), 194
Nepal: Brahmanical structure, 74–77; citizenship act, 167; constitution of, 13, 76–77, 167–78; indigenous cuisines, 74–77; right to food policy, 170–78
New Deal Federal Writers' Project (FWP), 53–56
Ntelioglou, Burcu Wayman, 90
Nutbeam, Don, 89

Ogallala Commons, 11, 110–16; and food summits, 116–20; and Local Llano project, 120–26
O'Pioneers (Cather), 214
Orr, David, 209
Owens, Derek, 250–51

Pandey, Dr. Binda, 169, 173
Pascua Yaqui people, 43
pedagogy: antiracist, 244; centering BIPOC authors, 252–56, 260; and civic engagement, 210–11, 217–21; community-engaged, 130, 151–52, 250; critical, 13, 205–7; food, 207–9; food justice, 214–16; centering Indigenous scholarship in, 149–50; land as, 162; with personal food practices, 211–13; place-based, 250; and transnational contexts, 6, 248–54
Peña, Devon, 248
Penniman, Leah, 61, 72, 101, 215, 246–47, 255
permaculture, 243–45
Phillips-Merriman, Andrea, 56
Poulakos, Paul, 141

Prendergast, Neil, 218–19
Prospect Park, *67*
Proust, Marcel, 72

Quinney, Richard, 77

Rai, Candice, 131, 146n2
Ravitch, Diane, 246
reciprocal being. *See* kapwa
reciprocity, 5, 12, 149–55, 256; and foragers, 156–61
Reclaiming the Rural (Donehower, Hogg, and Schell), 250
Refugee English as a Second Language (RESLA), 20–22
Regeneración, 42
Reign of Error: The Hoax of the Privatization Movement and the Danger to America's Public Schools (Ravitch), 246
repatriation, 150, 160–61, 163
resilience, 11; and agricultural resistance, 60; creative, 91; in education and thinking, 210; and food justice, 113, 169; and food literacy, 19, 32, 102
RESLA. *See* Refugee English as a Second Language
Reynolds, Nedra, 250–51
right to food (RtF), 10, 12, 72, 168–72, 177; and "the smell of the other," 80–81
Riina-Ferrie, Joseph, 98
Robb, Hattie, 120
Rodricks, Dirks, J., 91, 93, 97
Rodriguez, Claudio, 42
Romer, Nancy, 64
Rosomoff, Richard Nicholas, 101
Rothschild, Mayor Jonathan, 45
Royster, Jacqueline Jones, 131–32
Ruiz, Iris, D. 150–513, 154
Ruiz, Nelda, 42
Rural Literacies (Donehower, Hogg, and Schell), 7, 22–23
rural otherness, 23

sack yogurt. *See* labneh
A Sacramento Valley Kitchen Garden blog (Thaiss), 259
safartas, *31*
Samuels, Kathryn Lafrenz, 39
Schell, Eileen, 7, 23, 124, 128n3, 116, 198–99, 248, 250–51
Schlosser, Eric, 213–14
Schwartz, Robin Lovrien, 21
settler colonialism, 42–44, 160–61
Shiva, Vandana, 194
Shively, Vince, 113
Simpson, Leanne Betasamosake, 162
Song of Solomon (Morrison), 61
Soul Fire Farms, 215, 252
sustainability, 7, 9, 13, 46, 73; and agrifood industrial complex, 186–87, 189–90, 192–96, 198; ecological, 109, 115, 207; and environmental economics, 216, 219; and rural literacy, 22–23, 28; urban, 65
Syrian refugee women: and food making, 24–25, 28; food preservation practices, 24, 28–30; gendered literacy practices, 20–22; literacy development, 21–22; narratives of, 19–20

Texas Hunger Initiative, 111
Thaiss, Chris, 259
Thorp, Laurie, 94
tiffin carrier, *31*
Todd, Zoe, 149
Tohono O'odham people, 42–43
transgenic, 188, 192, 194, 203n6
Trouillot, Michael-Rolph, 37–38
Tucson, Arizona: as Creative City of Gastronomy, 37–38
Twitty, Michael, 101

UCCN. *See* United Nations Educational, Scientific, and Cultural Organization Creative Cities Network
Under the Feet of Jesus (Viramontes), 212

UNESCO. *See* United Nations Educational, Scientific, and Cultural Organization
United Nations Educational, Scientific, and Cultural Organization (UNESCO), 9, 37–40, 45
United Nations Educational, Scientific, and Cultural Organization Creative Cities Network (UCCN), 9, 37–42, 45–46
The Unsettling of America (Berry), 245
urban renewal, 44, 59, 69n1. *See also* gentrification

Vasudevan, Lalitha, 98
Vidgen, Helen Anna, 88
Viebrock, Margaret, 138–42
Viramontes, Helena Maria, 212
Voices of Lefferts Community History Project (VoL), 52–58, 65–67
VoL. *See* Voices of Lefferts Community History Project

Wabanaki people, 249–51
war: and food shortages, 29; impacts on women, 29–30

Washington State University Women in Ag workshops, 129–30, 132–33, 142
Wessels, Anne, 90
Whitehorse DeLaune, Dorothy, 161–62
Whitelaw, Jessica, 92
Wilson, Fergus, 78–79
Winslow, Dianna, 88
Women LEAD Nepal, 175
writing: in academic courses, 185–99, 205–21, 243–60; Afrofuturist prompts, 96–95; with Black youth, 90–96; community, 51–67, 150, 161, 247–49; community engaged, 149–50, 243, 247; creative, 90–91, 104–6; collaborative, 91–93; and Kiowa approach (community listening), 151–52
writing assignments: from community gardening projects, 251–58; on food justice, 223–42; instructor feedback, *257*

Yagelski, Robert, P., 92

zero hunger, 171, 181n8

About the Contributors

Deborah Adelman is professor of English and film studies at the College of DuPage in Glen Ellyn, Illinois. For thirty years, she has taught writing, literature, and film classes, including interdisciplinary seminars combining the humanities and environmental science perspectives. She is co-founder of the campus garden that has developed into the Food Security Initiative—a collaborative project between Academic Affairs and Student Life to address student hunger by growing food and educating the campus community on food system issues. She has presented nationally and internationally and published academic work and creative writing, including poetry, fiction, and nonfiction.

Shamili Ajgaonkar is professor of biology and environmental science at the College of DuPage in Glen Ellyn, Illinois. For thirty years, she has taught biology and environmental science courses in various modalities including traditional classroom, online, field-based, and interdisciplinary seminars. She has developed environmental science courses for local, national, and international settings. In her teaching practice as well as co-curricular work, she is deeply committed to advancing ecoliteracy by engaging students in experiential learning and civic engagement to encourage critical analysis of ecological systems in human society and participation in the problem-solving of pressing environmental challenges.

OreOluwa Badaki is a postdoctoral fellow at Teachers College, Columbia University. She earned her PhD from the Literacy, Culture, and International Education Division at the University of Pennsylvania Graduate School of Education. Her dissertation work, which focused on the critical and creative literacy practices of youth of color working in urban agriculture, received the Ralph C. Preston Award for Scholarship and Teaching Contributing to Social Justice. She is currently working on a book project about the pedagogical and methodological possibilities of collaborative and creative writing in environmental justice education.

About the Contributors

Cori Brewster is professor of writing and rhetoric at Eastern Oregon University and a founding member of Oregon Rural Action, a grassroots organization working for social and environmental justice in northeast Oregon. Her work on rural rhetorics and literacies has appeared in several collections, including *Reclaiming the Rural* (ed. Donehower, Hogg, and Schell), *The Ecopolitics of Consumption* (ed. Davis, Pilgrim, and Sinha), *Crossing Borders, Drawing Boundaries: The Rhetoric of Lines Across America* (ed. Wojahn and Couture), and *Class in the Composition Classroom* (ed. Carter and Thelin). Her article "Basic Writing through the Back Door: Community-Engaged Courses in the Rush-to-Credit Age" was selected for inclusion in the *Best of the Independent Rhetoric and Composition Journals*, 2015. Her current research focuses on rhetorics of place, access, and privatization in public higher education.

Abby M. Dubisar is associate professor of English and an affiliate faculty member in women's and gender studies and sustainable agriculture at Iowa State University, where she teaches classes on feminist rhetoric, gender and communication, and popular culture analysis. Her recent research addresses rhetorical strategies in a variety of food and farming contexts. These studies address a woman farmer's strategies to cultivate legitimacy, pedagogies to address food waste, and an archival study on linking rural women historically through a theory of postwar global citizenship. Her work has been published in *College English*, *Community Literacy Journal*, *Computers and Writing*, and other venues.

Nabila Hijazi is a teaching assistant professor of writing at the George Washington University.. Her research interests include Muslim and refugee women's rhetorics and literacy practices. Drawing on community-based work with Syrian refugee women in the Washington, DC, region, Hijazi examines the cultural, economic, and political dimensions of their Arabic literacy practices and English literacy learning in the United States. Currently, she is at work on a book that focuses on Syrian refugee women's literacy. She has received multiple awards and scholarships, including the 2020 President's Dissertation Award by the Coalition of Feminist Scholars in the History of Rhetoric and Composition.

Veronica House teaches and writes about food localization and food justice efforts in Colorado. She is the founding executive director of the Coalition for Community Writing, director of the Conference on Community Writing, and co-editor of the *Community Literacy Journal*. Veronica is a professor in the University Writing Program at the University of Denver.

Callie F. Kostelich is assistant professor of English at Texas Tech University. Her primary research areas include rural literacies, agricultural literacy, feminist rhetorics, and first-year writing. She recently published "'You Are What You Eat': Oprah, Amarillo, and Food Politics" in *Veg(etari)an Arguments in Culture, History, and Practice: The V Word* and is currently working on her book project, "Sponsoring Agricultural Literacy: Literacies, Ideologies, and the FFA."

Deborah Mutnick is professor of English at Long Island University's Brooklyn campus. She is author of *Writing in an Alien World: Basic Writing and the Struggle for Equality in Higher Education* (Boynton/Cook 1996); co-editor with Shannon Carter, Steven Parks, and Jessica Pauszek of *Writing Democracy: The Political Turn In and Beyond the Trump Era* (Routledge 2019); and co-editor with Margaret Cuonzo, Carole Griffiths, Timothy Leslie, and Jay Shuttleworth of *The City Is an Ecosystem: Sustainable Education, Practices, and Policy* (Routledge 2022). She also directs the Voices of Lefferts Community History Project, which she helped spearhead in 2015.

Ellen Platts is a PhD candidate in the Department of Anthropology at the University of Maryland. Her research interests focus on the use of culture and heritage for sustainability and social justice in responses to climate change and urban development. Ellen was a 2020 National Science Foundation Global STEWARDS Fellow at the University of Maryland, working to incorporate social science methodologies and social justice into research at the food-energy-water nexus.

Bibhushana Poudyal is a PhD candidate in the Rhetoric and Writing Studies Program at the University of Texas at El Paso. Her research and teaching interests emerge from the intersections of anti-oppressive theories, criticisms, pedagogies, critical archival studies, critical digital humanities, and technical communication. Her work explores ways to use intellectual labor, technologies, and research methodologies in the service of underrepresented communities and intersectionally disadvantaged groups to build healing spaces in and through academia. She serves as an honorary digital humanities consultant at the Center for Advanced Studies in South Asia (CASSA).

Mala Rai is an indigenous feminist scholar from Nepal. She has been a faculty member of the Gender Studies Department at Tribhuvan University since 2011, where she teaches a variety of classes on feminist theory, discourse, and methods, including "Feminist Discourse as a Part of Life" and "Feminist Political Agendas in Gender Studies." Her research and teaching are situated at the intersection of gender, intersectionality, migration, indigenous feminism, and indigenous women's movements in Nepal, and violence against women (VAW). She is a member of TEWA Nepal, which is a self-sustained women-led organization for the development and empowerment of women, and works as a consultant for Kathmandu-based indigenous women's groups.

Eileen E. Schell is professor of writing and rhetoric and Laura J. and L. Douglas Meredith Professor of Teaching Excellence and faculty affiliate in women's and gender studies at Syracuse University. Schell is the author and editor of six books and co-edited collections that address labor studies, rural rhetorics and literacies, feminist rhetorics, and veteran studies. In her work with collaborators Dr. Kim Donehower and Charlotte Hogg, Schell addresses the intersections of food rhetorics and agricultural literacies, strands of which emerge in her co-authored book *Rural Literacies* (SIUP, 2007) and co-edited collection *Reclaiming the Rural* (SIUP, 2011). Schell also leads two longstanding community writing groups for senior citizens and veterans in the greater Syracuse, New York, area.

Pritisha Shrestha is a PhD candidate in the Composition and Cultural and Rhetoric (CCR) Program at Syracuse University. She also has a certificate in advanced studies in food studies from Falk College at Syracuse University. Her research interests and pedagogies are related to rhetorics of food, public policies, and transnational feminisms.

Stephanie Wade teaches in the Program in Writing and Rhetoric at Stony Brook University. Formerly, she taught community-engaged writing and humanities classes that center food justice, language rights, and ecological literacy at Searsport District High School, Bates College, and Unity College. Her research uses permaculture and ecological approaches to literacy to illustrate the material, aesthetic, and ethical significance of making space for multiple genres and multiple dialectics in college writing. She serves on the Board of Directors of the Coalition for Community Writing and recently launched "Coda," a new section of the *Community Literacy Journal* devoted to community writing and creative work.

Dianna Winslow is assistant director and writing instruction specialist for the Center for Teaching, Learning, and Technology at California Polytechnic, San Luis Obispo. Her work for the center promotes writing across the curriculum and writing in the disciplines. She also facilitates workshops and retreats for faculty scholarly writing. Dianna's research addresses community-engaged approaches to teaching and research on alternative agri-food systems, food justice movements, environmental justice, and teaching for social change.

Kelly Zepelin works with wild plant foragers in Southwest Colorado to study wild food cultures, ethics, soil microbiology, decolonization, and the connection between ecological and human health. She graduated with her PhD from the University of Colorado–Boulder in 2022 and works full-time as a mother and on local food projects in Durango, Colorado.

www.ingramcontent.com/pod-product-compliance
Lightning Source LLC
Chambersburg PA
CBHW020112010526
44115CB00008B/801